CONTENTS

Introduction	vii
1 Trigonometry 1	**1**
Right-angled triangles	1
Types and measures of angles	3
Length of an arc and area of a sector	6
The unit circle	8
Angles greater than 360°	10
General solutions of trigonometric equations	12
Graphs of trigonometric functions	13
Checklist	21
2 Trigonometry 2	**22**
Area of a triangle	22
Area of a segment	23
Sine rule and cosine rule	24
3D problems	33
Trigonometric formulae and identities	37
Checklist	42
3 Co-ordinate Geometry of the Line	**43**
Co-ordinate geometry formulae	43
Linear relationships and graphs	49
Area of a triangle	51
Dividing a line segment in a given ratio	54
Perpendicular distance from a point to a line	55
Angle between two lines	57
Checklist	60

Contents iii

4 Synthetic Geometry 1 — 61

Logic and deductive reasoning	61
Axioms 1 to 5	62
Theorems 1 to 21	65
Proofs of Theorems 11, 12 and 13	71
Checklist	74

5 Synthetic Geometry 2 — 75

Application of Theorems 1 to 21	75
Constructions	77
Triangle centres	80
Transformations	87
Checklist	99

6 The Circle — 100

Properties of a circle	100
The equation of a circle	101
Testing points	104
Intersection of a line and circle	105
Equations of tangents to a circle	108
Touching circles	112
Common chord and tangent	113
Circles touching axes	115
Circle problems	118
Checklist	120

7 Statistics 1 — 121

Introduction	121
Sampling techniques	125
Surveys and questionnaires	132
Checklist	133

8 Probability 1 — 134

Introduction and key words	134
Fundamental principle of counting	135
Permutations	137
Combinations	140
Probability rules	144
Checklist	155

9 Statistics 2 — 156

Measures of location (central tendency)	157
Measures of variability	161
Statistical diagrams	168
Bivariate data	179
Checklist	190

10 Further Probability and Statistics — 191

Probability distribution	192
Expected value	192
Bernoulli trials AFL 1.	194
Normal distribution	198
Confidence interval	208
Checklist	224

Appendix: Questions to Practise — 225

Introduction

This book covers the material needed for Paper 2 of the Leaving Certificate Higher Level mathematics examination. The examination consists of two written papers, each carrying 300 marks.

Paper 2 generally tests the material in strands 1 and 2 of the syllabus (statistics and probability, and geometry and trigonometry), along with material from section 3.4 in strand 3 (length, area and volume). Any synthetic geometry examined on the paper will be based on the geometry set out in the syllabus. The paper is split into two sections:

- Section A: Concepts and Skills, worth 150 marks
- Section B: Contexts and Applications, worth 150 marks.

The book contains numerous questions of the type that you will see in the exam, with worked solutions. Attempt each question yourself before looking at the solution. Make a note of any that you can't do by yourself and try again in your next revision session. That way, you will make the most of your revision time by focusing on the areas you find hardest.

Make sure to practise your basic skills in geometry, co-ordinate geometry, statistics, and so on. These skills will be needed in many different contexts. You should know them well.

When you get into the exam, take five minutes at the start to read through the paper. Allow 70 minutes for Section A, and 70 for Section B, with five minutes at the end to check that you haven't missed anything.

Be prepared for the unfamiliar. Section B in particular involves problem solving skills, and will be challenging. Don't give up if a problem is not working out.

Read each question carefully before starting. The first step might involve stating a correct formula, drawing a graph or completing a table. Make sure that the axes and points on graphs are clearly labelled. Use a pencil for graphs, diagrams and constructions, so that you can easily rub them out if necessary. Make sure that any arcs drawn as part of a construction are shown clearly.

Double check what the question has asked for. Give your answer to the correct number of decimal places or in the correct form, and in the simplest form if relevant.

Show all your work clearly, and make your final answer clear. You will lose marks if you haven't shown all the necessary work, or if the examiner cannot read or make sense of what you have written. Minus signs can sometimes be hard to read on squared paper, so take extra care to make them obvious. Don't forget units of measurement if applicable – you will lose marks if you leave them out.

Don't leave any question blank. If you don't write anything you can't get any marks. Write down any formulae that you think are relevant, even if you don't know how to use them. You will get partial credit for any work of merit. Avoid crossing out work if you can – anything you have written might be worth marks.

If you are struggling with a particular question, leave it and move on to the next one. You can always come back to it at the end if you have time.

The *Formulae and Tables* booklet is your friend! Study it carefully before the exam and make sure you know how to find the information you need. Practise using your calculator. Read the manual and ensure that you know how to calculate indices and logarithms, trigonometric functions and functions such as ^nC_r.

There are many websites that are useful for revision. Here are just a few.

- **www.projectmaths.ie** has a wealth of activities in the student area, including tips for getting the most out of your calculator. This is particularly useful for statistics.

- **www.examinations.ie** contains lots of information about the examinations. The most relevant part for students is the examination material archive, where you can find past papers and marking schemes.

- **www.betterexaminations.ie** also makes past papers available.

- **www.ncca.ie** gives information about the Leaving Certificate Mathematics Syllabus.

- **www.mathopenref.com** is an easy to use maths reference site with animations and interactive tools that illustrate key concepts.

Trigonometry 1

Learning objectives

In this chapter you will learn how to:
- Use Pythagoras' theorem to solve 2D problems
- Use the radian measure of angles
- Solve problems involving the area of a sector and the length of an arc of a circle
- Understand the properties and uses of the unit circle
- Solve trigonometric equations giving all solutions
- Graph the trigonometric functions sine, cosine and tangent
- Graph trigonometric functions of the form $f(\theta) = a + b\sin c\theta$ and $g(\theta) = a + b\cos c\theta$ for $a, b, c \in \mathbb{R}$
- Recognise the period and range of the above trigonometric functions and the effect of changing the values of a, b and c.

Right-angled triangles

Pythagoras' theorem and trigonometric ratios

The formula for **Pythagoras' theorem** is on page 16 of the *Formulae and Tables* booklet.

$c^2 = a^2 + b^2$

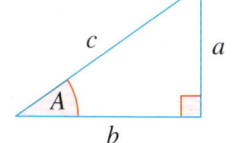

The same page also shows three **trigonometric ratios**.

$\sin A = \dfrac{a}{c}$, $\cos A = \dfrac{b}{c}$, $\tan A = \dfrac{a}{b}$

In the diagram, c is the **hypotenuse** of the triangle. The hypotenuse is the longest side, and is always opposite the right angle.

Side a is the **opposite** side, because it is opposite the angle being calculated. Side b is the **adjacent** side, because it is adjacent to (next to) the angle being calculated.

Point to note

The opposite and adjacent sides interchange depending on which angle we are working with. If we wanted to calculate the blank angle in the diagram, then b would be the opposite side and a would be the adjacent side.

Top Tip

The trigonometric ratios can also be written as

$$\sin A = \frac{opposite}{hypotenuse}, \cos A = \frac{adjacent}{hypotenuse}, \tan A = \frac{opposite}{adjacent}.$$

The acronym SOH-CAH-TOA gives an easy way to remember the ratios.

Examples

In the given diagram:
(a) find the value for c correct to 2 decimal places
(b) find the measure of the other two angles to the nearest degree.

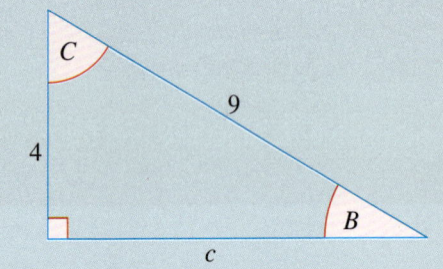

Solutions

(a) Using Pythagoras' theorem, $9^2 = c^2 + 4^2 \Rightarrow c^2 = 9^2 - 4^2 = 81 - 16 = 65$
$c^2 = 65 \Rightarrow c = \sqrt{65} = 8\cdot06$ units

(b) Find angle C using SOH-CAH-TOA.
$\cos C = \dfrac{a}{h} = \dfrac{4}{9} \Rightarrow C = \cos^{-1}\dfrac{4}{9} = 63\cdot61° \approx 64°$
$B = 180° - (90° + 64°) = 26°$

Top Tip

We could have calculated angle B first using $\sin B = \dfrac{o}{h}$. The result would be the same.

Types and measures of angles

Types of angles

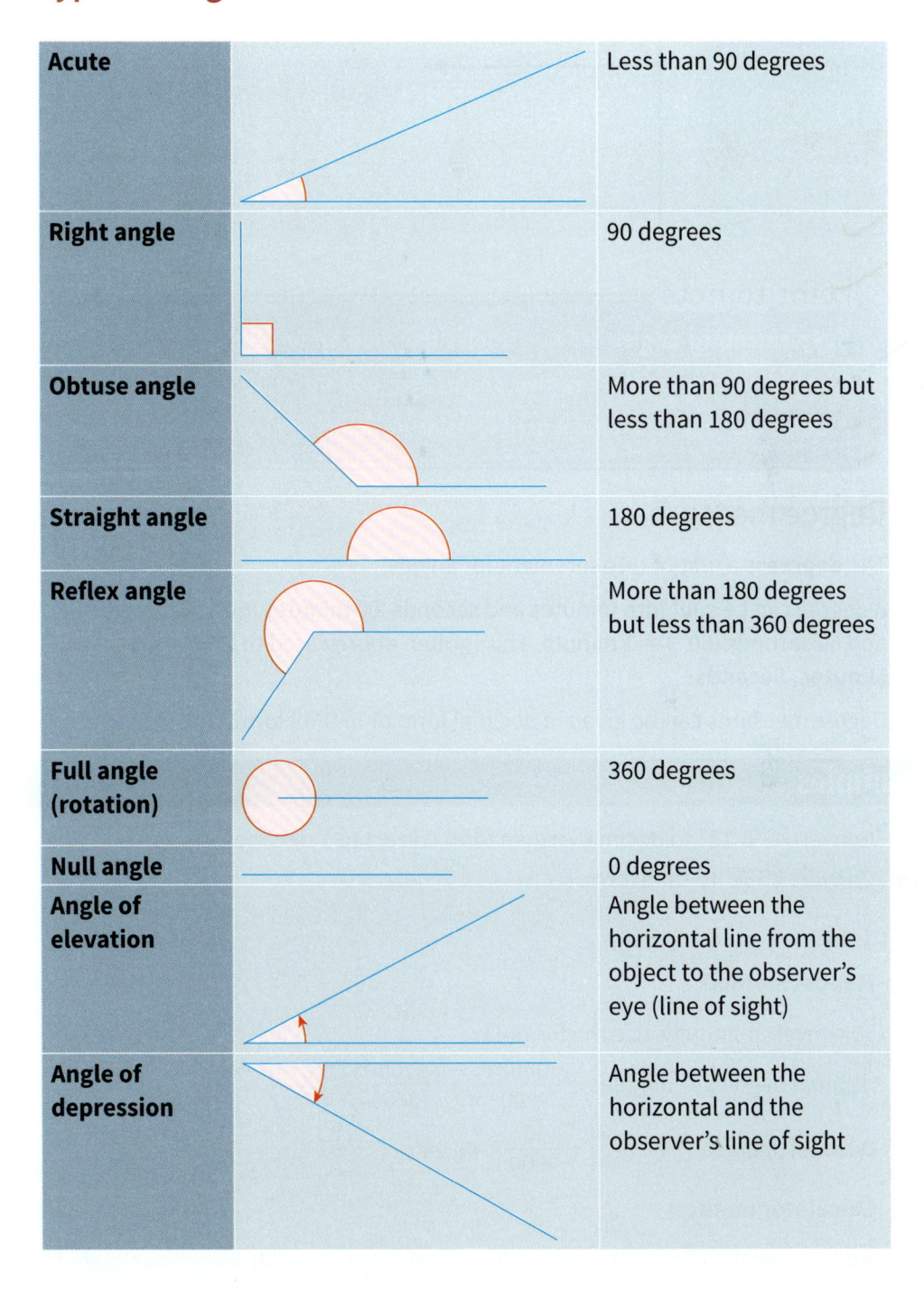

Acute		Less than 90 degrees
Right angle		90 degrees
Obtuse angle		More than 90 degrees but less than 180 degrees
Straight angle		180 degrees
Reflex angle		More than 180 degrees but less than 360 degrees
Full angle (rotation)		360 degrees
Null angle		0 degrees
Angle of elevation		Angle between the horizontal line from the object to the observer's eye (line of sight)
Angle of depression		Angle between the horizontal and the observer's line of sight

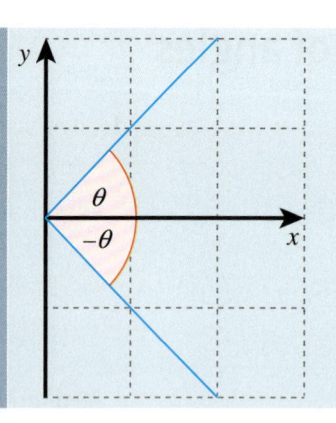

Negative angle — Angle created by moving clockwise from the positive side of the *x*-axis

> **Point to note**
> **Supplementary angles** are two angles that add up to 180°.
> **Complementary angles** are two angles that add up to 90°.
> A **clinometer** is an instrument used to measure angles of elevation or depression.

Degree measure

The **degree** is a unit of measurement for angles.

A degree can be split into minutes and seconds. 60 minutes (60′) = 1 degree and 60 seconds (60″) = 1 minute. This is often abbreviated to **DMS = Degrees, Minutes, Seconds**.

Degree measures can be given in decimal form or in DMS form.

Examples

(a) Convert 43°8′12″ to decimal degree form correct to 2 decimal places.
(b) Convert 35·36° to DMS form.

Solutions

(a) Manual method

To convert manually, use the formula

$$\text{decimal degrees} = \text{degrees} + \frac{\text{minutes}}{60} + \frac{\text{seconds}}{3600}.$$

$$\text{Decimal degrees} = 43 + \frac{8}{60} + \frac{12}{3600} = 43\cdot14°$$

Calculator method

You can use the DMS button on your calculator to convert between decimal and DMS form. The button should look something like this D°M′S or this ° ′ ″, depending on what type of calculator you have.

To enter 43°8'12" into your calculator, enter 43, then [°'''], then 8, then [°'''], then 12, then [°''']. Press the equals button to display the number in DMS form. Then press the [°'''] button again to display the result in decimal form. The answer is 43·14°.

(b) Manual method

When you convert from decimal to DMS form, the whole number part is the number of degrees. To find the number of minutes, multiply the decimal part of the number by 60; the number of minutes is the whole number part of the result. To find the number of seconds, multiply the decimal part of the minutes by 60.

For 35·36°,

degrees = 35

0·36 × 60 = 21·6, so minutes = 21

0·6 × 60 = 36, so seconds = 36

The answer is 35°21'36".

Calculator method

To convert a decimal to DMS form with a calculator, simply type in the decimal, then press the [°'''] button followed by the equals button.

The answer is 35°21'36".

Radian measure

Radian measure is a circular measure based on the unit circle. A radian is defined by an arc of a circle. One radian is the angle made at the centre of a circle by an arc whose length is equal to the radius of the circle.

The diagram shows a circle with radius r. The length of the arc is r, and the angle subtended at the centre of the circle is 1 radian.

The circumference of a circle is $2\pi r$. Therefore the number of radians in a full circle is $\dfrac{2\pi r}{r} = 2\pi \approx 6\cdot 28$ radians.

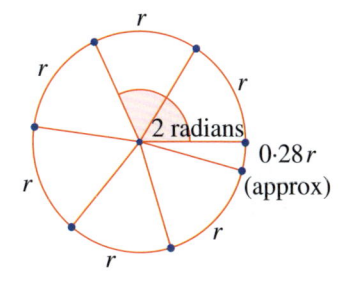

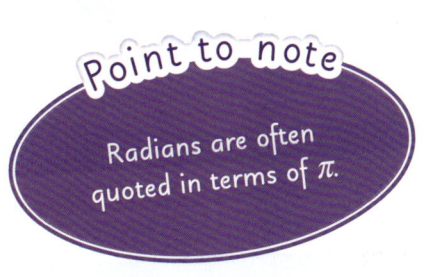

Point to note

Radians are often quoted in terms of π.

1. Trigonometry 1

Converting between degrees and radians

2π radians = a full circle = 360°, and π radians = a half circle = 180°.

Therefore, 1 radian = $\dfrac{360°}{2\pi} \approx 57\cdot296°$ and $1° = \dfrac{2\pi}{360°} \approx 0\cdot01745$ radians.

It is more accurate to use $\dfrac{180}{\pi}$ to convert from radians to degrees, and $\dfrac{\pi}{180}$ to convert from degrees to radians.

Radians	Degrees
Angle	Angle × $\dfrac{180}{\pi}$
$\dfrac{7}{36}\pi$	$\dfrac{7\pi}{36}\left(\dfrac{180}{\pi}\right) = 35°$
$\dfrac{7}{6}\pi$	$\dfrac{7\pi}{6}\left(\dfrac{180}{\pi}\right) = 210°$

Degrees	Radians
Angle	Angle × $\dfrac{\pi}{180}$ (simplify if possible)
35°	$35 \times \dfrac{\pi}{180} = \dfrac{35}{180}\pi = \dfrac{7}{36}\pi$
210°	$210 \times \dfrac{\pi}{180} = \dfrac{210}{180}\pi = \dfrac{7}{6}\pi$

Length of an arc and area of a sector

The formulae for the length of an arc and the area of a sector are on page 9 of the *Formulae and Tables* booklet.

If the angle is in radians:
- length of arc = $l = r\theta$
- area of sector = $A = \dfrac{1}{2}r^2\theta$.

If the angle is in degrees:
- length of arc = $l = 2\pi r\left(\dfrac{\theta}{360°}\right)$
- area of sector = $A = \pi r^2\left(\dfrac{\theta}{360°}\right)$.

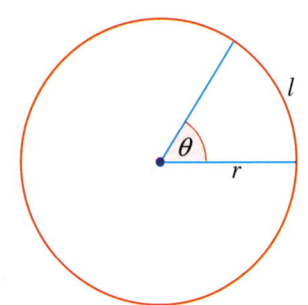

> **Top Tip**
> Check if the angle given in the question is in degrees or radians, and make sure to use the correct formula for finding length of arc and area of sector.

Degrees → radians: Angle × π/180

Radians → degrees: Angle × 180/π

Examples

A company is considering a new logo. The design of the logo is shown in the diagram.

O is the centre of the circle, and the radius of the circle is 9 cm. The angle about the centre is $\frac{\pi}{3}$ radians.

(a) Find the perimeter of the shaded region $BCDE$ correct to 2 decimal places.

(b) Find the area of the shaded region $BCDE$ in terms of π.

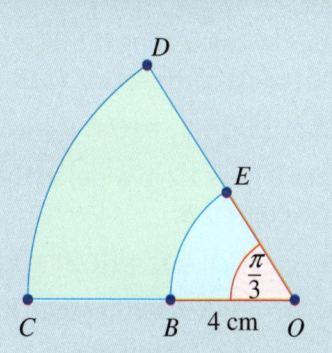

Solutions

(a) Perimeter of $BCDE = |BC| + |ED|$ + length of arc CD + length of arc BE

Length of arc CD (angle in radians) $= r\theta = 9\left(\frac{\pi}{3}\right) = 3\pi$ cm

Length of arc BE (angle in radians) $= r\theta = 4\left(\frac{\pi}{3}\right) = \frac{4\pi}{3}$ cm

Perimeter of shaded region $= 5 + 5 + 3\pi + \frac{4\pi}{3} = 10 + \frac{13\pi}{3} = 23 \cdot 61$ cm

(b) Area of shaded region = area of sector OCD − area of sector OBE

Area of sector OCD (angle in radians) $= \frac{1}{2}r^2\theta = \frac{1}{2}9^2\left(\frac{\pi}{3}\right) = \frac{81\pi}{6}$ cm^2

Area of sector OBE (angle in radians) $= \frac{1}{2}r^2\theta = \frac{1}{2}4^2\left(\frac{\pi}{3}\right) = \frac{16\pi}{6}$ cm^2

Area of shaded region $= \frac{81\pi}{6} - \frac{16\pi}{6} = \frac{65\pi}{6}$ cm^2

Example

The diagram shows part of the circular end of a running track with three running lanes shown. The centre of each of the circular boundaries of the lanes is at O.

Kate runs in the middle of lane 1, from A to B as shown.

Helen runs in the middle of lane 2, from C to D as shown.

Helen runs 3 m further than Kate.

$|\angle AOB| = |\angle COD| = \theta$ radians.

If each lane is 1·2 m wide, find θ.

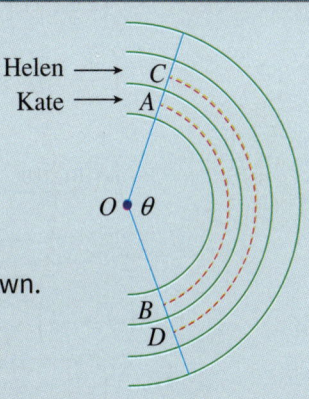

(SEC 2014)

Solution

Start by calculating the distance covered by each runner in terms of r, where r is the radius of the sector OAB.

Kate: $|AB| = s_1 = |OA|\theta = r\theta$

Each lane is 1·2 m wide, so the radius of sector OCD is 1·2 m longer than the radius of sector OAB.

Helen: $|CD| = s_2 = (|OA| + 1·2)\theta = (r + 1·2)\theta$

Helen runs 3 m further than Kate, so $s_1 + 3 = s_2$

$\Rightarrow r\theta + 3 = r\theta + 1·2\theta$

$\Rightarrow 1·2\theta = 3$

$\Rightarrow \theta = 2·5$ radians

The unit circle

This diagram shows the signs of trigonometric functions in each of the four quadrants. This information can be useful for evaluating trigonometric equations.

You can see that in the first quadrant, All the functions are positive. In the second quadrant, only Sin is positive. In the third quadrant, only Tan is positive, and in the fourth quadrant only Cos is positive.

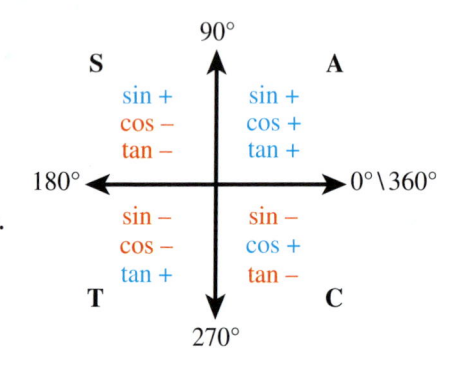

$(x, y) = (\cos A, \sin A) = $ (Christian name, surname)

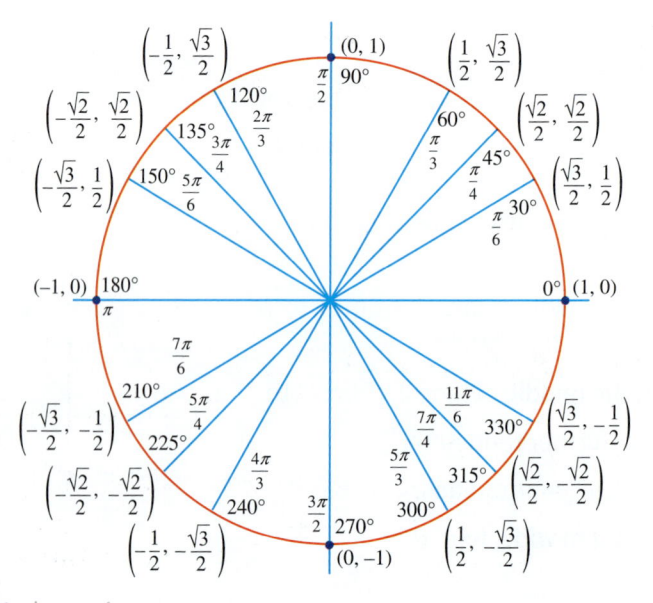

The unit circle diagram on page 8 gives x and y values on a circle of radius 1 at key angles. At any point on the unit circle, the x co-ordinate is equal to the cos of the angle produced and the y co-ordinate is equal to the sin of the angle produced. Using this diagram, we can see the pattern of sines and cosines of angles that occur frequently in trigonometric problems.

Example

If $\sin \theta = \dfrac{1}{2}$, find two values of θ, where $0° \leq \theta \leq 360°$.

Solution

The required angles are in the first and second quadrants, since $\sin \theta$ is positive in both quadrants.

From the unit circle diagram we can see that the required angles are 30° and $180° - 30° = 50°$.

30° is the reference angle in this example.

> **Point to note**
>
> The reference angle is the trigonometric inverse of the positive value of the angle.

The method for solving simple trigonometric equations is:
1. Identify the quadrants that contain the solutions.
2. Find the reference angle in the first quadrant.
3. Use the key diagram to find the angles.
4. Check if angles required are in degrees or radians, and give the answer to the specified precision (nearest degree, etc.).

Example

If $\tan A = \dfrac{-1}{\sqrt{3}}$, find values for $\sin A$, where $0 \leq A \leq 2\pi$.

Solution

1. Identify the quadrants that contain the solutions.

   $\tan A$ is negative in the second and fourth quadrants.

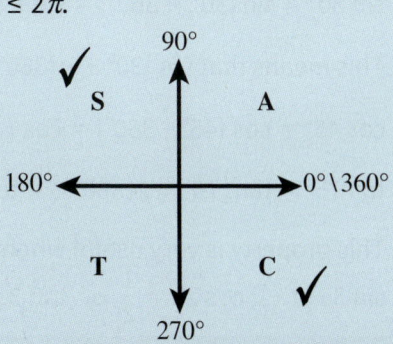

2. Find the reference angle in the first quadrant.

Reference angle = trigonometric inverse of positive value

$$= \tan^{-1}\frac{1}{\sqrt{3}} = \frac{\pi}{6}$$

3. Use the key diagram to find the angles.

> **Top Tip**
> Learn this key diagram.

We need the values in the second and fourth quadrants.

$$A = \pi - \frac{\pi}{6} = \frac{5\pi}{6} \text{ and } A = 2\pi - \frac{\pi}{6} = \frac{11\pi}{6}$$

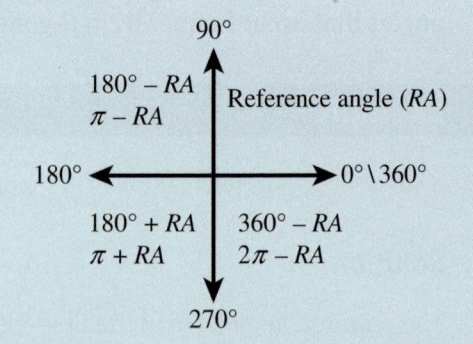

4. Check if angles required are in degrees or radians, and give the answer to the specified precision (nearest degree, etc.).

The question asks for the values of sin A.

$$\sin\frac{5\pi}{6} = \frac{1}{2}, \sin\frac{11\pi}{6} = -\frac{1}{2}$$

> **Top Tip**
> If you are evaluating trigonometric ratios where the angle is given in radians, either use your calculator in radian mode or convert the angle to degrees and use your calculator in degree mode (which can be easier).

Angles greater than 360°

Consider that sin 30° = $\frac{1}{2}$. If we add or subtract 360°, or whole number multiples of 360°, to the original angle we get the same result. The same applies to the two other basic trigonometric functions.

sin 30° = sin (30° + 360°) = sin (390°) = $\frac{1}{2}$

This means that sin [30° + n(360°)] = $\frac{1}{2}$, where $n \in \mathbb{Z}$.

cos 45° = cos (45° − 360°) = cos (−315°) = $\frac{\sqrt{2}}{2}$

tan 75° = tan [75° + 2(360°)] = tan (795°) = 2 + $\sqrt{3}$

This property is very useful when solving trigonometric equations of the type

sin 3x = −1, cos 2x = $\frac{1}{2}$ or tan 3x = 0.

Example

Solve $\cos 2x = \frac{1}{2}$, where $0° \leq x \leq 360°$.

Solution

We are solving for x here, where x is an angle in degrees.

$0° \leq x \leq 360° \Rightarrow 0° \leq 2x \leq 720°$

We now know that we must include angles greater than 360° to solve for x in this question.

Solve as shown in the previous example.

1. Identify the quadrants that contain the solutions.

   $\cos 2x$ is positive in the first and fourth quadrants.

2. Find the reference angle in the first quadrant.

   Reference angle = $\cos^{-1} \frac{1}{2} = 60°$

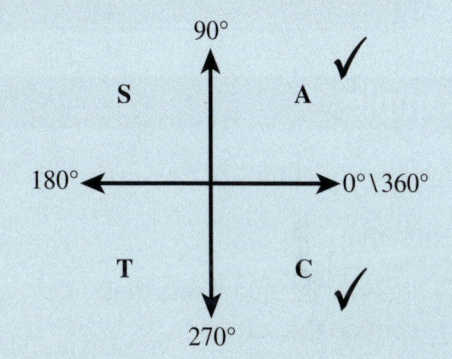

3. Use the key diagram to find the angles.

   We need the values in the first and fourth quadrants.

   $2x = 60°$ or $2x = 360 - 60 = 300°$

4. Check if angles required are in degrees or radians, and give the answer to the specified precision (nearest degree, etc.).

   The question asks for all solutions where $0° \leq x \leq 360°$. To find all solutions, add $n(360°)$ to each angle, where $n = 0, 1, 2, \ldots$

   $2x = 60 \Rightarrow x = 30°$

   $2x = 60 + 360 = 420 \Rightarrow x = 210°$

   $2x = 300 \Rightarrow x = 150°$

   $2x = 300 + 360 = 660 \Rightarrow x = 330°$

   Further multiples of 360° produce values of x that are outside the required range, so the values of x are 30°, 120°, 150°, 330°.

> **Point to note**
>
> This question could also be asked as a graph question, where $f(x) = \cos 2x$, $g(x) = \frac{1}{2}$ and we are asked to solve for x from the graph where $f(x) = g(x)$.

1. Trigonometry 1

General solutions of trigonometric equations

sin x	cos x	tan x
$x + n(360°)$ where $n \in \mathbb{Z}$	$x + n(360°)$ where $n \in \mathbb{Z}$	$x + n(180°)$ where $n \in \mathbb{Z}$
$x + n(2\pi)$ where $n \in \mathbb{Z}$	$x + n(2\pi)$ where $n \in \mathbb{Z}$	$x + n(\pi)$ where $n \in \mathbb{Z}$

Point to note

If the given angle is $2x$, $3x$, etc. then divide the general solutions by 2, 3, etc.

Example

Solve the equation $\cos 3\theta = \dfrac{1}{2}$ for $\theta \in \mathbb{R}$ (where θ is in radians). *(SEC 2010)*

Solution

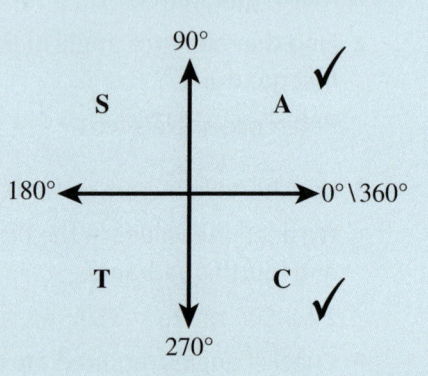

1. Identify the quadrants that contain the solutions.

   $\cos 3\theta$ is positive in the first and fourth quadrants.

2. Find the reference angle in the first quadrant.

   Reference angle $= \cos^{-1}\dfrac{1}{2} = \dfrac{\pi}{3}$

3. Use the key diagram to find the angles.

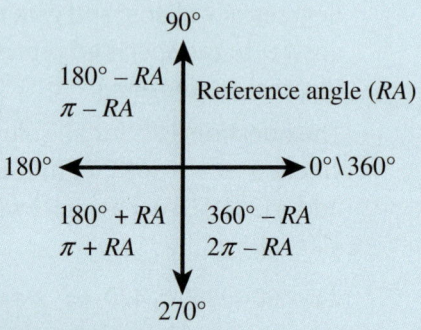

   We need the values in the first and fourth quadrants.

   $3\theta = \dfrac{\pi}{3}$ or $3\theta = 2\pi - \dfrac{\pi}{3} = \dfrac{5\pi}{3}$

4. Check if angles required are in degrees or radians, and give the answer to the specified precision (nearest degree, etc.).

   The question asks for all solutions in $\mathbb{R}$, so we need to give the solutions in the general form.

   $3\theta = \dfrac{\pi}{3} + 2n\pi \Rightarrow \theta = \dfrac{\pi}{9} + \dfrac{2n\pi}{3}$, where $n \in \mathbb{Z}$

   $3\theta = \dfrac{5\pi}{3} + 2n\pi \Rightarrow \theta = \dfrac{5\pi}{9} + \dfrac{2n\pi}{3}$, where $n \in \mathbb{Z}$

12 Revise Wise • Mathematics

Graphs of trigonometric functions

Period and range

There are many naturally occurring wave patterns, such as ocean waves, sound waves and light waves. There are also wave patterns in science and engineering, such as the pattern in the voltage of an electric circuit.

Graphs of trigonometric functions, e.g. sine and cosine graphs, have a wave pattern called a **sinusoid**. They are **periodic functions**, also called **oscillating functions (wave-type)**, which means that they repeat a pattern of y values at regular intervals. One complete repetition of the pattern is a called a **cycle**.

The **period** of a trigonometric function is the horizontal length of one complete cycle.

The **range** of a trigonometric function is the interval from the minimum (lowest y value) to the maximum (highest y value).

The **amplitude** of a sinusoidal function is the height of the graph = $\frac{1}{2}|\max - \min|$.

Consider the sine function shown below.

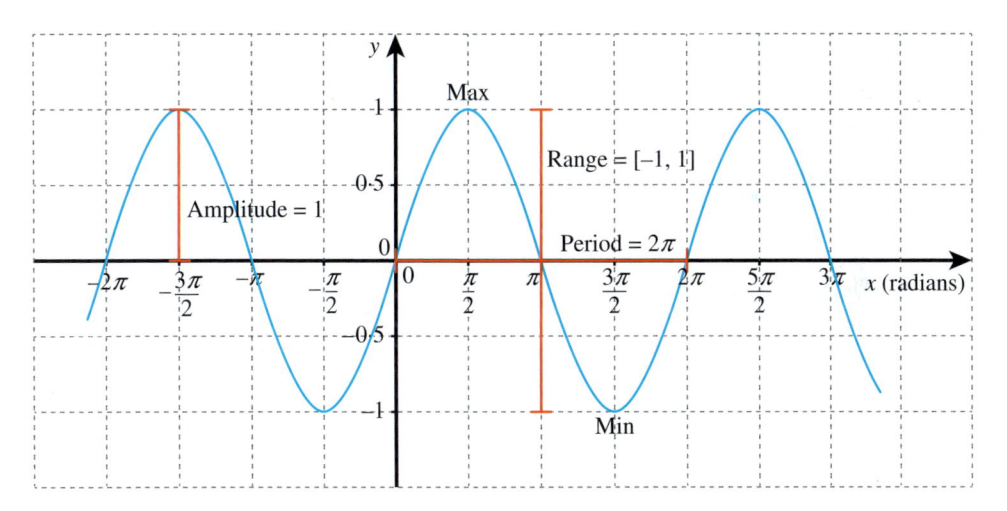

For $f(x) = \sin x$:
- period = 2π = 360°
- domain = $(-\infty, \infty)$ (all real numbers)
- x intercepts ..., $-2\pi, -\pi, 0, \pi, 2\pi, ...$ = $n\pi$, where $n \in \mathbb{Z}$
- range = $[-1, 1]$
- amplitude = 1
- rotational symmetry about the origin.

Consider the cosine function shown below.

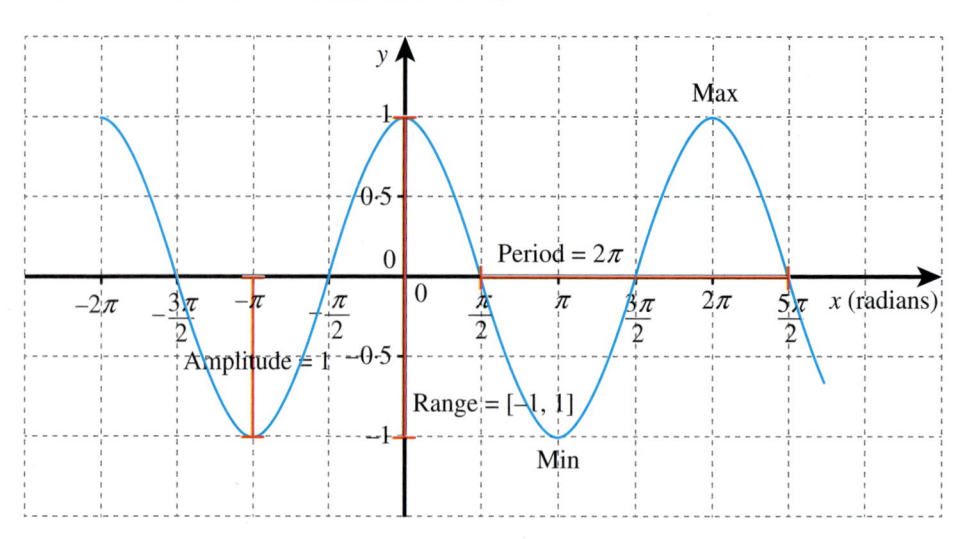

For $f(x) = \cos x$:
- period = 2π = 360°
- domain = $(-\infty, \infty)$ (all real numbers)
- x intercepts ..., $-\dfrac{3\pi}{2}, -\dfrac{\pi}{2}, \dfrac{\pi}{2}, \dfrac{3\pi}{2}$, ... = $\dfrac{n\pi}{2}$, where $n \in \mathbb{Z}$, n is odd
- range = $[-1, 1]$
- amplitude = 1
- reflectional symmetry in the y-axis.

Consider the tangent function shown below.

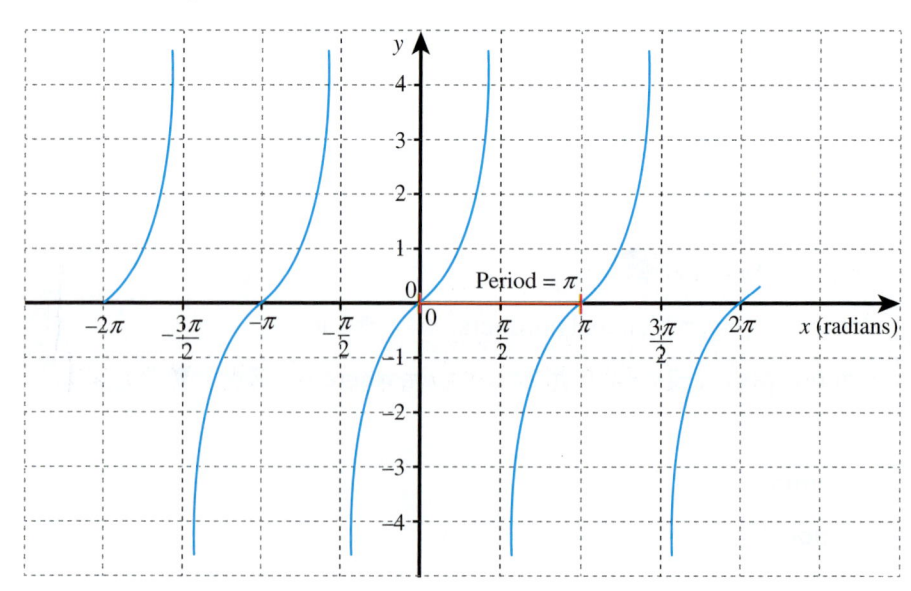

For $f(x) = \tan x$:

- period = π = 180°
- domain = $(-\infty, \infty)$ (all real numbers)
- x intercepts ..., $-2\pi, -\pi, 0, \pi, 2\pi, ... = n\pi$, where $n \in \mathbb{Z}$
- range = $\mathbb{R}$ (real numbers)
- undefined at the vertical asymptotes $x = ..., -\dfrac{3\pi}{2}, -\dfrac{\pi}{2}, \dfrac{\pi}{2}, \dfrac{3\pi}{2}, ...$
- rotational symmetry about the origin.

Consider the graphs of $\sin x$, $2\sin x$ and $3\sin x$ as shown in the diagram. If we take $\sin x$ as the parent or basic graph, the range of the other graphs changes. The graphs are stretched vertically but the period of all three graphs remains the same.

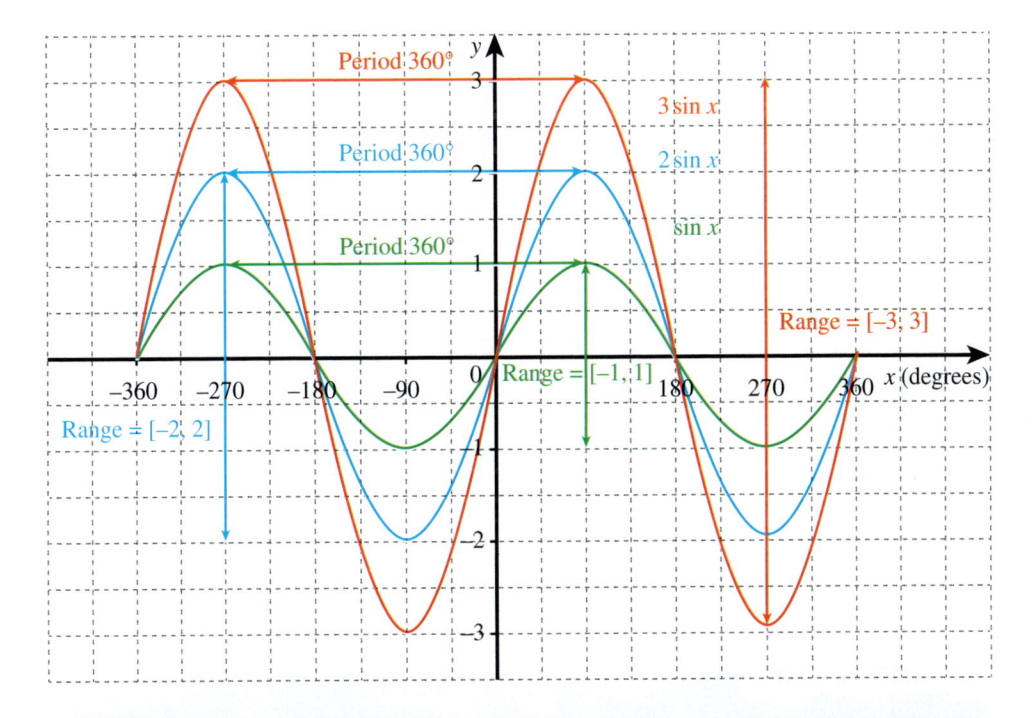

> **Point to note**
>
> $b \sin x$ has period 2π = 360° and range $[-b, b]$.
>
> $b \cos x$ has period 2π = 360° and range $[-b, b]$.

What happens to $b \sin x$ or $b \cos x$ if b is negative?

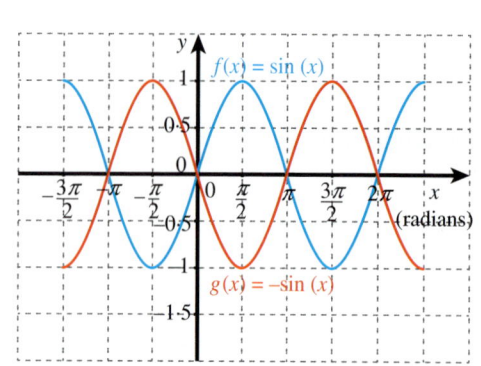

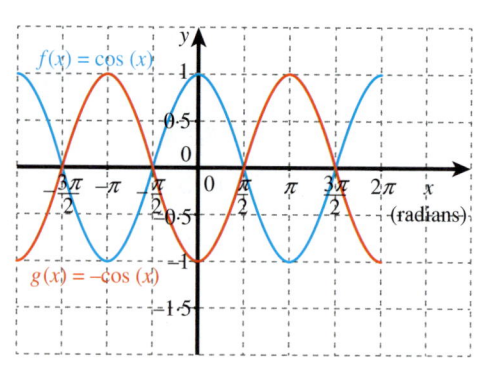

$b = -1 \Rightarrow b \sin x = -\sin x$, the reflection of $\sin x$ in the x-axis.

$b = -1 \Rightarrow b \cos x = -\cos x$, the reflection of $\cos x$ in the x-axis.

Consider the graphs of $\sin x$, $\sin(2x)$ and $\sin\left(\dfrac{x}{2}\right)$ as shown in the diagram.

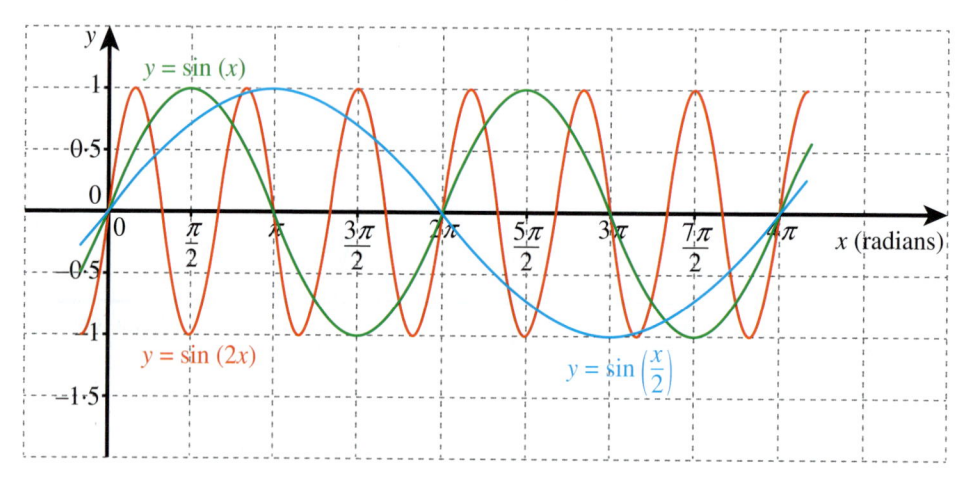

If we take $\sin x$ as the parent or basic graph, the range does not change but the period does. The graph is stretched or shrunk horizontally.

Point to note

$\sin(cx)$ has period $\dfrac{2\pi}{c}$ and range $[-1, 1]$.

$\cos(cx)$ has period $\dfrac{2\pi}{c}$ and range $[-1, 1]$.

Summary

Function	Period	Range
$b \sin(c\theta)$	$\frac{2\pi}{c}$	$[-b, b]$
$b \cos(c\theta)$	$\frac{2\pi}{c}$	$[-b, b]$
$b \tan(c\theta)$	$\frac{\pi}{c}$	$\mathbb{R}$ (real numbers)

Example

The graphs of three functions are shown on the diagram below. The scales on the axes are not labelled. The three functions are:

$x \mapsto \cos 3x$

$x \mapsto 2 \cos 3x$

$x \mapsto 3 \cos 2x$

Identify which function is which.

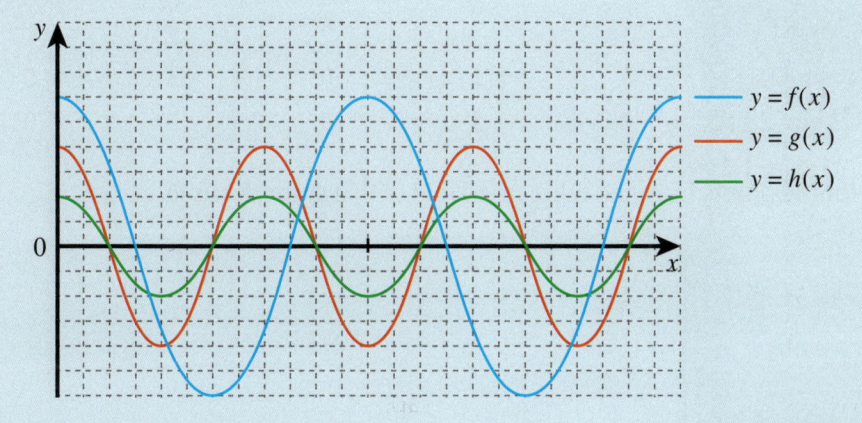

(SEC 2010)

Solution

$\cos 3x$ and $2 \cos 3x$ have the same period, but $2 \cos 3x$ has twice the range of $\cos 3x$.

$g(x)$ and $h(x)$ have the same period, and $g(x)$ has twice the range of $h(x)$. Therefore, $g(x) = 2 \cos 3x$ and $h(x) = \cos 3x$.

$f(x)$ has a different period to the other two functions, so $f(x) = 3 \cos 2x$.

Examples

The function $f(x) = 3\sin(2x)$ is defined for $x \in \mathbb{R}$.

(a) Complete the table below.

x	0	$\frac{\pi}{4}$	$\frac{\pi}{2}$	$\frac{3\pi}{4}$	π
$2x$					
$\sin(2x)$					
$3\sin(2x)$					

(b) Draw the graph of $y = f(x)$ in the domain $0 \leq x \leq \pi$, $x \in \mathbb{R}$.

(c) Write down the range and period of f.

(SEC Sample 2010)

Solutions

(a)

x	0	$\frac{\pi}{4}$	$\frac{\pi}{2}$	$\frac{3\pi}{4}$	π
$2x$	0	$\frac{\pi}{2}$	π	$\frac{3\pi}{2}$	2π
$\sin(2x)$	0	1	0	-1	0
$3\sin(2x)$	0	3	0	-3	0

(b) Plot the points from the table, then join with a smooth curve.

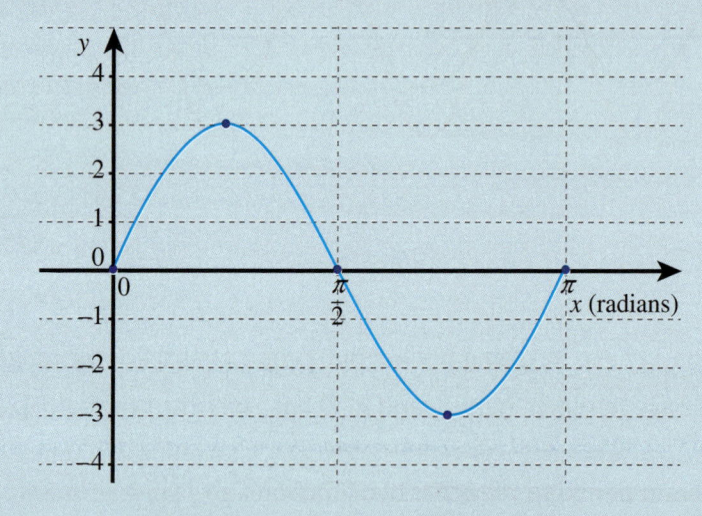

(c) $b \sin cx$ has a range of $[-b, b]$ and a period of $\frac{2\pi}{c}$.

Therefore, $3 \sin 2x$ has a range of $[-3, 3]$ and a period of $\frac{2\pi}{2} = \pi$.

Graphs of trigonometric functions plus a constant

Consider graphs of the form $f(\theta) = a + b\sin(c\theta)$ and $g(\theta) = a + b\cos(c\theta)$ for $a, b, c \in \mathbb{R}$.

We have already seen that b changes the range and c changes the period.

The effect of a on trigonometric graphs is to move or translate the graphs vertically.

Examples

Find the period and range of the following trigonometric functions:

(a) $f(x) = 3\sin(2\theta)$

(b) $g(x) = 2\cos(3\theta)$

(c) $h(x) = 4\tan\left(\dfrac{\theta}{2}\right)$

(d) $f(x) + 3$.

Solutions

(a) Period = $\dfrac{2\pi}{2} = \pi$, Range = $[-3, 3]$

(b) Period = $\dfrac{2\pi}{3}$, Range = $[-2, 2]$

(c) Period = $\dfrac{\pi}{\frac{1}{2}} = 2\pi$, Range = $\mathbb{R}$

(d) $f(x) + 3$ is $f(x)$ moved 3 units up (vertically), so the range changes but the period does not.

Period = π, Range = $[-3 + 3, 3 + 3] = [0, 6]$

Summary

Function	Period	Range
$a + b\sin c\theta$	$\dfrac{2\pi}{c}$	$[-b + a, b + a]$
$a + b\cos c\theta$	$\dfrac{2\pi}{c}$	$[-b + a, b + a]$

Examples

The graph below shows the voltage, V, in an electric circuit as a function of time, t. The voltage is given by the formula $V = 311 \sin(100\pi t)$, where V is in volts and t is in seconds.

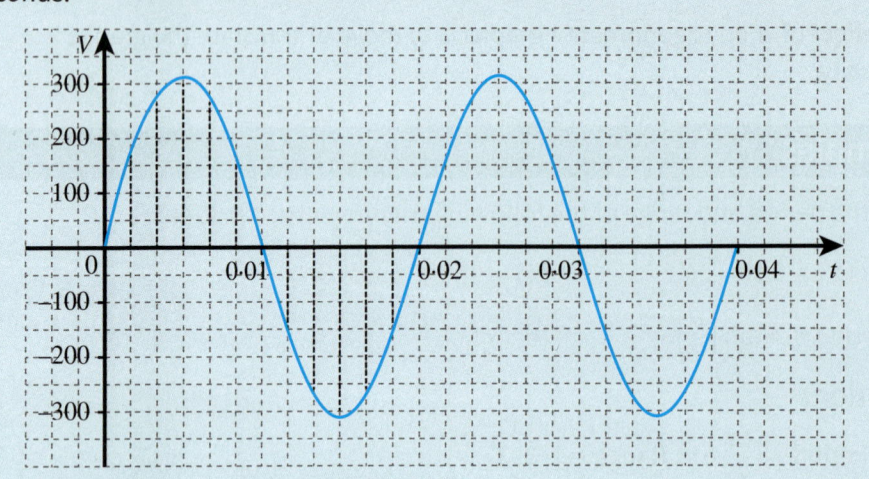

(a) (i) Write down the range of the function.

   (ii) How many complete periods are there in one second?

(b) (i) The table below gives the voltage, correct to the nearest whole number, at equally spaced intervals from t_0 to t_{12} over one complete period (as shown by the dashed lines on the diagram). Use the entries given in the table and the properties of the function to complete the table.

T	t_1	t_2	t_3	t_4	t_5	$t_6 = 0.01$	t_7	t_8	t_9	t_{10}	t_{11}	$t_{12} = 0.02$
V	156	269	311									

   (ii) Using a calculator, or otherwise, calculate the standard deviation, σ, of the twelve values of V in the table, correct to the nearest whole number.

(c) (i) The standard deviation, σ, of closely spaced values of any function of the form $V = a\sin(bt)$, over 1 full period, is given by $k\sigma = V_{max}$, where k is a constant that does not depend on a or b, and V_{max} is the maximum value of the function. Use the function $V = 311\sin(100\pi t)$ to find an approximate value for k correct to 3 decimal places.

   (ii) Using your answer in part (c) (i), or otherwise, find the value of b required so that the function $V = a\sin(bt)$ has 60 complete periods in one second and the approximate value of a so that it has a standard deviation of 110 volts.

(SEC 2014)

Solutions

(a) (i) Range = [−311, 311]

(ii) **Method one**

Period = $\dfrac{2\pi}{100\pi} = \dfrac{1}{50}$ seconds

Periods per second = 50

Method two

From the graph, 1 period = 0·02 seconds.

Periods per second = $\dfrac{1}{0\cdot 02} = 50$.

(b) (i) Given the first three values in the table, the other values can be deduced by looking at the pattern of the graph.

T	t_1	t_2	t_3	t_4	t_5	$t_6 = 0\cdot01$	t_7	t_8	t_9	t_{10}	t_{11}	$t_{12} = 0\cdot02$
V	156	269	311	269	156	0	−156	−269	−311	−269	−156	0

(ii) $\sigma = 219\cdot 89 = 220$

(c) (i) $k = \dfrac{V_{max}}{\sigma} = \dfrac{311}{220} \approx 1\cdot 414$

(ii) The number of complete periods in one second is $\dfrac{b}{2\pi}$.

$\dfrac{b}{2\pi} = 60 \Rightarrow b = 120\pi = 377$

$k\sigma = V_{max} \Rightarrow V_{max} = 1\cdot 414 \times 110 = 155\cdot 54$

The range of the function is [−a, a] so $V_{max} = 155\cdot 54 \Rightarrow a = 155\cdot 54 \approx 156$

Checklist

✓ Be familiar with the relevant pages on trigonometry in the *Formulae and Tables* booklet.

✓ Make sure your calculator is in the correct mode: degrees or radians.

✓ Draw trigonometry graphs using a pencil.

✓ Make sure that graph scales are correct. Check if the *x*-axis is in degrees or radians.

✓ Remember the key diagrams for solving trigonometric equations and the summaries for trigonometric graphs.

✓ Read the question carefully for the final answer: is it to the nearest degree, correct to 1 decimal place, in terms of π, etc.?

2 Trigonometry 2

Learning objectives

In this chapter you will learn how to:
- Use the formula $A = \frac{1}{2}ab \sin C$ for the area of a triangle to solve problems and find the area of a segment
- Solve 2D problems using the sine and cosine rules, including the ambiguous case
- Use trigonometry to solve problems in 3D
- Derive trigonometric formulae 1–8
- Apply trigonometric formulae 1–24.

Area of a triangle

The formulae for the area of a triangle are on page 9 of the *Formulae and Tables* booklet.

If you have the perpendicular height and length of base of the triangle use $A = \frac{1}{2}ah$.

If you have the length of two sides and the included angle between the sides use $A = \frac{1}{2}ab \sin C$. You can use this formula to find the area of non-right-angled triangles where the perpendicular height is not given.

Given a triangle with sides a, b and c, the area, A, is given by the formula $A = \sqrt{s(s-a)(s-b)(s-c)}$, where $s = \frac{a+b+c}{2}$.

Examples

Find the area of the following triangles correct to one decimal place:

(a) Triangle with $AB = \sqrt{20}$, $BC = 4$, $AC = x$, right angle at C.

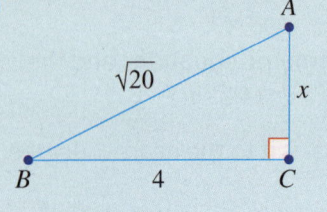

(b) Triangle XYZ with $XY = 6$ cm, $XZ = 10$ cm, angle $X = 35°$.

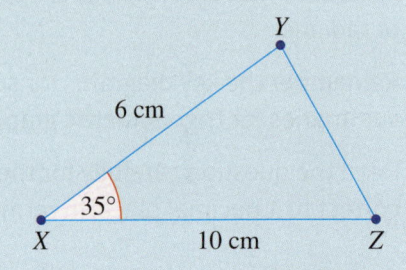

Solutions

(a) First find length x, which is the perpendicular height of the triangle. It is a right-angled triangle, so we can use Pythagoras' theorem.

$(\sqrt{20})^2 = x^2 + 4^2$

$\Rightarrow x^2 = 20 - 16 = 4$

$\Rightarrow x = 2$

Now use the formula $A = \frac{1}{2}ah$.

$A = \frac{1}{2}(4)(2) = 4$ square units

(b) We don't have the perpendicular height, but we do have two sides and the included angle, so use $A = \frac{1}{2}ab \sin C$.

$A = \frac{1}{2}(6)(10) \sin(35°)$

$= 30 \sin 35° = 17 \cdot 21$ cm²

Area of a segment

Area of segment = area of sector − area of triangle

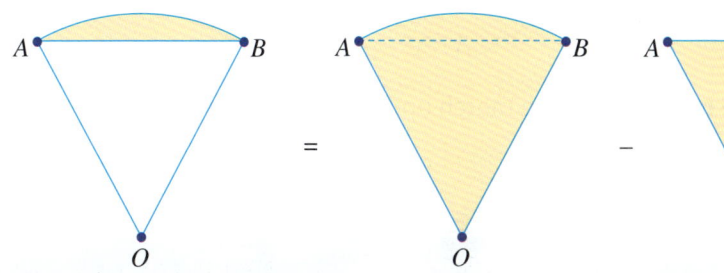

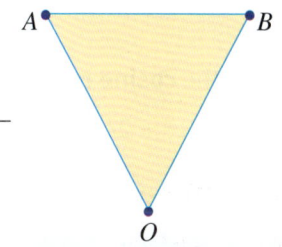

Example

O is the centre of a circle. OA is the radius of the circle. Find the area of the segment (shaded region) correct to 2 decimal places.

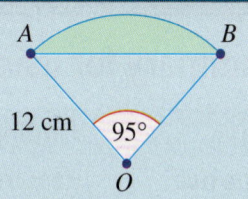

Solution

Area of segment = area of sector OAB − area of triangle OAB

Area of sector $OAB = \frac{\theta}{360} \times \pi r^2 = \frac{95}{360} \times \pi(12)^2 = 38\pi = 119 \cdot 38$ cm²

Area of triangle $OAB = \frac{1}{2}ab \sin C = \frac{1}{2}(12)(12) \sin 95° = \frac{1}{2}(144) \sin 95°$

$= 71 \cdot 73$ cm²

Area of segment = $119 \cdot 38 - 71 \cdot 73 = 47 \cdot 65$ cm²

Sine rule and cosine rule

The **sine and cosine rules** are on page 16 of the *Formulae and Tables* booklet. We use these formulae to solve non-right-angled triangles. It is very important to label the triangle carefully.

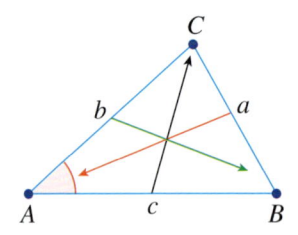

To use the **sine rule** you need a **matching pair** of **side with angle**. You need to know one angle, and the side opposite it.

$$\frac{a}{\sin A} = \frac{b}{\sin B} = \frac{c}{\sin C}$$

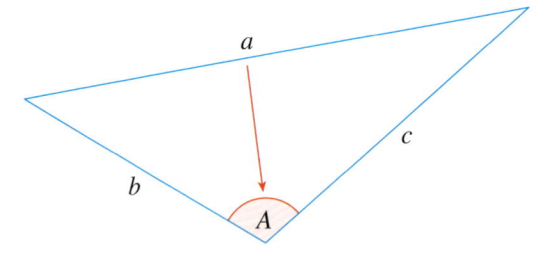

To use the **cosine rule** you need to match up **angle A with side a**.

$$a^2 = b^2 + c^2 - 2bc \cos A$$

> **Point to note**
>
> In a triangle the shortest side is opposite the smallest angle, and the longest side is opposite the largest angle.

Summary for using sine rule and cosine rule

Rule	Finding sides	Finding angles
Sine rule	Require two angles and any side	Require two sides and a non-included angle
Cosine rule	Require two sides and included angle	Require all three sides

Example

Find ∠PRQ correct to 2 decimal places.

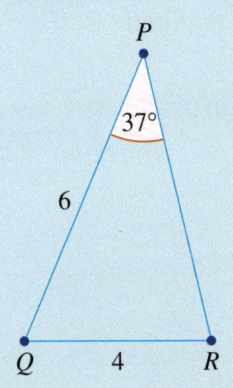

Solution

Label the required angle, and match sides to angles.

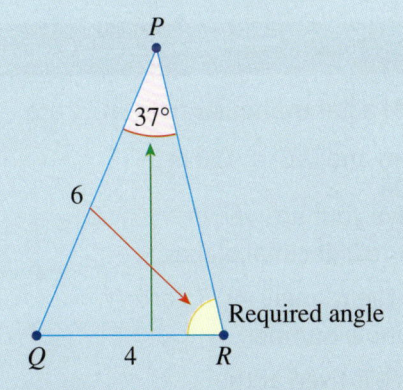

We have two sides and a non-included angle, so we can use the sine rule.

$$\frac{a}{\sin A} = \frac{b}{\sin B} \Rightarrow \frac{(4)}{\sin(37°)} = \frac{(6)}{\sin(R)}$$

$\Rightarrow 4 \sin R = 6 \sin 37°$

$\Rightarrow \sin R = \dfrac{6 \sin 37°}{4} = 0.902723$

$\Rightarrow R = \sin^{-1}(0.902723) = 64.52°$

Example

Find the largest angle in $\triangle ABC$ given the lengths of the three sides. Give your answer to the nearest degree.

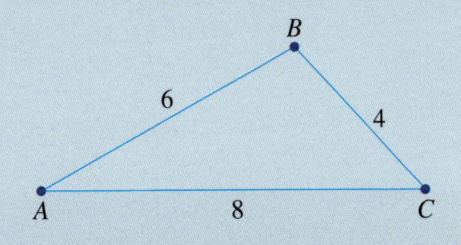

2. Trigonometry 2

Solution

The largest angle is the angle opposite the longest side, angle B. Label the required angle, and label each side.

We have all three sides, so we can use the cosine rule.

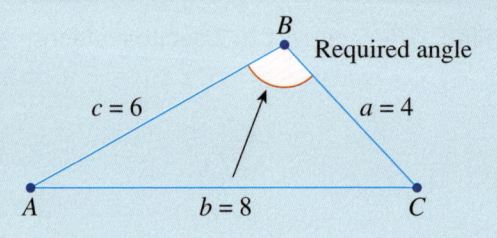

$b^2 = a^2 + c^2 - 2ac \cos B$

$\Rightarrow \cos B = \dfrac{a^2 + c^2 - b^2}{2ac}$

$\cos B = \dfrac{(4)^2 + (6)^2 - (8)^2}{2(4)(6)} = -\dfrac{12}{48} = -\dfrac{1}{4}$

$\Rightarrow B = \cos^{-1}\left(-\dfrac{1}{4}\right) = 104\cdot4775 = 104°$ to the nearest degree

Examples

The lengths of the sides of a flat triangular field ACB are $|AB| = 120$ m, $|BC| = 134$ m and $|AC| = 150$ m.

(a) (i) Find $|\angle CBA|$. Give your answer, in degrees, correct to 2 decimal places.

(ii) Find the area of the triangle ACB correct to the nearest whole number.

(b) A vertical mast, $[DE]$, is fixed at the circumcentre, D, of the triangle. The mast is held in place by three taut cables $[EA]$, $[EB]$ and $[EC]$. Explain why the three cables are equal in length.

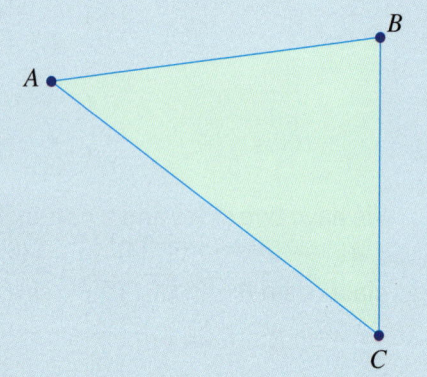

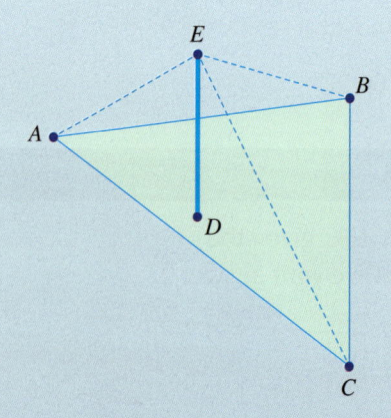

(SEC 2014)

Solutions

(a) (i) We know the lengths of the three sides, so we can use the cosine rule. We need to find angle B. The sides are $c = |AB| = 120$ m, $a = |BC| = 134$ m and $b = |AC| = 150$ m.

$$\cos B = \frac{a^2 + c^2 - b^2}{2ac}$$

$$= \frac{(134)^2 + (120)^2 - (150)^2}{2(134)(120)}$$

$$= \frac{9856}{32\,160} = 0 \cdot 306468$$

$\Rightarrow B = \cos^{-1} 0 \cdot 306468 = 72 \cdot 15°$

(ii) Method one: Use two sides and included angle

$$A = \frac{1}{2} ac \sin B = \frac{1}{2}(134)(120) \sin 72 \cdot 15°$$

$$= 7652 \cdot 97 = 7653 \text{ m}^2$$

Method two: Use three sides

$A = \sqrt{s(s-a)(s-b)(s-c)}$ where $s = \dfrac{a+b+c}{2}$.

$$s = \frac{134 + 150 + 120}{2} = 202$$

$$A = \sqrt{202(202-134)(202-150)(202-120)} = \sqrt{58\,570\,304}$$

$$= 7653 \cdot 12 = 7653 \text{ m}^2$$

(b) Circumcentre at $D \Rightarrow |AD| = |BD| = |CD|$

> **Remember**
> The circumcentre of a triangle is the place where the perpendicular bisectors of all three sides intersect. This point is the same distance from all three vertices.

Each of the triangles EAD, EBD and ECD is right-angled at D and has two sides (the base and the perpendicular) equal. Hence, by Pythagoras' theorem, the third side of each (the cables) must be equal.

Examples

The diagram is a representation of a robotic arm that can move in a vertical plane. The point P is fixed, and so are the lengths of the two segments of the arm. The controller can vary the angles α and β from $0°$ to $180°$.

(a) Given that $|PQ| = 20$ cm and $|QR| = 12$ cm, determine the values of the angles α and β so as to locate R, the tip of the arm, at a point that is 24 cm to the right of P, and 7 cm higher than P.

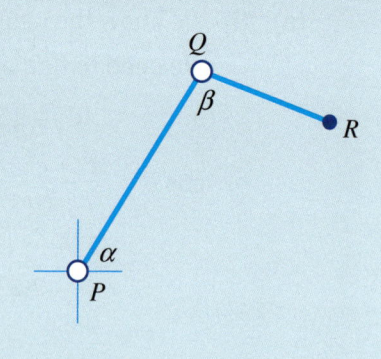

Give your answers correct to the nearest degree.

(b) In setting the arm to the position described in part (a), which will cause the greater error in the location of R: an error of $1°$ in the value of α or an error of $1°$ in the value of β?

Justify your answer. You may assume that if a point moves along a circle through a small angle, then its distance from its starting point is equal to the length of the arc travelled.

(c) The answer to part (b) above depends on the particular position of the arm. That is, in certain positions, the location of R is more sensitive to small errors in α than to small errors in β, while in other positions, the reverse is true. Describe, with justification, the conditions under which each of these two situations arises.

(d) Illustrate the set of all possible locations of the point R on a co-ordinate diagram. Take P as the origin and take each unit in the diagram to represent a centimetre in reality.

Note that α and β can vary only from $0°$ to $180°$. (SEC 2012)

Solutions

(a) Draw a diagram including the extra information given in the question.

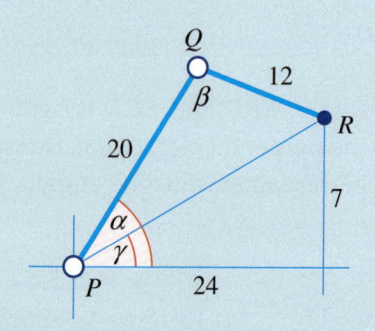

The distance $|PR|$ is the hypotenuse of a right-angled triangle, with the other two sides being the given horizontal and vertical distances of R from P. Therefore, we can use Pythagoras' theorem to calculate $|PR|$.

$|PR|^2 = 7^2 + 24^2 \Rightarrow |PR| = 25$

Now we have the three sides of triangle PQR we can use the cosine rule to calculate angles α and β.

$\cos A = \dfrac{b^2 + c^2 - a^2}{2bc}$ where $A = (\alpha - \gamma)$, $a = |QR|$, $b = |PR|$, $c = |PQ|$

$\Rightarrow \cos(\alpha - \gamma) = \dfrac{(25)^2 + (20)^2 - (12)^2}{2(25)(20)} = 0.881$

$\Rightarrow \alpha - \gamma = \cos^{-1} 0.881 = 28.237°$

We can find γ using basic trigonometry.

$\tan \gamma = \dfrac{7}{24} \Rightarrow \gamma = 16.260°$

$\alpha = 28.237 + 16.260 = 44.497 \approx 44°$

$\cos B = \dfrac{a^2 + c^2 - b^2}{2ac}$ where $B = \beta$, $a = |QR|$, $b = |PR|$, $c = |PQ|$

$\Rightarrow \cos \beta = \dfrac{(12)^2 + (20)^2 - (25)^2}{2(12)(20)} = -0.16875$

$\Rightarrow \beta = \cos^{-1} -0.16875 = 99.72 \approx 100°$

So $\alpha = 44°$, $\beta = 100°$

(b) Answer: an error of 1° in the value of α will cause a greater error in the position of R.

Reason: a 1° error in the value of α causes R to move along an arc of radius 25. A 1° error in the value of β causes R to move along an arc of radius 12. Since $l = r\theta$, and θ is 1° in each case, the point moves further in the first case.

(c) The location of R is more sensitive to errors in α when $|PR| > 12$, and more sensitive to errors in β when $|PR| < 12$. This can be justified by the explanation in part (b).

$|PR| > 12$ when $\beta > \cos^{-1}\left(\dfrac{(20)^2 + (12)^2 - (12)^2}{2(20)(12)}\right) = \cos^{-1}\left(\dfrac{5}{6}\right) \approx 33.6°$

(d) To draw the diagram, think about the possible locations for R given different options for α and β.

- If $\beta = 0°$ then the possible locations of R form a semicircle of radius $20 - 12 = 8$ cm, centre P, above the x-axis.
- If $\beta = 180°$ then the possible locations of R form a semicircle above the x-axis of radius $20 + 12 = 32$ cm, centre P.

- If $\alpha = 0°$ then the possible locations of R form a semicircle below the x-axis of radius 12 cm, centre 20 cm to the right of P.
- If $\alpha = 180°$ then the possible locations of R form a semicircle above the x-axis of radius 12 cm, centre 20 cm to the left of P.

The four semicircles form a boundary for the possible locations of R.

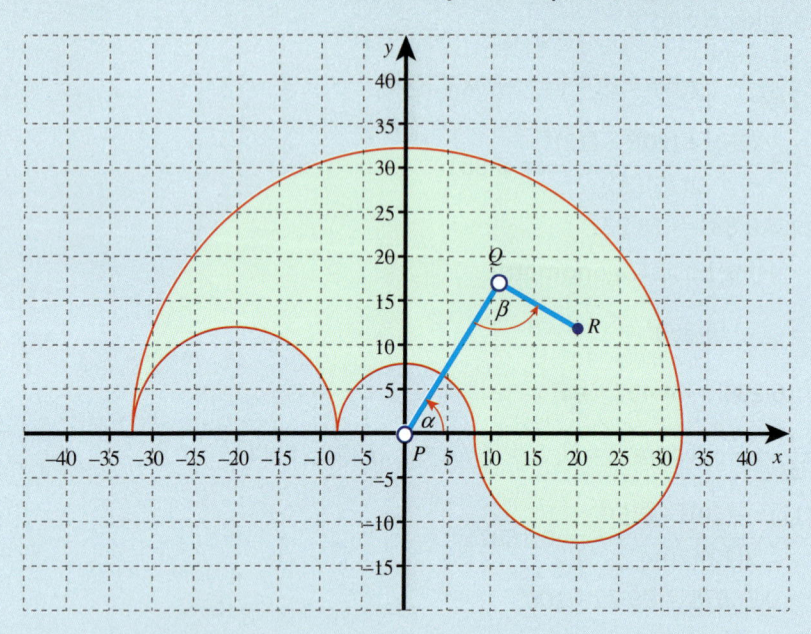

Example

ABC is a triangle and D is a point on $[BC]$.
The lengths $|AB|$, $|AD|$, $|AC|$ and $|BD|$ are as shown in the diagram.

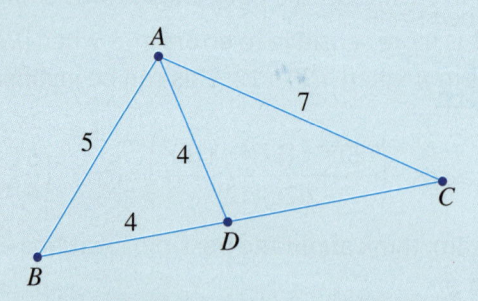

Find $|DC|$, correct to 1 decimal place.

(SEC Sample 2010)

Solution

Label the sides of the triangles as shown in the diagram.

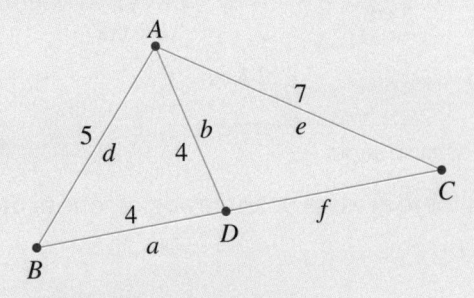

In triangle ABD, $(d)^2 = (a)^2 + (b)^2 - 2(a)(b)\cos D$

$\Rightarrow (5)^2 = (4)^2 + (4)^2 - 2(4)(4)\cos D$

$\Rightarrow \cos D = \dfrac{7}{32}$

We can use this in triangle ABD, remembering that $\cos(180° - \theta) = -\cos(\theta)$.

$(e)^2 = (f)^2 + (b)^2 - 2(f)(b)\cos(180° - D)$

$\Rightarrow (7)^2 = (f)^2 + (4)^2 - 2(f)(4)\left(-\dfrac{7}{32}\right)$

$\Rightarrow 0 = f^2 + \dfrac{7}{4}f - 33$

This doesn't factorise, so use the formula: $f = \dfrac{-1 \cdot 75 \pm \sqrt{1 \cdot 75^2 + 132}}{2}$

$\Rightarrow f = 4 \cdot 94$ or $f = -6 \cdot 69$

We can ignore the negative value, so $|DC| = 4 \cdot 9$ to 1 decimal place.

The **ambiguous case** occurs when we are given two sides of a triangle and an angle *not* between them.

Example

Consider a triangle ABC where $AB = 5$ cm, $AC = 3 \cdot 5$ cm and $\angle ABC = 35°$. Find two possible values of $\angle ACB$.

Solution

To visualise this problem, use a ruler and compass to draw triangle ABC.
1. Construct $\angle ABC = 35°$.
2. Use a ruler to find point A, 5 cm from B on one of the lines that make the angle.
3. Use a compass to draw an arc of radius $3 \cdot 5$ cm centred at A. The points where this arc intersects the other line that makes the angle give the two possible locations of C.

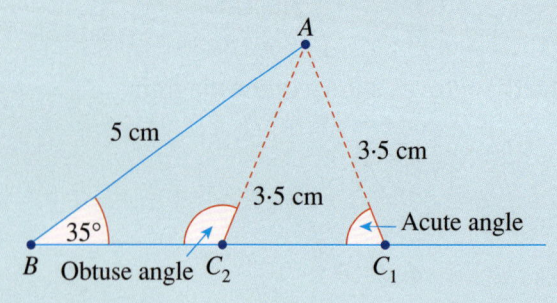

We can see clearly that there are two possible angles, one acute and one obtuse.

$$\frac{3 \cdot 5}{\sin 35°} = \frac{5}{\sin C_1}$$

$$\Rightarrow \sin C_1 = \frac{5 \sin 35°}{3 \cdot 5} = 0 \cdot 819395$$

$$\Rightarrow C_1 = 55° \text{ to the nearest degree.}$$

AC_1C_2 is an isosceles triangle, so $\angle AC_2C_1 = AC_1C_2 = 55°$.
Therefore, $\angle AC_2B = 180 - 55 = 125°$.
The two possible values of $\angle ACB$ are 55° and 125°.

Examples

(a) In a triangle ABC, the lengths of the sides are a, b and c.
Using a formula for the area of a triangle, or otherwise, prove that
$$\frac{a}{\sin \angle A} = \frac{b}{\sin \angle B} = \frac{c}{\sin \angle C}.$$

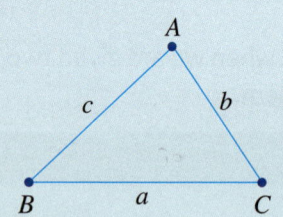

(b) In a triangle XYZ, $|XY| = 5$ cm, $|XZ| = 3$ cm and $|\angle XYZ| = 27°$.

  (i) Find the two possible values of $|\angle XZY|$. Give your answers correct to the nearest degree.

  (ii) Draw a sketch of the triangle XYZ, showing the two possible positions of the point Z.

(c) In the case that $|\angle XZY| < 90°$, write down $|\angle ZXY|$, and hence find the area of the triangle XYZ, correct to the nearest integer.

(SEC 2013)

Solutions

(a) $\frac{1}{2}ac \sin B = \frac{1}{2}ab \sin C$

Divide both sides by $\frac{1}{2}abc$ to get

$\frac{\sin B}{b} = \frac{\sin C}{c} \Rightarrow \frac{b}{\sin B} = \frac{c}{\sin C}.$

The same argument can be used to prove that $\frac{a}{\sin \angle A}$ is also equal to $\frac{b}{\sin \angle B}$ and $\frac{c}{\sin \angle C}.$

(b) (i) $\frac{3}{\sin 27°} = \frac{5}{\sin Z} \Rightarrow \sin Z = \frac{5 \sin 27°}{3} = 0.36$

$\Rightarrow |\angle Z| = 49°$ or $|\angle Z| = 180 - 49 = 131°$

(ii)

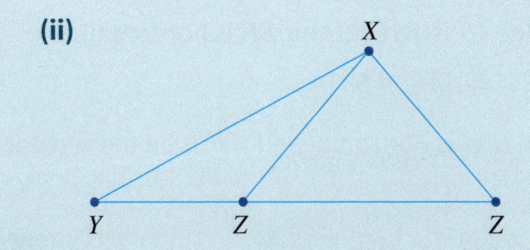

(c) $|\angle ZXY| = 180 - (27 + 49) = 104°$

Area $= \frac{1}{2}ab \sin C = \frac{1}{2}(5)(3) \sin 104° = 7.28 = 7 \text{ cm}^2$

3D problems

When dealing with a 3D problem in trigonometry, remember the following guidelines.

1. Identify the angles and sides you need to find.
2. Draw out right-angled triangles and non-right-angled triangles separately. Be careful to label the triangles correctly.
3. Identify right-angled triangles (where vertical meets horizontal). Use Pythagoras' theorem or SOH-CAH-TOA to find sides or angles.
4. Identify non-right-angled triangles and use the sine rule or cosine rule to find angles or sides.

Examples

The diagram shows a rectangular box. Rectangle *ABCD* is the top of the box and rectangle *EFGH* is the base of the box.

$|AB|$ = 4 cm, $|BF|$ = 3 cm, $|FG|$ = 12 cm.

(a) Find $|AF|$.

(b) Find $|AG|$.

(c) Find the measure of the acute angle between $[AG]$ and $[DF]$. Give your answer correct to the nearest degree.

(LCHL 2004)

Solutions

(a) *ABF* forms a right-angled triangle (*AB* is vertical and *BF* is horizontal). So
$|AF|^2 = |AB|^2 + |BF|^2 = 16 + 9 = 25 \Rightarrow |AF| = 5$

(b) *AGF* forms a right-angled triangle (*FG* is horizontal and *AF* is on the vertical plane). So
$|AG|^2 = |AF|^2 + |FG|^2 = 25 + 144 = 169 \Rightarrow |AG| = 13$

(c) Let *AG* and *FD* intersect at the point *r*.

As the two lines bisect each other, $|AR| = |FR| = 6.5$.

$$\cos ARF = \frac{|AR|^2 + |FR|^2 - |AF|^2}{2|AR||FR|} = \frac{(6.5)^2 + (6.5)^2 - (5)^2}{2(6.5)(6.5)}$$

$$= \frac{59.5}{84.5} \Rightarrow |\angle ARF| = 45.2 = 45°$$

Example

P, *Q* and *R* are three points on horizontal ground.

[*SR*] is a vertical pole of height *h* m.

The angle of elevation of *S* from *P* is 60° and the angle of elevation of *S* from *Q* is 30°.

$|PQ|$ = *c* m.

Given that $3c^2 = 13h^2$, find $|\angle PRQ|$.

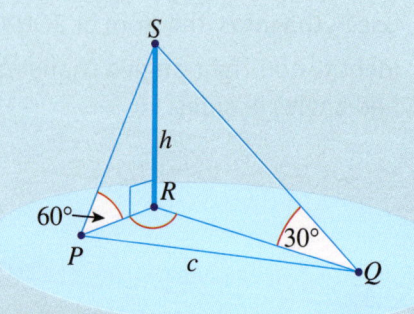

(LCHL 2007)

Solution

$\tan 60° = \dfrac{h}{|PR|} \Rightarrow |PR| = \dfrac{h}{\tan 60°} = \dfrac{h}{\sqrt{3}}$ From PRS, a right-angled triangle.

$\tan 30° = \dfrac{h}{|RQ|} \Rightarrow |RQ| = \dfrac{h}{\tan 30°} = \dfrac{h}{\frac{1}{\sqrt{3}}} = h\sqrt{3}$ From RQS, a right-angled triangle.

$\cos(\angle PRQ) = \dfrac{|PR|^2 + |RQ|^2 - |PQ|^2}{2|PR||RQ|} = \dfrac{\left(\frac{h}{\sqrt{3}}\right)^2 + (h\sqrt{3})^2 - (c)^2}{2\left(\frac{h}{\sqrt{3}}\right)(h\sqrt{3})}$ Use cosine rule and substitute in values in terms of h.

$= \dfrac{\frac{h^2}{3} + 3h^2 - c^2}{2h^2} = \dfrac{10h^2 - 3c^2}{6h^2} = \dfrac{10h^2 - 13h^2}{6h^2} = -\dfrac{1}{2}$

$\Rightarrow |\angle PRQ| = \cos^{-1}\left(-\dfrac{1}{2}\right) = 120°$

Examples

A square-based pyramid has a base with a side of length 4 cm and perpendicular height 12 cm as shown in the diagram.

Find:

(a) $|AC|$ in surd form

(b) the angle θ between a face of the pyramid and the base of the pyramid, correct to 2 decimal places

(c) the length of a sloping edge in the form $a\sqrt{b}$, where $a, b \in \mathbb{N}$

(d) the angle between an edge and the base, correct to 1 decimal place.

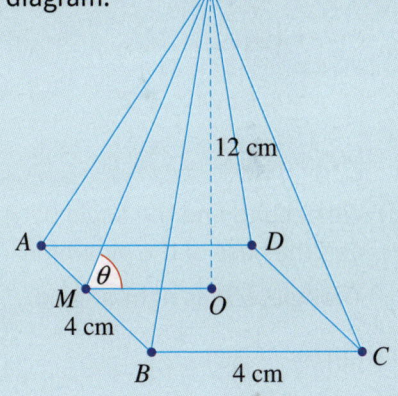

Solutions

(a)

$AC^2 = AB^2 + BC^2$ Triangle ABC is right angled.
$\Rightarrow AC^2 = 4^2 + 4^2 = 32$
$\Rightarrow |AC| = \sqrt{32}$ cm

2. Trigonometry 2   35

(b)

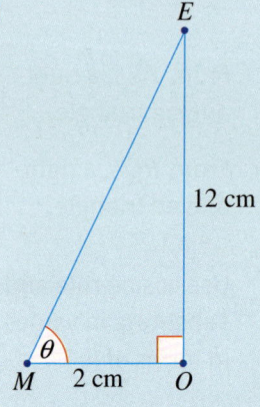

In triangle MOE, $\tan\theta = \dfrac{12}{2} = 6 \Rightarrow \theta = \tan^{-1} 6 = 80\cdot 54°$.

(c) We want to find the length of a sloping edge, say $|AE|$.
In triangle AOE, we need to find $|AO|$ first.
From part (a) we know that $|AC| = \sqrt{32}$ cm,
so $|AO| = \dfrac{1}{2}|AC| = \dfrac{1}{2}\sqrt{32} = \dfrac{1}{2} 4\sqrt{2} = 2\sqrt{2}$ cm.

Using Pythagoras' theorem,

$AE^2 = AO^2 + OE^2$

$= \left(2\sqrt{2}\right)^2 + 12^2$

$= 8 + 144 = 152$

$|AE| = \sqrt{152} = 2\sqrt{38}$ cm

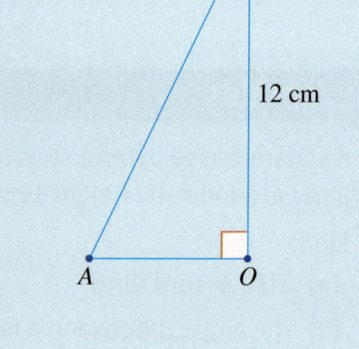

(d) We need to find the angle between the edge AE and the base of the pyramid.
Triangle AOE is right-angled.

$\tan\theta = \dfrac{12}{2\sqrt{2}} = \dfrac{6}{\sqrt{2}}$

$\Rightarrow \theta = \tan^{-1}\dfrac{6}{\sqrt{2}} = 76\cdot 7°$

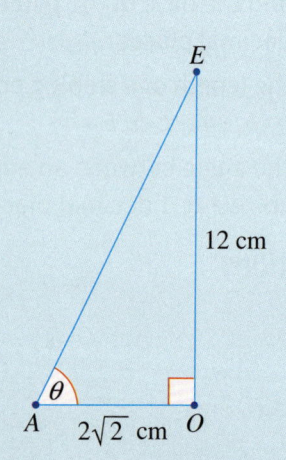

Trigonometric formulae and identities

You need to know how to prove the following trigonometric formulae. The proofs are covered in your textbook, or can be found in the *Teacher Handbook LC HL*, 'Appendix F: Sample derivations of some trigonometric formulae' on the www.projectmaths.ie website.

1. $\cos^2 A + \sin^2 A = 1$
2. sine rule: $\dfrac{a}{\sin A} = \dfrac{b}{\sin B} = \dfrac{c}{\sin C}$
3. cosine rule: $a^2 = b^2 + c^2 - 2bc\cos A$
4. $\cos(A - B) = \cos A \cos B + \sin A \sin B$
5. $\cos(A + B) = \cos A \cos B - \sin A \sin B$
6. $\cos 2A = \cos^2 A - \sin^2 A$
7. $\sin(A + B) = \sin A \cos B + \cos A \sin B$
8. $\tan(A + B) = \dfrac{\tan A + \tan B}{1 - \tan A \tan B}$

Example

Prove that $\cos 2A = \cos^2 A - \sin^2 A$ (SEC 2014)

Solution

$\cos(A + B) = \cos A \cos B - \sin A \sin B$

$\cos 2A = \cos(A + A) = \cos A \cos A - \sin A \sin A = \cos^2 A - \sin^2 A$

> **Point to note**
> When you prove a trigonometric formula, you may make use of any formula that comes *before* it in the list above.

The remaining trigonometric formulae used at higher level are listed below. You don't need to prove these formulae, but you should be familiar with them and know how to use them.

9. $\sin(A - B) = \sin A \cos B - \cos A \sin B$
10. $\tan(A - B) = \dfrac{\tan A - \tan B}{1 + \tan A \tan B}$
11. $\sin 2A = 2 \sin A \cos A$
12. $\sin 2A = \dfrac{2 \tan A}{1 + \tan^2 A}$

13 $\cos 2A = \dfrac{1 - \tan^2 A}{1 + \tan^2 A}$

14 $\tan 2A = \dfrac{2 \tan A}{1 - \tan^2 A}$

15 $\cos^2 A = \dfrac{1}{2}(1 + \cos 2A)$

16 $\sin^2 A = \dfrac{1}{2}(1 - \cos 2A)$

17 $2 \cos A \cos B = \cos(A + B) + \cos(A - B)$

18 $2 \sin A \cos B = \sin(A + B) + \sin(A - B)$

19 $2 \sin A \sin B = \cos(A - B) - \cos(A + B)$

20 $2 \cos A \sin B = \sin(A + B) - \sin(A - B)$

21 $\cos A + \cos B = 2 \cos\left(\dfrac{A + B}{2}\right) \cos\left(\dfrac{A - B}{2}\right)$

22 $\cos A - \cos B = -2 \sin\left(\dfrac{A + B}{2}\right) \sin\left(\dfrac{A - B}{2}\right)$

23 $\sin A + \sin B = 2 \sin\left(\dfrac{A + B}{2}\right) \cos\left(\dfrac{A - B}{2}\right)$

24 $\sin A - \sin B = 2 \cos\left(\dfrac{A + B}{2}\right) \sin\left(\dfrac{A - B}{2}\right)$

Point to note

The 24 trigonometric formulae are all listed in the *Formulae and Tables* booklet.

Formula 1 is on page 13. Formulae 2 and 3 are on page 16. The remaining formulae are on pages 14 and 15, arranged in the sections:

- compound angle formulae
- double angle formulae
- products to sums and differences
- sums and differences to products.

The formulae for negative angles are on page 13 of the *Formulae and Tables* booklet.

$\cos(-A) = \cos(A)$, e.g. $\cos(-20°) = \cos 20° = 0{\cdot}9397$

$\sin(-A) = -\sin(A)$, e.g. $\sin(-2\pi) = \sin(2\pi) = 0$

$\tan(-A) = -\tan(A)$, e.g. $\tan(-45°) = \tan 45° = 1$

Application of trigonometric formulae

Example

Prove that $\dfrac{\sqrt{1-\cos^2 x}}{\tan x} = \cos x$.

Solution

We usually prove identities working from left to right.

In this example we can use formula 1: $\cos^2 x + \sin^2 x = 1 \Rightarrow \sin^2 x = 1 - \cos^2 x$.

Substitute this into the identity to be proved and simplify.

$$\dfrac{\sqrt{1-\cos^2 x}}{\tan x} = \dfrac{\sqrt{\sin^2 x}}{\tan x} = \dfrac{\sin x}{\left(\dfrac{\sin x}{\cos x}\right)} = \cos x$$

Examples

Consider the diagram below.

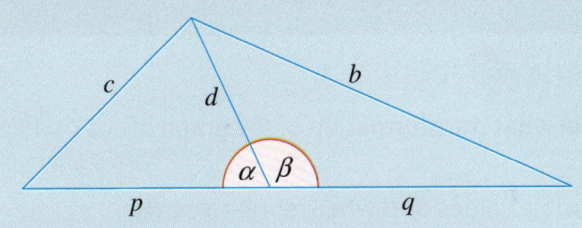

(a) Express $\cos \alpha$ and $\cos \beta$ in terms of the labelled lengths.

(b) Show that $pb^2 + qc^2 = (p+q)(pq + d^2)$.

(Pre-leaving paper 2010)

Solutions

(a) Use the cosine rule on each triangle.

$$c^2 = p^2 + d^2 - 2pd\cos\alpha \Rightarrow \cos\alpha = \dfrac{c^2 - p^2 - d^2}{-2pd}$$

$$b^2 = d^2 + q^2 - 2dq\cos\beta \Rightarrow \cos\beta = \dfrac{b^2 - d^2 - q^2}{-2dq}$$

(b) α and β are supplementary angles (they add up to 180°) so $\cos\alpha = -\cos\beta$.
Use this fact to equate the two expressions from part (a).

$$\dfrac{c^2 - p^2 - d^2}{-2pd} = -\left(\dfrac{b^2 - d^2 - q^2}{-2dq}\right)$$

Now simplify to obtain the required equation.

$\Rightarrow -2dqc^2 + 2dqp^2 + 2d^2q = 2pdb^2 - 2pd^2 - 2pdq^2$ Multiply both sides by $-2pd^2q$.

$\Rightarrow qp^2 + qd^2 + pd^2 + pq^2 = pb^2 + qc^2$ Divide both sides by 2, and rearrange so that each term is positive.

$\Rightarrow p(pq + d^2) + q(pq + d^2) = pb^2 + qc^2$ Factorise the left-hand side.

$\Rightarrow (p + q)(pq + d^2) = pb^2 + qc^2$ as required.

Point to note

In formulae such as $\cos(A - B) = \cos A \cos B + \sin A \sin B$ and $\cos(A + B) = \cos A \cos B - \sin A \sin B$, the angles $A \pm B$ are called compound angles.

Examples

(a) Prove that $\cos\left(\theta - \dfrac{\pi}{2}\right) = \sin\theta$.

(b) Hence explain what transformation of the graph of $\cos\theta$ will produce the graph of $\sin\theta$.

(c) Give two possible values of θ where $\sin\theta = \cos\theta$.

Solutions

(a) Use the compound angle formula: $\cos(A - B) = \cos A \cos B + \sin A \sin B$.

$\cos\left(\theta - \dfrac{\pi}{2}\right) = \cos\theta \cos\dfrac{\pi}{2} + \sin\theta \sin\dfrac{\pi}{2}$

$= \cos\theta(0) + \sin\theta(1) = \sin\theta$

(b) $\cos\left(\theta - \dfrac{\pi}{2}\right)$ is a translation of $\cos\theta$ by $\dfrac{\pi}{2}$ radians. Therefore, if we translate the graph of $\cos\theta$ to the left by $\dfrac{\pi}{2}$ radians it will produce the graph of $\sin\theta$.

(c) $\sin\theta = \cos\theta \Rightarrow \sin^2\theta = \cos^2\theta$ Square both sides of the equation.

$\Rightarrow \sin^2\theta = 1 - \sin^2\theta$ Use the identity $\sin^2\theta + \cos^2\theta = 1$.

$\Rightarrow 2\sin^2\theta = 1 \Rightarrow \sin^2\theta = \dfrac{1}{2} \Rightarrow \sin\theta = \pm\dfrac{1}{\sqrt{2}}$

$\Rightarrow \theta = \sin^{-1}\left(\pm\dfrac{1}{\sqrt{2}}\right) \Rightarrow \theta = 45°$ or $\theta = -45°$.

Examples

A is an acute angle such that $\tan A = \dfrac{8}{15}$.

Without evaluating A, find:

(a) $\cos A$

(b) $\sin 2A$.

Solutions

(a) Assume that A is an angle in a right-angled triangle, so $\tan A = \dfrac{8}{15} = \dfrac{o}{a}$.
We can use this to find the length of the hypotenuse.
$h^2 = o^2 + a^2$
$\Rightarrow h^2 = 8^2 + 15^2 = 289 \Rightarrow h = \sqrt{289} = 17$
Therefore, $\cos A = \dfrac{a}{h} = \dfrac{15}{17}$.

(b) Use the identity $\sin 2A = 2 \sin A \cos A$.
From part (a), $\sin A = \dfrac{o}{h} = \dfrac{8}{17}$. So $\sin 2A = 2\left(\dfrac{8}{17}\right)\left(\dfrac{15}{17}\right) = \dfrac{240}{289}$

Examples

Express as a sum or a difference and simplify:

(a) $2 \sin 45° \cos 75°$

(b) $\cos \dfrac{x}{2} \cos \dfrac{x}{4}$.

Solutions

(a) Use the formula $2 \sin A \cos B = \sin(A + B) + \sin(A - B)$.

$2 \sin 45° \cos 75° = \sin(45° + 75°) + \sin(45° - 75°)$

$= \sin(120°) + \sin(-30°) = \sin 120° - \sin 30°$

$= \dfrac{\sqrt{3}}{2} - \dfrac{1}{2} = \dfrac{\sqrt{3} - 1}{2}$

(b) Use the formula $2 \cos A \cos B = \cos(A + B) + \cos(A - B)$

$\cos A \cos B = \dfrac{1}{2}[\cos(A + B) + \cos(A - B)]$ Divide both sides by 2.

$\cos \dfrac{x}{2} \cos \dfrac{x}{4} = \dfrac{1}{2}\left[\cos\left(\dfrac{x}{2} + \dfrac{x}{4}\right) + \cos\left(\dfrac{x}{2} - \dfrac{x}{4}\right)\right]$

$= \dfrac{1}{2}\left[\cos\left(\dfrac{3x}{4}\right) + \cos\left(\dfrac{x}{4}\right)\right]$

Examples

(a) Express $\cos(2\theta) + \cos(-2\theta)$ as a product in the form $k \cos k\theta$, where $k \in \mathbb{N}$.

(b) Hence, find all solutions of the trigonometric equation $\cos(2\theta) + \cos(-2\theta) = 0$, where $\theta \in \mathbb{R}$ and θ in radians.

Solutions

(a) We know that $\cos(-A) = \cos(A)$ so

$\cos(2\theta) + \cos(-2\theta) = \cos(2\theta) + \cos(2\theta) = 2\cos 2\theta$.

(b) Solve $2\cos 2\theta = 0$.

$\cos 2\theta = 0$ Divide both sides by 2.

$\Rightarrow 2\theta = \cos^{-1} 0 = \dfrac{\pi}{2}$ or $\dfrac{3\pi}{2}$.

To find *all* solutions, include $2n\pi$.

$2\theta = \dfrac{\pi}{2} + 2n\pi$ or $2\theta = \dfrac{3\pi}{2} + 2n\pi$

$\Rightarrow \theta = \dfrac{\pi}{4} + n\pi$ or $\theta = \dfrac{3\pi}{4} + n\pi$, where $n \in \mathbb{Z}$.

Checklist

- ✓ Practise questions using the sine rule and cosine rule. Know when to use each rule and where the formulae are in the *Formulae and Tables* booklet.
- ✓ Practise questions on areas of triangles, areas of sectors and areas of segments.
- ✓ Practise questions on 3D problems.
- ✓ Be familiar with the trigonometric identities in the *Formulae and Tables* booklet.
- ✓ Label triangles carefully and mark the angles or sides you need to find.
- ✓ Identify right-angled and non-right-angled triangles.
- ✓ Check you are using the correct mode in your calculator – degrees or radians.
- ✓ Check what form is required for the answer – surd form, decimal form, fraction, etc.
- ✓ Check if the angle is required in degrees or radians.
- ✓ Check units.

Co-ordinate Geometry of the Line   3

Learning objectives

In this chapter you will learn how to:
- Use formulae for co-ordinate geometry of the line
- Use slopes to show that two lines are
  - Parallel
  - Perpendicular
- Recognise the fact that the relationship $ax + by + c = 0$ is linear
- Solve problems involving slopes of lines
- Calculate the area of a triangle using co-ordinates
- Divide a line segment internally in the ratio $m : n$
- Solve problems involving
  - The perpendicular distance from a point to a line
  - The angle between two lines.

Co-ordinate geometry formulae

The formulae for co-ordinate geometry of the line are on pages 18 and 19 of the *Formulae and Tables* booklet. You need to be familiar with and practise using these formulae.

Slope of line

Slope $(m) = \dfrac{\text{rise}}{\text{run}} = \dfrac{y_2 - y_1}{x_2 - x_1}$ = rate of change of y with respect to x.

Parallel lines have equal slopes. If two lines l_1 and l_2 are parallel then $m_1 = m_2$.

If two lines l_1 and l_2 are perpendicular then $m_1 \times m_2 = -1$, so $m_1 = \dfrac{-1}{m_2}$.

Consider the diagram shown.

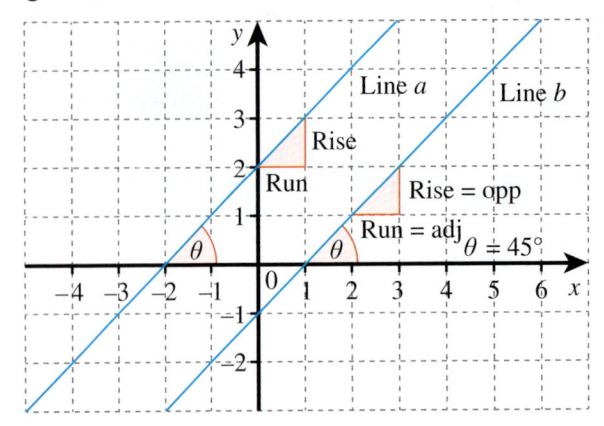

We can see that the slopes are equal ($m = 1$) for line a and line b. We can also see that the angle of inclination (θ) is the same for both lines.

slope $= \dfrac{\text{opp}}{\text{adj}} = \tan \theta$

In the diagram, slope $= 1 = \tan \theta \Rightarrow \theta = \tan^{-1} 1 = 45°$.

> **Point to note**
>
> The **angle of inclination** is the angle that the line makes with positive x-axis.

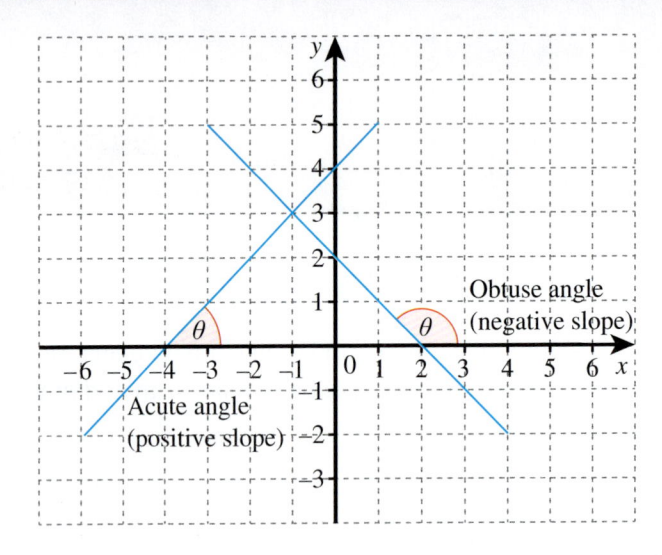

If the slope of a line is positive then line climbs from left to right and the angle of inclination θ is acute.

If the slope of a line is negative then line climbs from right to left and the angle of inclination θ is obtuse.

> **Point to note**
> For lines parallel to the x-axis the equation is of the form $y = k$, where $k \in \mathbb{R}$, and the slope $= 0$.
>
> For lines parallel to the y-axis the equation is of the form $x = k$, where $k \in \mathbb{R}$, and the slope is undefined.

x and y intercepts

The x **intercept** of a line is the point where it meets the x-axis, and the y **intercept** is the point where it meets the y-axis.

To find the x intercept, let $y = 0$ and solve for x.

To find the y intercept, let $x = 0$ and solve for y.

Examples

Find the intercepts of the lines:

(a) $2x - 3y + 3 = 0$

(b) $x + y - 6 = 0$.

Does either line have intercepts with equal values?

Solutions

(a) $y = 0 \Rightarrow 2x - 3(0) + 3 = 0 \Rightarrow 2x = -3 \Rightarrow x = \dfrac{-3}{2}$

$x = 0 \Rightarrow 2(0) - 3y + 3 = 0 \Rightarrow 3y = 3 \Rightarrow y = 1$

The x intercept is $x = \dfrac{-3}{2}$ and the y intercept is $y = 1$. The intercepts are not equal in value.

(b) $y = 0 \Rightarrow x + (0) - 6 = 0 \Rightarrow x = 6$

$x = 0 \Rightarrow (0) + y - 6 = 0 \Rightarrow y = 6$

The x intercept is $x = 6$ and the y intercept is $y = 6$. The intercepts have equal values.

Equation of a line

There are several ways of writing the equation of a line. Which one is most appropriate will depend on the information you have available.

Slope–intercept $y = mx + c$ (m is the slope and c is the y intercept)

Slope–point $y - y_1 = m(x - x_1)$ (m is the slope and (x_1, y_1) is a point on the line)

Standard form $ax + by + c = 0$ $\left(a, b, c \in \mathbb{R}, m = \text{slope} = \dfrac{-a}{b}\right)$

3. Co-ordinate Geometry of the Line

Example

Complete the table by finding the equation of each line in slope–intercept form.

Slope m	y intercept	Equation $y = mx + c$
3	4	
−4	0	
$\frac{1}{3}$	−2	
$\sqrt{2}$	1	

Solution

Slope m	y intercept	Equation $y = mx + c$
3	4	$y = 3x + 4$
−4	0	$y = -4x$
$\frac{1}{3}$	−2	$y = \frac{1}{3}x - 2$
$\sqrt{2}$	1	$y = \sqrt{2}x - 1$

Example

Complete the table by finding the slope, intercept and angle of inclination for each equation.

Equation $ax + by + c = 0$	Slope $\frac{-a}{b}$	x intercept $(y = 0)$	y intercept $(x = 0)$	Angle $\left(\tan^{-1}\left(\frac{-a}{b}\right)\right)$
$x - 2y + 3 = 0$				
$4x - y = 0$				
$3x + 6y - 4 = 0$				

Solution

Equation $ax + by + c = 0$	Slope $\frac{-a}{b}$	x intercept $(y = 0)$	y intercept $(x = 0)$	Angle $\left(\tan^{-1}\left(\frac{-a}{b}\right)\right)$
$x - 2y + 3 = 0$	$\frac{-1}{-2} = \frac{1}{2}$	−3	$\frac{3}{2}$	27° approx (acute)
$4x - y = 0$	4	0	0	76° approx (acute)
$3x + 6y - 4 = 0$	$\frac{-3}{6} = \frac{-1}{2}$	$\frac{4}{3}$	$\frac{4}{6} = \frac{2}{3}$	153° approx (obtuse ⇒ negative slope)

Example

The equations of six lines are given:

Line	Equation
h	$x = 3 - y$
i	$2x - 4y = 3$
k	$y = -\dfrac{1}{4}(2x - 7)$
l	$4x - 2y - 5 = 0$
m	$x + \sqrt{3}y - 10 = 0$
n	$\sqrt{3}x + y - 10 = 0$

Complete the table below by matching each description given to one or more of the lines.

Description	Line(s)
A line with a slope of 2.	
A line which intersects the y-axis at $\left(0, -2\dfrac{1}{2}\right)$.	
A line which makes equal intercepts on the axes.	
A line which makes an angle of 150° with the positive sense of the x-axis	
Two lines which are perpendicular to each other.	

(SEC 2013)

Solution

Start by finding the slope and intercepts of each line. Write each line in either slope–intercept form or standard form, and use this equation to find the slope.

Lines h, i and k can be expressed in slope–intercept form.

Line	Slope–intercept form	Slope	x intercept ($y = 0$)	y intercept ($x = 0$)
h	$y = -x + 3$	-1	$x - 3 - (0) \Rightarrow x = 3$	$y = 3$
i	$y = \dfrac{1}{2}x + \dfrac{3}{4}$	$\dfrac{1}{2}$	$2x - 4(0) = 3 \Rightarrow x = \dfrac{3}{2}$	$y = \dfrac{3}{4}$
k	$y = -\dfrac{1}{2}x + \dfrac{7}{4}$	$-\dfrac{1}{2}$	$(0) = -\dfrac{1}{2}x + \dfrac{7}{4} \Rightarrow x = \dfrac{7}{2}$	$y = \dfrac{7}{4}$

Lines *l*, *m* and *n* are more easily written in standard form.

Line	Standard form	Slope	x intercept (y = 0)	y intercept (x = 0)
l	$4x - 2y - 5 = 0$	$\dfrac{-(4)}{(-2)} = 2$	$4x - 2(0) - 5 = 0$ $\Rightarrow x = \dfrac{5}{4}$	$4(0) - 2y - 5 = 0$ $\Rightarrow y = -\dfrac{5}{2}$
m	$x + \sqrt{3}y - 10 = 0$	$\dfrac{-(1)}{\sqrt{3}} = -\dfrac{1}{\sqrt{3}}$	$x + \sqrt{3}(0) - 10 = 0$ $\Rightarrow x = 10$	$(0) + \sqrt{3}y - 10 = 0$ $\Rightarrow y = \dfrac{10}{\sqrt{3}}$
n	$\sqrt{3} + y - 10 = 0$	$\dfrac{-(\sqrt{3})}{1} = -\sqrt{3}$	$\sqrt{3}x + (0) - 10 = 0$ $\Rightarrow x = \dfrac{10}{\sqrt{3}}$	$\sqrt{3}(0) + y - 10 = 0$ $\Rightarrow y = 10$

We can now complete the first three lines of the table easily. The final two lines require a little more work.

150° is obtuse, so a line which makes an angle of 150° with the *x*-axis must have a negative slope. This rules out lines *i* and *l*. Find the angle of inclination of the remaining lines by taking the inverse tan of the slope.

h: $\theta = \tan^{-1}(-1) = -45°$

k: $\theta = \tan^{-1}\left(-\dfrac{1}{2}\right) = -26\cdot6°$

m: $\theta = \tan^{-1}\left(\dfrac{-1}{\sqrt{3}}\right) = -30°$

n: $\theta = \tan^{-1}(-\sqrt{3}) = -60°$

An angle of −30° with the *x*-axis is the same as an angle of 150°, so line *m* makes this angle.

If two lines are perpendicular then the products of their slopes is −1, so *k* and *l* are perpendicular.

Thus the table can be completed as follows.

Description	Line(s)
A line with a slope of 2.	*l*
A line which intersects the *y*-axis at $\left(0, -2\dfrac{1}{2}\right)$.	*l*
A line which makes equal intercepts on the axes.	*h*
A line which makes an angle of 150° with the positive sense of the *x*-axis	*m*
Two lines which are perpendicular to each other.	*k* and *l*

Linear relationships and graphs

Linear relationships can be given in words, as data in a table, as a formula or as a graph.

It is important to be able to recognise linear relationships and find the slope, y intercept and other points on the graph. You also need to be able to interpret the meaning of the slope in real-life problems.

> **Point to note**
>
> In a linear relationship, x is the **independent variable** and y is the **dependent variable**. Other variables are sometimes used.

Examples

A cylinder of cold liquid was heated in a lab. The temperature was recorded at 10-minute intervals as shown in the table.

Time (minutes)	Temperature (°C)
0	−5
10	0
20	5
30	10
40	15

(a) Draw a linear graph to represent the data in the table.

(b) What is the slope of the graph and what does the slope of the graph represent? Is this a constant rate of change?

(c) Find a formula to represent the linear relationship.

(d) Use your graph to estimate the time taken for the temperature to rise from 0° to 15 °C.

(e) What does the y intercept represent?

(f) Assuming that the temperature of the liquid is increasing at the same rate, use your graph to predict the temperature of the liquid after 29 minutes. Check your answer using your formula.

Solutions
(a)

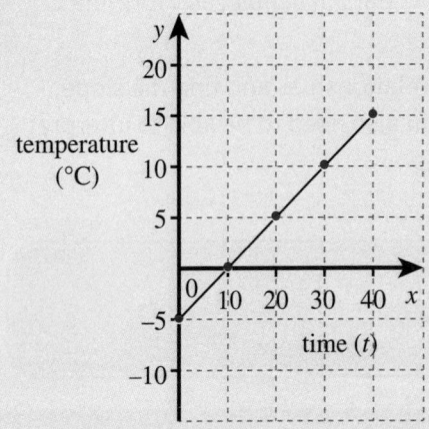

[Graph showing temperature (°C) on y-axis vs time (t) on x-axis, with a line passing through points and y-intercept at -5]

(b) $m = \dfrac{\text{rise}}{\text{run}} = \dfrac{5}{10} = \dfrac{1}{2}$.

This means that the temperature rises by 1 °C every 2 minutes.

(c) $m = \dfrac{1}{2}$ and the y intercept is -5

so $y = mx + c \Rightarrow y = \dfrac{1}{2}x - 5$.

(d) 30 minutes

(e) The y intercept co-ordinates are $(0, -5)$.
When time = 0 the temperature is -5 °C.
This is the initial temperature of the liquid.

(f) From the graph it is 9·5 minutes.
With the formula, $C = \dfrac{1}{2}(29) - 5 = 9\cdot5$ minutes

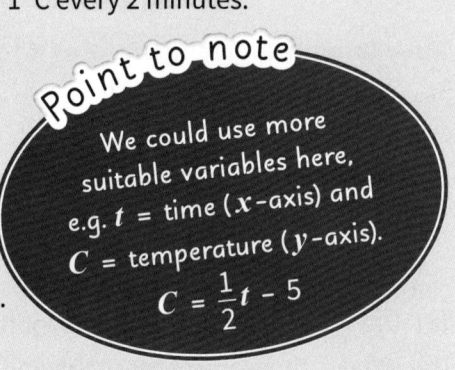

Point to note

We could use more suitable variables here, e.g. t = time (x-axis) and C = temperature (y-axis).
$C = \dfrac{1}{2}t - 5$

Examples

Jonathan started a business selling custom bikes. The fixed cost of setting up the business is €3000. Each bike costs €150 to make. He hopes to sell the bikes for €230 each.
(a) Write a formula to represent the fixed cost, denoted by $F(x)$.
(b) Write a formula to represent $C(x)$ = variable cost + fixed cost.
(c) Draw a graph of $F(x)$ and $C(x)$.
(d) On the same diagram, draw $R(x) = 230(x)$. What does this linear graph represent?
(e) Using the graph, find out how many bikes Jonathan will need to sell in order to break even. Check this algebraically.

Solutions

(a) The fixed cost is a constant. It doesn't vary with x. $F(x) = 3000$

(b) The variable cost is the cost of each bike multiplied by the number of bikes built. $C(x) = 150x + 3000$

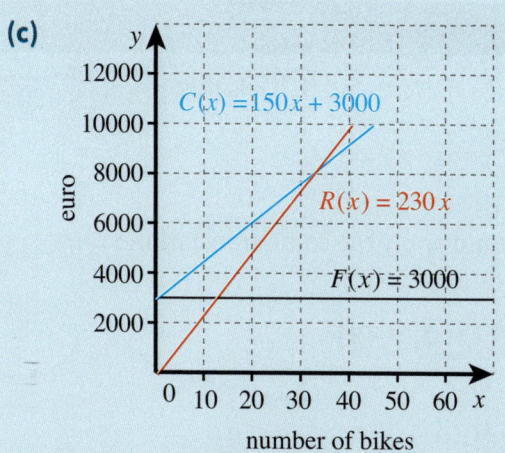

(c)

(d) $R(x)$ is the total revenue = selling price multiplied by the number of bikes sold.

(e) Jonathan breaks even when $R(x) = C(x)$. From the graph, this occurs when about 38 bikes are sold.

Algebraically, Jonathan breaks even when $230x = 150x + 3000$

$\Rightarrow 80x = 3000 \Rightarrow x = 37 \cdot 5$.

He can't sell half a bike, so he will need to sell 38 bikes to break even (which will make a small profit).

Area of a triangle

Given the three vertices of a triangle, there are two ways to calculate its area.

Case 1: One of the vertices is (0, 0).

Denote the other two vertices by (x_1, y_1) and (x_2, y_2).

Area $= \dfrac{1}{2} |x_1 y_2 - x_2 y_1|$

This formula is on page 18 of the *Formulae and Tables* booklet.

Case 2: (0, 0) is not one of the vertices.

In this case, translate one of the vertices to the origin and then **apply the same translation** to the other two vertices. You can then use the same formula as in Case 1.

3. Co-ordinate Geometry of the Line

> **Top Tip**
> If you know the perpendicular height and the length of the base, you could also use the formula Area = $\frac{1}{2}bh$.

Example

Find the area of the triangle with vertices (2, 3), (7, 4) and (7, 1). Is this a right-angled triangle?

Solution

Translate one of the vertices to the origin, and apply the same translation to the other vertices.

Vertex	(x, y)	Translation = $(x - 2, y - 3)$
A	(2, 3)	(0, 0)
B	(7, 4)	(5, 1)
C	(6, 2)	(4, −1)

Area of triangle $ABC = \frac{1}{2}|x_1 y_2 - x_2 y_1| = \frac{1}{2}|(5)(-1) - (4)(1)| = \frac{1}{2}|-5 - 4|$

$= \frac{1}{2}(9) = 4\cdot 5$ square units

Find the slope of AB, BC and CA.

Slope of $AB = m_1 = \frac{4-3}{7-2} = \frac{1}{5}$

Slope of $BC = m_2 = \frac{2-4}{6-7} = \frac{-2}{-1} = 2$

Slope of $CA = m_3 = \frac{3-2}{2-6} = -\frac{1}{4}$

$m_1 \times m_2 = \frac{1}{5} \times \frac{2}{1} = \frac{2}{5} \neq -1$

$m_2 \times m_3 = 2 \times -\frac{1}{4} = -\frac{1}{2} \neq -1$

$m_3 \times m_1 = -\frac{1}{4} \times \frac{1}{5} = -\frac{1}{20} \neq -1$

> **Remember**
> Area is always positive.

No two pairs of lines are perpendicular, so triangle ABC is not right angled.

> **Point to note**
> To prove that three points are collinear, show that the area of the triangle = 0.

Examples

The line RS cuts the x-axis at the point R and the y-axis at the point $S\ (0, 10)$, as shown. The area of the triangle ROS, where O is the origin, is $\frac{125}{3}$.

(a) Find the co-ordinates of R.

(b) Show that the point $E(-5, 4)$ is on the line RS.

(c) A second line $y = mx + c$, where m and c are positive constants, passes through the point E and again makes a triangle of area $\frac{125}{3}$ with the axes. Find the value of m and the value of c.

(SEC 2014)

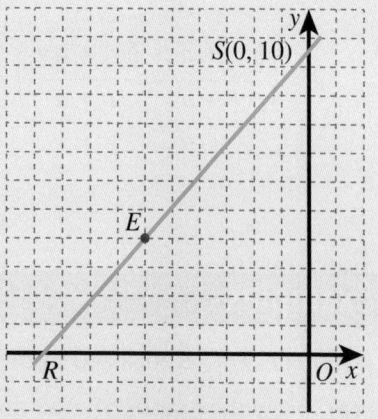

Solutions

(a) Substitute the given values into the formula for the area of a triangle, and rearrange to find the length of RO.

Area $ROS = \frac{1}{2}|RO||OS| = \frac{125}{3} \Rightarrow \frac{1}{2}|RO|(10) = \frac{125}{3} \Rightarrow |RO| = \frac{25}{3}$

We can see from the diagram that R is a point on the negative x-axis, therefore $R = \left(-\frac{25}{3}, 0\right)$.

(b) Slope $RS = \dfrac{10 - 0}{0 + \frac{25}{3}} = \dfrac{6}{5}$ Slope $RE = \dfrac{10 - 4}{0 + 5} = \dfrac{6}{5}$ Slope $ES = \dfrac{4 - 0}{-5 + \frac{25}{3}} = \dfrac{6}{5}$

The slopes of RS, RE and ES are the same, so ES must lie on RS.

(c) $y = mx + c$ cuts the x-axis at $P\left(\frac{-c}{m}, 0\right)$ and the y-axis at $Q(0, c)$. This gives us two vertices of the triangle, with the third vertex being the origin. We can now use the area of a triangle formula, and rearrange to find m and c.

Area $POQ = \frac{1}{2}\left|(0)(0) - \left(\frac{-c}{m}\right)(c)\right| = \frac{1}{2}\left|\frac{c^2}{m}\right| = \frac{125}{3} \Rightarrow m = \frac{3c^2}{250}$

The line passes through the point $E\ (-5, 4)$, so $4 = -5m + c$

$\Rightarrow 4 = -5\left(\dfrac{3c^2}{250}\right) + c \Rightarrow 3c^2 - 50c + 200 = 0$

$\Rightarrow (3c - 20)(c - 10) = 0 \Rightarrow c = \dfrac{20}{3}$ or $c = 10$

$c = 10$ gives a point on the original line, so on the new line $c = \dfrac{20}{3}$

Hence, $m = \dfrac{3c^2}{250} = \dfrac{3\left(\frac{20}{3}\right)^2}{250} = \dfrac{400}{750} = \dfrac{8}{15}$

Dividing a line segment in a given ratio

The formula to find the point that divides a line segment in a given ratio $a : b$ is on page 18 of the *Formulae and Tables* booklet.

$$R = \left(\frac{bx_1 + ax_2}{b + a}, \frac{by_1 + ay_2}{b + a} \right)$$

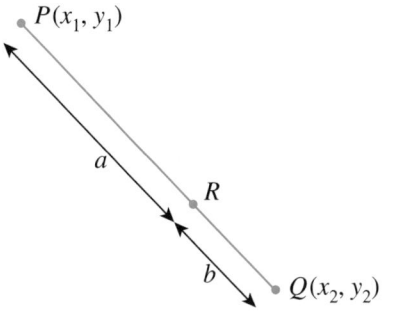

Examples

A triangle ABC is enclosed by the functions $f(x) = |x - 8|$ and $g(x) = 6$.

(a) Draw the graphs of $f(x)$ and $g(x)$ on the same diagram and label points A, B and C, where A is on the x-axis and B, C are points of intersection of $f(x)$ and $g(x)$.

(b) Find the co-ordinates of the point D on $[AB]$ if D divides the side in the ratio $2 : 1$.

(c) Given that triangles ABC and ADE are similar, find the co-ordinates of E.

(d) Calculate the ratio Area ABC : Area ADE.

(e) Hence, or otherwise, find the area of the quadrilateral $BCED$.

Solutions

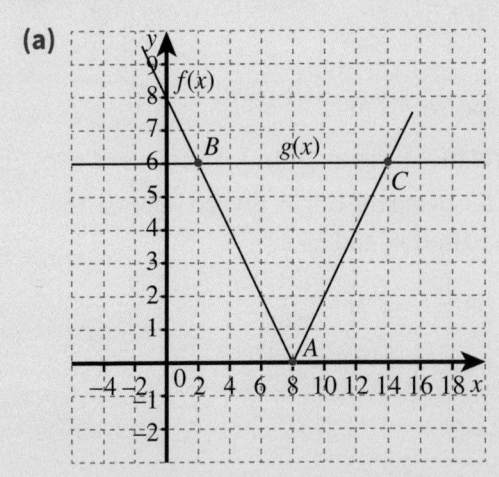

(a)

(b) The ratio is $2 : 1$, so $a = 2$ and $b = 1$.

$(x_1, y_1) = (8, 0)$ and $(x_2, y_2) = (2, 6)$

$$D = \left(\frac{(1)(8) + (2)(2)}{(1) + (2)}, \frac{(1)(0) + (2)(6)}{(1) + (2)} \right) = \left(\frac{12}{3}, \frac{12}{3} \right) = (4, 4)$$

(c) As the triangles are similar, E must divide $[AC]$ in the same ratio. Using the formula.

$$E = \left(\frac{(1)(8) + (2)(14)}{(1) + (2)}, \frac{(1)(0) + (2)(6)}{(1) + (2)} \right)$$

$$= \left(\frac{36}{3}, \frac{12}{3} \right) = (12, 4)$$

(d) Area of $ABC = \frac{1}{2}bh = \frac{1}{2}(12)(6) = \frac{1}{2}(72) = 36$ square units

Area of $ADE = \frac{1}{2}bh = \frac{1}{2}(8)(4) = \frac{1}{2}(32) = 16$ square units

Ratio is $36 : 16 = 9 : 4$

(e) Area of quadrilateral = area of triangle ABC − area of triangle ADE
$= 36 − 16 = 20$ square units

> **Point to note**
> We could also use the formula for the area of a trapezium, since DE is parallel to BC.

Perpendicular distance from a point to a line

The formula for the perpendicular distance from a point to a line is on page 19 of the *Formulae and Tables* booklet.

For a line $ax + by + c = 0$, the perpendicular distance to a point (x_1, y_1) is given by

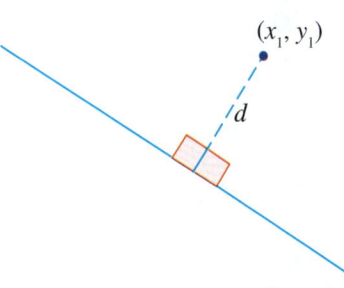

$$d = \frac{|ax_1 + by_1 + c|}{\sqrt{a^2 + b^2}}$$

Examples

(a) Show that $(4, −2)$ is equidistant from the lines $3x + y = 0$ and $x − 3y = 0$.

(b) Another line, p, is drawn from the point of intersection of the lines in part (a) through $(4, −2)$, to bisect the angle between the two lines. Find the equation of this line.

(c) Find the measure of the angle at the point of intersection.

Solutions

(a) First line: $(x_1, y_1) = (4, -2)$, $3x + y = 0 \Rightarrow a = 3, b = 1, c = 0$

$$d = \frac{|(3)(4) + (1)(-2) + 0|}{\sqrt{(3)^2 + (1)^2}} = \frac{|10|}{\sqrt{10}} = \sqrt{10} \text{ units}$$

Second line: $(x_1, y_1) = (4, -2)$, $x - 3y = 0 \Rightarrow a = 1, b = -3, c = 0$

$$d = \frac{|(1)(4) + (-3)(-2) + 0|}{\sqrt{(3)^2 + (1)^2}} = \frac{|10|}{\sqrt{10}} = \sqrt{10} \text{ units}$$

Therefore $(4, -2)$ is equidistant from both lines.

(b) Draw a diagram of the two lines in part (a) and p.

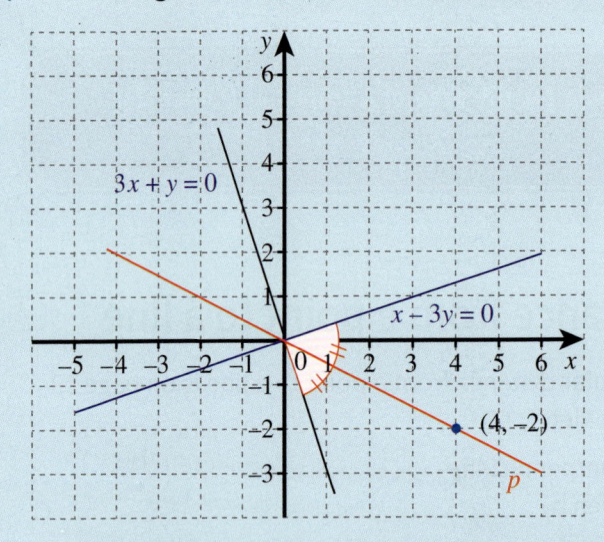

We know two points on p: $(4, -2)$ and, from the diagram, $(0, 0)$.

Therefore the y intercept is 0, and the slope is $\dfrac{(0) - (-2)}{(0) - (4)} = \dfrac{-2}{4} = -\dfrac{1}{2}$.

$y = mx + c \Rightarrow y = -\dfrac{1}{2}x + 0 \Rightarrow 2y = -x \Rightarrow x + 2y = 0$ is the equation of the bisector p.

(c) The slope of $3x + y = 0$ is -3 and the slope of $x - 3y = 0$ is $\dfrac{1}{3}$. The product of slopes is -1, so the two lines are perpendicular. The angle is $90°$.

> **Point to note**
> You could also use the angle between two lines formula to find the measure of the angle.

Angle between two lines

The formula for the angle between two lines is on page 19 of the *Formulae and Tables* booklet.

To find the angles between two lines of slopes m_1 and m_2, use the formula

$$\tan \theta = \pm \frac{m_1 - m_2}{1 + m_1 m_2}$$

or the absolute value version

$$\tan \theta = \left| \frac{m_1 - m_2}{1 + m_1 m_2} \right|.$$

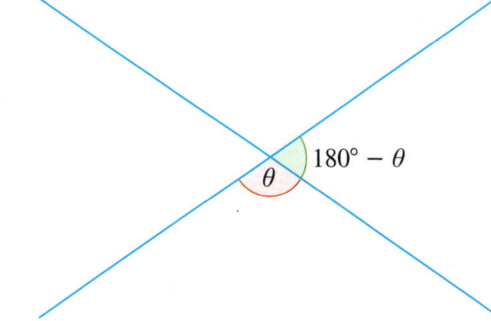

Point to note
We find the acute angle first ($\tan \theta$ is positive) and then subtract the angle from 180° to find the obtuse angle.

Examples

A pool table measures 10 feet by 5 feet, as shown in the diagram. The white ball is located at A and the black ball is located at B. Corner pockets are located at D and E. A pool player wants to pot the black ball into the corner pocket at D, and the path of the shot is shown in the diagram.

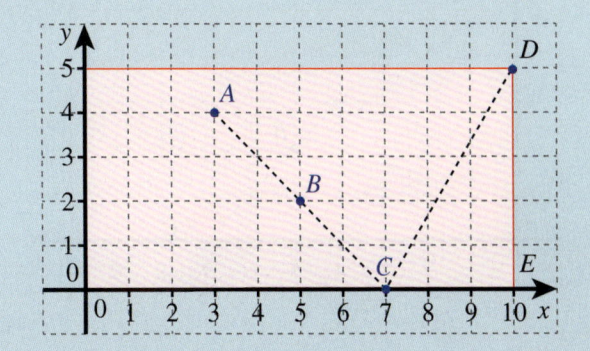

3. Co-ordinate Geometry of the Line

(a) Find, to the nearest degree, the measure of the acute angle in the path of the black ball when it hits the cushion at C.

(b) If the black ball hits the cushion at a right angle at C, suggest a possible location for where the black ball might finish. Give a reason for your answer.

Solutions

(a) We can use the diagram to find the slopes of the two sections of the path, then use the formula $\tan \theta = \left| \dfrac{m_1 - m_2}{1 + m_1 m_2} \right|$ to find the angle of the path at C.

Slope of $[AC] = \dfrac{\text{rise}}{\text{run}} = -\dfrac{4}{4} = -1 = m_1$

Slope of $[CD] = \dfrac{\text{rise}}{\text{run}} = \dfrac{5}{3} = m_2$

So $\tan \theta = \left| \dfrac{(-1) - \left(\dfrac{5}{3}\right)}{1 + (-1)\left(\dfrac{5}{3}\right)} \right| = \left| \dfrac{-\dfrac{8}{3}}{\dfrac{-2}{3}} \right| = |-4| = 4$

$\Rightarrow \theta = \tan^{-1} 4 \approx 76°$ to the nearest degree

(b) $[AC]$ is perpendicular to $[CX]$ (path of black ball after hitting cushion).

Let X be a point on the path of the black ball after hitting the cushion. The slope of $[AC] = -1$, so the slope of $[CX] = 1$, because the lines are perpendicular. C is a point on the line, so we can use the slope–intercept formula for the equation of a line, where slope $= 1$ and $(x_1, y_1) = (7, 0)$.

$y - y_1 = m(x - x_1) \Rightarrow y - 0 = 1(x - 7) \Rightarrow x - y = 7$ represents the path of the black ball.

Assuming that the ball is not hit hard enough to bounce off the end cushion, it could end up at any point on the line $x - y = 7$, for example $(10, 3)$ or $(9, 2)$.

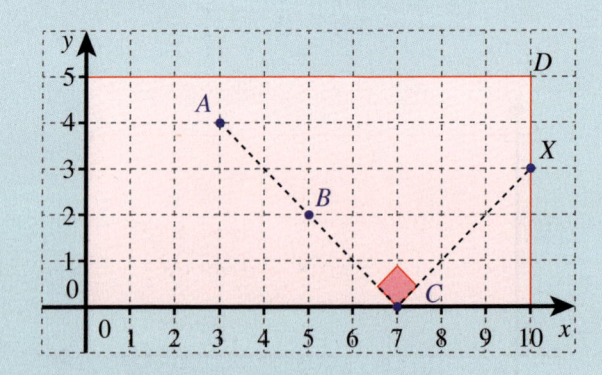

Examples

(a) Find, correct to 1 decimal place, the measures of the angles between the line $j: 3x - 2y - 6 = 0$ and the line $k: 3x + y - 24 = 0$.

(b) A triangle PQR is enclosed between lines j and k and the x-axis. $[PR]$ is on the x-axis. Find the acute angle $|\angle PQR|$.

(c) The point R is moved to a new position on the x-axis and labelled R_1. If $|\angle PQR_1| = 45°$, find the co-ordinates of R_1.

Solutions

Start by drawing a graph to visualise the problem.

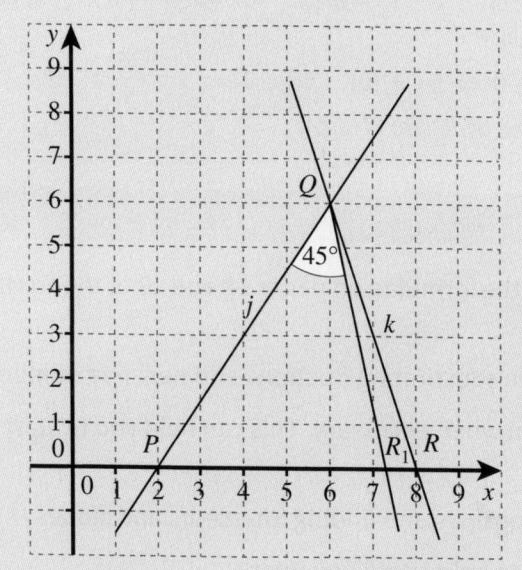

(a) Slope of line $j = \dfrac{-a}{b} = \dfrac{-(3)}{(-2)} = \dfrac{3}{2}$, slope of line $k = \dfrac{-a}{b} = \dfrac{-(3)}{(1)} = -3$

$$\tan\theta = \left|\dfrac{\left(\dfrac{3}{2}\right) - (-3)}{1 + \left(\dfrac{3}{2}\right)(-3)}\right| = \left|\dfrac{\dfrac{3}{2} + 3}{1 - \dfrac{9}{2}}\right| = \left|\dfrac{\dfrac{9}{2}}{\dfrac{-7}{2}}\right| = \left|-\dfrac{9}{7}\right| = \dfrac{9}{7} \Rightarrow \theta = \tan^{-1}\dfrac{9}{7} \approx 52.1°$$

This gives the acute angle. The obtuse angle is $180 - 52.1 = 127.9°$.

(b) $|\angle PQR| = 52.1°$

(c) Slope of PQ = slope of $j = \dfrac{3}{2}$. Let slope of $QR_1 = m$.

Use the formula to find the angle between two lines. Either slope could be m_1 and m_2 so there are two options:

$$\tan 45° = 1 = \left|\dfrac{\dfrac{3}{2} - m}{1 + \dfrac{3}{2}m}\right| \quad \text{or} \quad \tan 45° = 1 = \left|\dfrac{m - \dfrac{3}{2}}{1 + \dfrac{3}{2}m}\right|.$$

3. Co-ordinate Geometry of the Line

$$1 = \left|\dfrac{\frac{3}{2} - m}{1 + \frac{3}{2}m}\right| \Rightarrow 1 + \dfrac{3}{2}m = \dfrac{3}{2} - m \Rightarrow \dfrac{5}{2}m = \dfrac{1}{2} \Rightarrow m = \dfrac{1}{5}$$

$$1 = \left|\dfrac{m - \frac{3}{2}}{1 + \frac{3}{2}m}\right| \Rightarrow 1 + \dfrac{3}{2}m = m - \dfrac{3}{2} \Rightarrow \dfrac{3}{2}m - m = -\dfrac{3}{2} - 1 \Rightarrow m = -5$$

From the diagram, the slope of QR_1 is negative, so $m = -5$. We know one point on the line: $(x_1, y_1) = Q = (6, 6)$.

Equation of the line: $y - y_1 = m(x - x_1) \Rightarrow y - (6) = (-5)(x - (6))$
$\Rightarrow 5x + y - 36 = 0$

x intercept: $y = 0 \Rightarrow 5x + (0) - 36 = 0 \Rightarrow x = \dfrac{36}{5} = 7\cdot2$

The co-ordinates of R_1 are $(7\cdot2, 0)$.

Checklist

- ✓ Practise using the formulae on pages 18 and 19 of the *Formulae and Tables* booklet.
- ✓ Be careful when substituting fractions and negative numbers into formulae.
- ✓ Draw a diagram when necessary. This can help you to start working out a problem.
- ✓ Practise drawing lines and finding intercepts and slopes.
- ✓ Use GeoGebra to help check your work.
- ✓ Read the question carefully. Check the precision required (nearest degree, 1 decimal place, etc.) and don't forget units for distance and area.

Synthetic Geometry 1

4

Learning objectives

In this chapter you will learn how to:

- Use the terms theorem, proof, axiom, corollary, converse, implies, is equivalent to, if and only if, proof by contradiction
- Recognise Axioms 1 to 5
- Investigate Theorems 7, 8, 11, 12, 13, 16, 17, 18, 20 and 21, and Corollary 6
- Prove Theorems 11, 12 and 13, concerning ratios.

Logic and deductive reasoning

You are required to know the following definitions.

An **axiom** is a statement which is assumed to be true and is used as a basis for developing a system. For example, Axiom 1 states that there is exactly one line through any two given points.

A **theorem** is a statement which has been proved to be true.

A **proof** is a sequence of statements (made up of axioms and arguments) leading to the establishment of the truth of one final statement.

A **corollary** follows after a theorem and is a proposition which must be true because of that theorem. For example, Corollary 6 follows Theorem 20 and states that if two circles share a common tangent line at one point, then the centres and that point are collinear.

The **converse** of a theorem is formed by taking the conclusion as the starting point and having the starting point as the conclusion. For example, Theorem 2 states that in an isosceles triangle the angles opposite the equal sides are equal. The converse of Theorem 2 states that if two angles are equal, then the triangle is isosceles.

The word **implies** indicates a logical relationship between two statements, such that if the first is true then the second must also be true.

The phrase **is equivalent to**, or **if and only if**, means that the truth of either one of the connected statements implies the truth of the other, i.e. they are either both true or both false. This is often shortened to **iff** or $\Leftrightarrow$.

A **proof by contradiction** is a proof in which one assumption is made. Then, by using valid arguments, a statement is arrived at which is clearly false, so the original assumption must be false. For example, in the method used in Chapter 1 of Book 1 to prove that $\sqrt{2}$ is irrational we start by assuming that $\sqrt{2}$ is rational.

Axioms 1 to 5

Axiom 1 (Two Points Axiom) There is exactly one line through any two given points.

Axiom 2 (Ruler Axiom) The distance between two points A and B has the following properties:

1. The distance $|AB|$ is never negative.
2. $|AB| = |BA|$
3.

   If C lies on AB, between A and B, then $|AB| = |AC| + |CB|$.

4.

   (Marking off a distance) Given any ray from A, and given any real number $k \geq 0$, there is a unique point B on the ray whose distance from A is k.

Axiom 3 (Protractor Axiom) The number of degrees in an angle (also known as its degree-measure) is always a number between 0° and 360°. The number of degrees of an ordinary angle is less than 180°. It has the following properties.

1. A straight angle has 180°.
2.

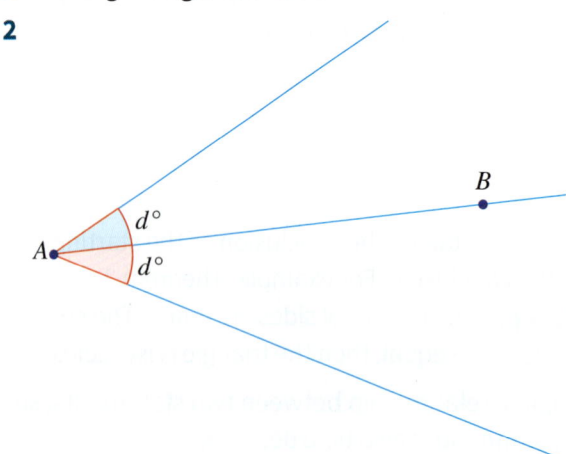

   Given a ray $[AB$, and a number d between 0 and 180, there is exactly one ray from A on each side of the line AB that makes an (ordinary) angle of d degrees with the ray $[AB$.

3

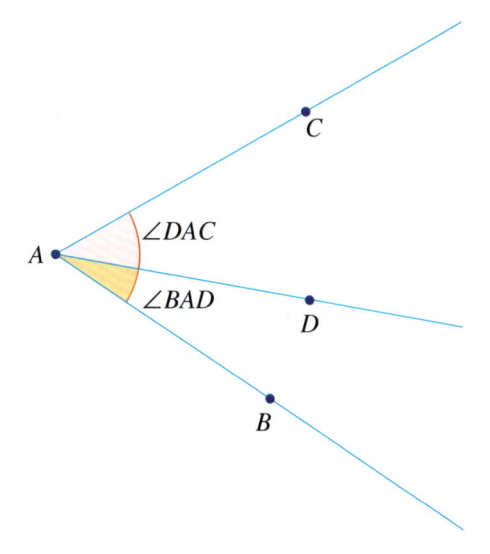

If D is a point inside an angle $\angle BAC$, then $|\angle BAC| = |\angle BAD| + |\angle DAC|$.

Axiom 4 (Congruent Triangles) Two triangles are congruent if

1. two sides and the angle between those sides are the same in both (**SAS**)

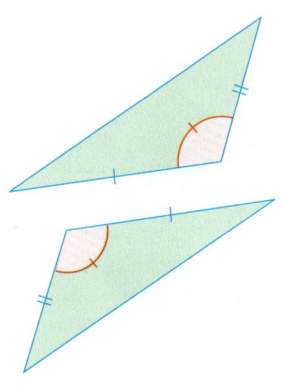

or

2. two angles and the side between them are the same in both (**ASA**)

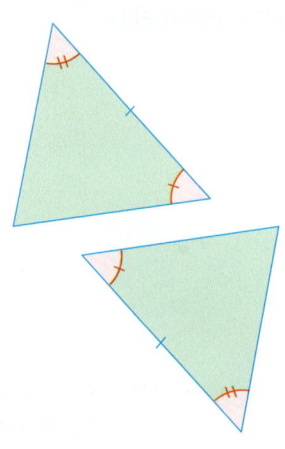

or

3 all three sides are equal in both (**SSS**)

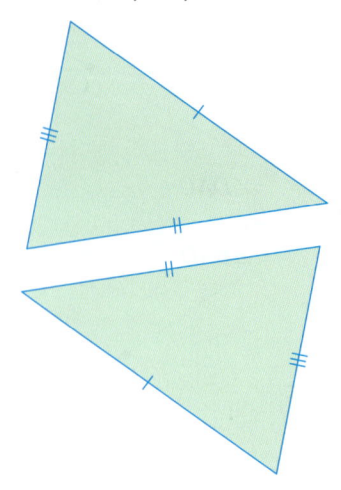

or

4 the triangles are right angled, and the hypotenuse and one other side are the same in both (**RHS**).

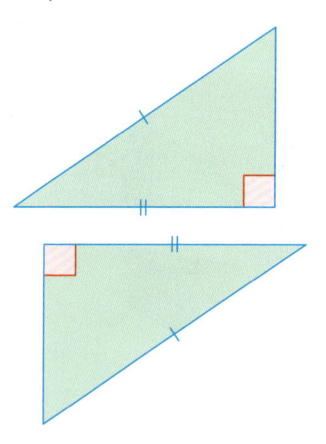

Axiom 5 (Axiom of Parallels) Given any line l and a point P not on l, there is exactly one line through P that is parallel to l.

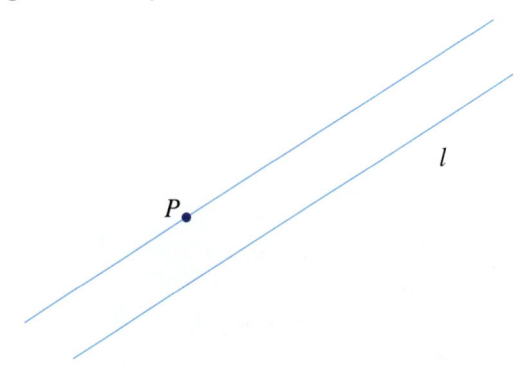

Theorems 1 to 21

Theorem 1 Vertically opposite angles are equal in measure.

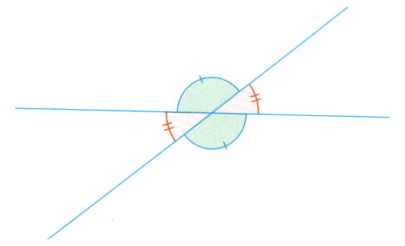

Theorem 2 In an isosceles triangle the angles opposite the equal sides are equal. Conversely, if two angles are equal, then the triangle is isosceles.

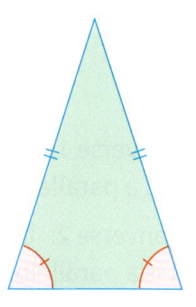

Theorem 3 (Alternate Angles) If a transversal makes equal alternate angles on two lines, then the lines are parallel. Conversely, if two lines are parallel, then any transversal makes equal angles on the lines.

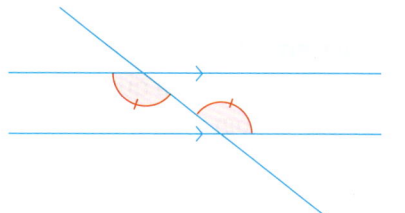

Theorem 4 The angles in a triangle add up to 180°.

Theorem 5 (Corresponding Angles) Two lines are parallel if and only if for any transversal, corresponding angles are equal.

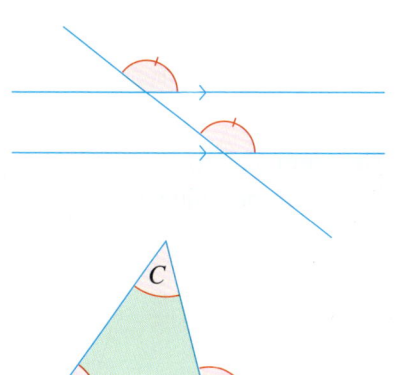

Theorem 6 (Exterior Angle) Each exterior angle of a triangle is equal to the sum of the interior opposite angles. $D = B + C$.

Theorem 7 The angle opposite the greater of two sides is greater than the angle opposite the lesser side. Conversely, the side opposite the greater of two angles is greater than the side opposite the lesser angle.
$|PR| > |PQ| \Leftrightarrow |\angle PQR| > |\angle PRQ|$.

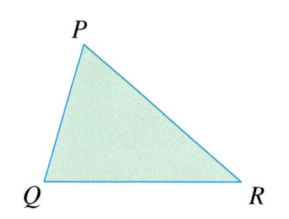

Theorem 8 (Triangle Inequality) The sum of any two sides of a triangle is greater than the length of the third side. $a + c > b, a + b > c, b + c > a.$

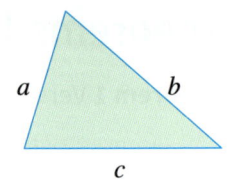

Theorem 9 In a parallelogram, opposite sides are equal, and opposite angles are equal.

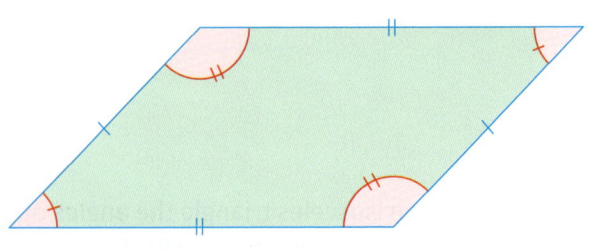

Converse 1: If the opposite angles of a quadrilateral are equal, then it is a parallelogram.

Converse 2: If the opposite sides of a quadrilateral are equal, then it is a parallelogram.

Corollary 1: A diagonal divides a parallelogram into two congruent triangles.

Theorem 10 The diagonals of a parallelogram bisect one another. Conversely, if the diagonals of a quadrilateral bisect one another, then the quadrilateral is a parallelogram.

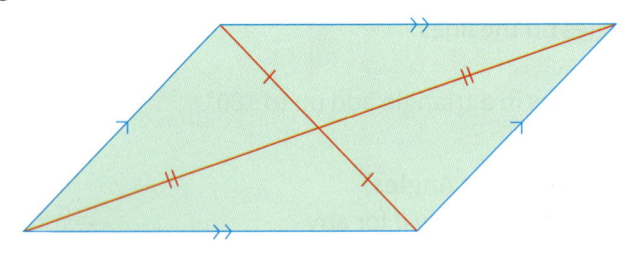

Theorem 11 If three parallel lines cut off equal segments on some transversal line, then they will cut off equal segments on any other transversal.

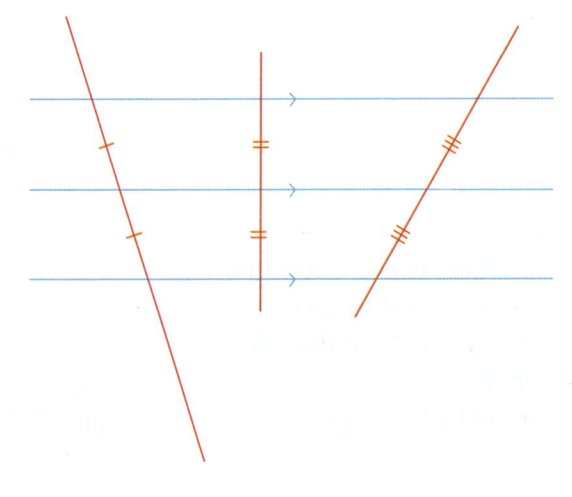

Theorem 12 Let ABC be a triangle. If a line l is parallel to BC and cuts $[AB]$ in the ratio $s:t$, then it also cuts $[AC]$ in the same ratio. $|AD|:|DB| = |AE|:|EC|$.

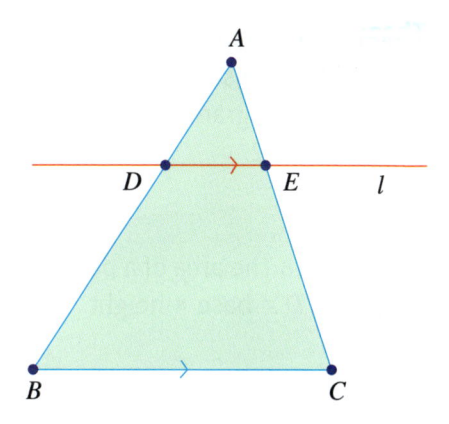

Theorem 13 If two triangles ABC and $A'B'C'$ are similar, then their sides are proportional, in order:

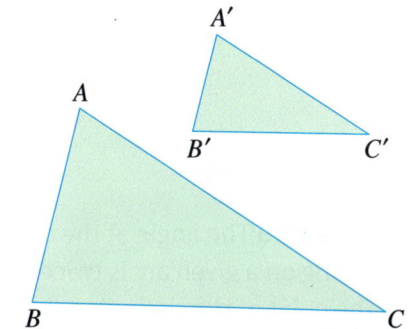

$$\frac{|AB|}{|A'B'|} = \frac{|BC|}{|B'C'|} = \frac{|CA|}{|C'A'|}.$$

Theorem 14 (Pythagoras) In a right-angled triangle the square of the hypotenuse is equal to the sum of the squares of the other two sides. $a^2 = b^2 + c^2$.

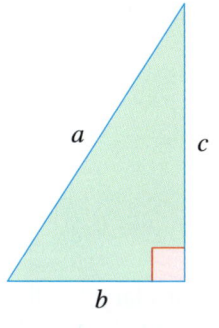

Theorem 15 (Converse to Pythagoras) If the square of one side of a triangle is equal to the sum of the squares of the other two sides, then the angle opposite the first side is a right angle.

Theorem 16 When calculating the area of a triangle using area = $\frac{1}{2}$ base × height, the result does not depend on the choice of base.

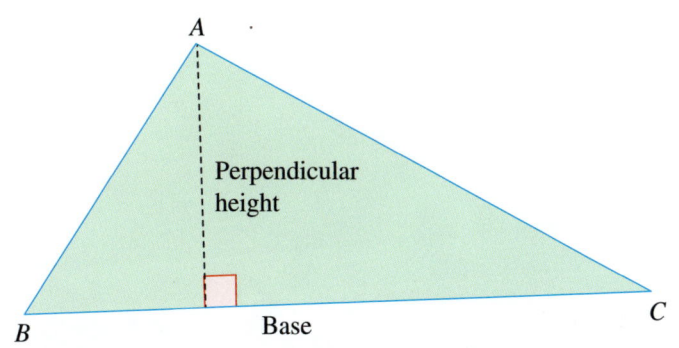

4. Synthetic Geometry 1

Theorem 17 A diagonal of a parallelogram bisects the area of the parallelogram.
Area 1 = Area 2.

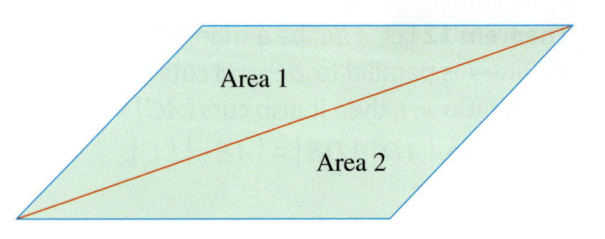

Theorem 18 The area of a parallelogram is the base multiplied by the height.
Area $ABCD$ = base × height.

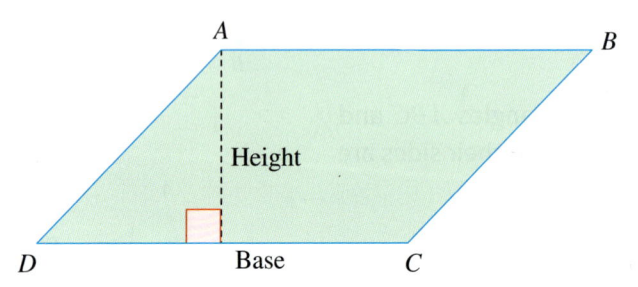

Theorem 19 The angle at the centre of a circle standing on a given arc is twice the angle at the point of the circle standing on the same arc.

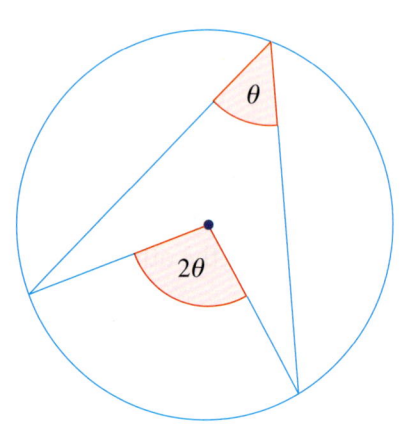

Corollary 2: All angles at points of a circle, standing on the same arc, are equal.

Corollary 3: Each angle in a semicircle is a right angle.

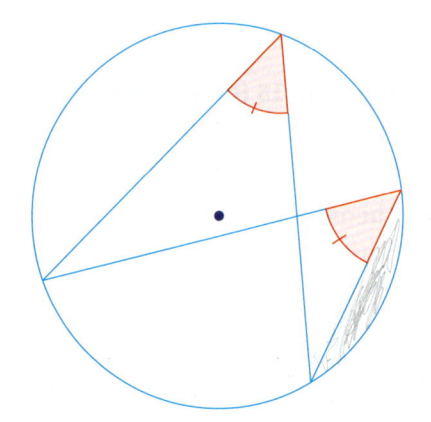

Corollary 4: If the angle standing on a chord $[BC]$ at some point of a circle is a right angle, then $[BC]$ is a diameter.

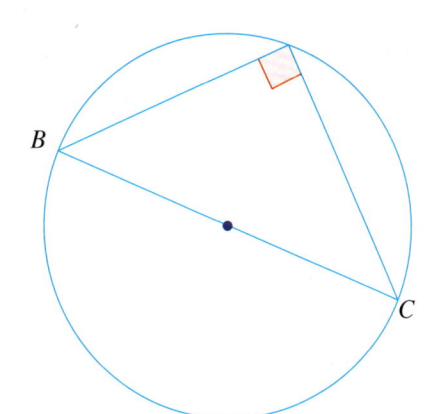

Corollary 5: If $ABCD$ is a cyclic quadrilateral, then opposite angles sum to 180°. Conversely, if the opposite angles of a quadrilateral sum to 180°, then the quadrilateral is cyclic.

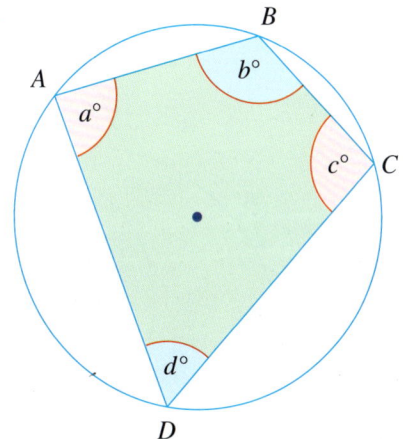

$a + c = 180°$, $b + d = 180°$, $a + b + c + d = 360°$

Theorem 20

1. Each tangent to a circle is perpendicular to the radius that goes to the point of contact.

2. If a point P lies on a circle s, and a line l through P is perpendicular to the radius to P, then l is a tangent to s.

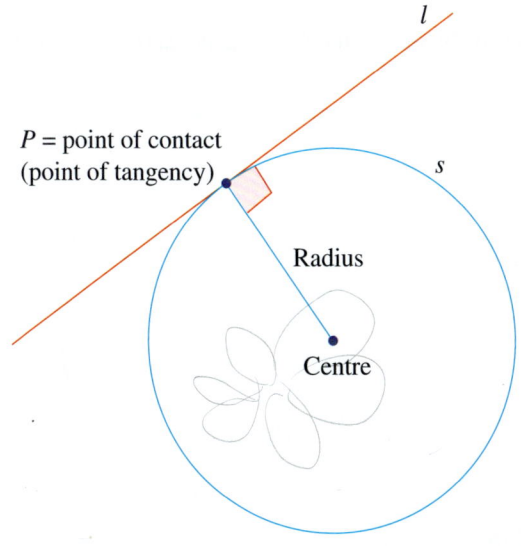

P = point of contact (point of tangency)

Corollary 6: If two circles intersect at one point only, then the two centres and the point of contact are collinear.

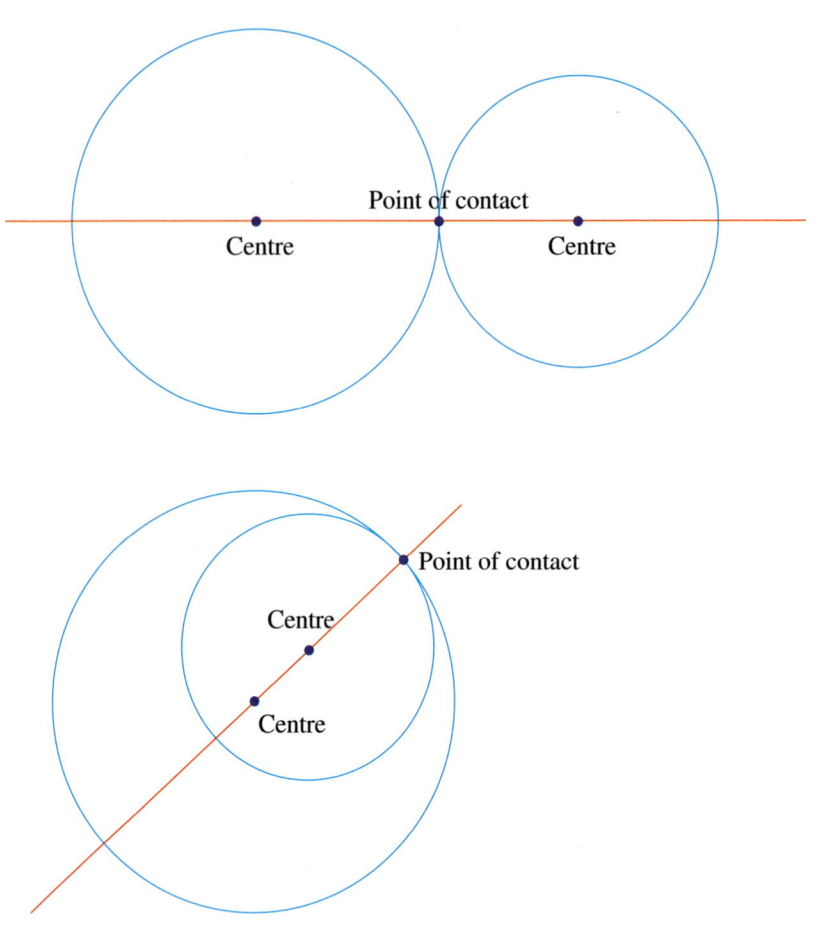

Theorem 21

1. The perpendicular from a chord to the centre of a circle bisects the chord.
2. The perpendicular bisector of a chord passes through the centre of the circle.

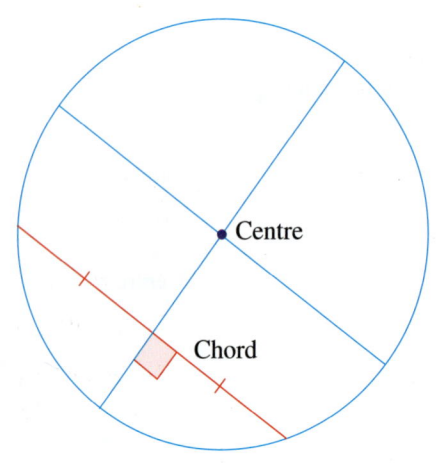

Proofs of Theorems 11, 12 and 13

> **Top Tip**
> If the proof of a theorem is asked for in an exam, include the sections 'Diagram', 'Given', 'To prove', 'Construction' and 'Proof' in your answer, as shown in the examples.

Proof of Theorem 11

Theorem: If three parallel lines cut off equal segments on some transversal line, then they will cut off equal segments on any other transversal.

Diagram:

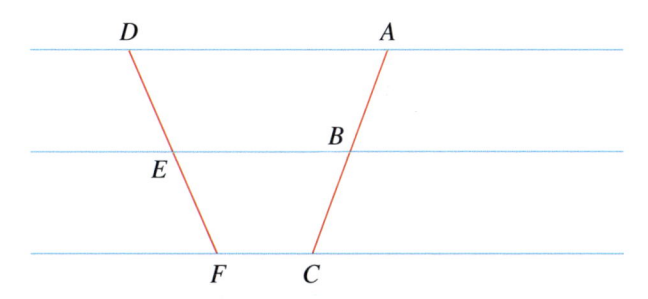

Given: Assume $AD \parallel BE \parallel CF$ and $|AB| = |BC|$. (This is another way of stating 'three parallel lines cut off equal segments on some transversal line'.)

To prove: $|DE| = |EF|$. (This is another way of stating 'they will cut off equal segments on any other transversal'.)

Construction: Draw $AE' \parallel DE$, cutting EB at E' and CF at F'.
Draw $F'B' \parallel AB$, cutting EB at B'.

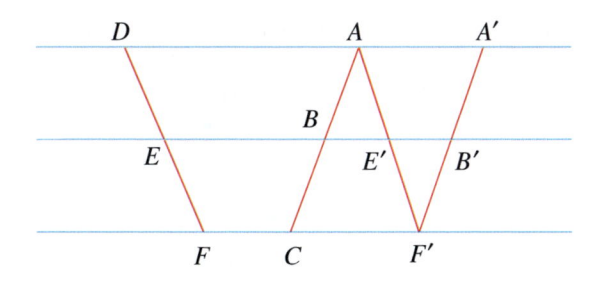

Proof:

$\|B'F'\| = \|BC\|$	By Theorem 9.
$= \|AB\|$	By assumption.
$\|\angle BAE'\| = \|\angle E'F'B'\|$	By the Alternate Angle theorem.
$\|\angle AE'B\| = \|\angle F'E'B'\|$	Because they are vertically opposite angles.

4. Synthetic Geometry 1

Therefore $\triangle ABE'$ is congruent to $\triangle F'B'E'$.   By ASA.
Therefore $|AE'| = |F'E'|$.
But $|AE'| = |DE|$ and $|F'E'| = |FE|$ By Theorem 9.
Therefore $|DE| = |EF|$ as required.

Proof of Theorem 12

Theorem: Let ABC be a triangle. If a line l is parallel to BC and cuts $[AB]$ in the ratio $s:t$, then it also cuts $[AC]$ in the same ratio. $|AD|:|DB| = |AE|:|EC|$.

Diagram:

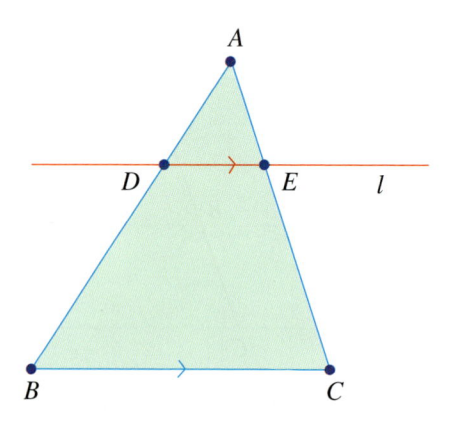

Given: $l \parallel BC$ and $|AD|:|DB| = s:t$.

To prove: $|AE|:|EC| = s:t$.

Construction: Let the points $D_0 = A$, $D_1, D_2, ..., D_{s-1}, D_s = D$, $D_{s+1}, ..., D_{s+t-1}, D_{s+t} = B$ be equally spaced along $[AB]$, i.e. the segments $[D_0, D_1], [D_1, D_2], ..., [D_i, D_{i+1}], ..., [D_{s+t-1}, D_{s+t}]$ have equal length.

Draw lines $D_1 E_1, D_2 E_2, ...$ parallel to BC with $E_1, E_2, ...$ on $[AC]$.

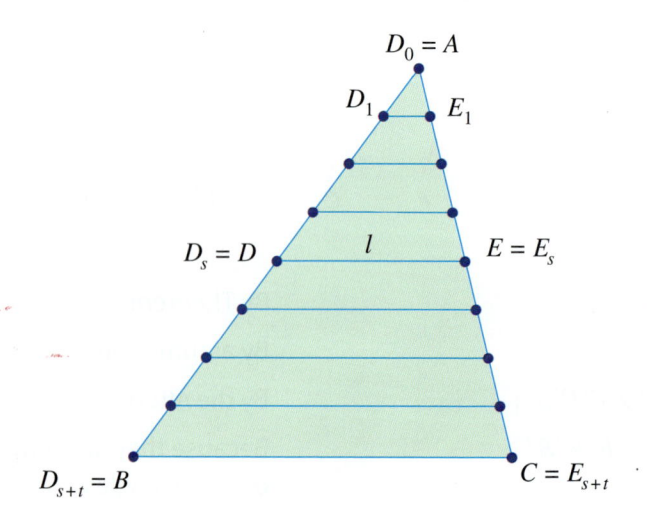

Proof: By Theorem 11, all the segments $[AE_1], [E_1E_2], [E_2E_3], ..., [E_{s+t-1}C]$ have the same length.

By the Axiom of Parallels, $E_s = E$ is the point where l cuts $[AC]$.

Therefore E divides $[AC]$ in the ratio $s:t$, so $|AE|:|EC| = s:t$, as required.

Proof of Theorem 13

Theorem: If two triangles ABC and $A'B'C'$ are similar, then their sides are proportional, in order:
$$\frac{|AB|}{|A'B'|} = \frac{|BC|}{|B'C'|} = \frac{|CA|}{|C'A'|}.$$

Diagram:

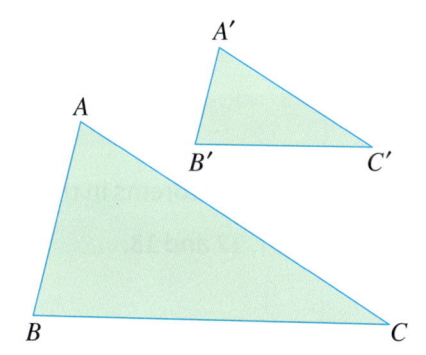

Given: Triangles ABC and $A'B'C'$ are similar.

To prove: $\frac{|AB|}{|A'B'|} = \frac{|BC|}{|B'C'|} = \frac{|CA|}{|C'A'|}.$

Construction: Mark B'' on $[AB]$ such that $|AB''| = |A'B'|$.

Mark C'' on $[AC]$ such that $|AC''| = |A'C'|$.

Join B'' and C''.

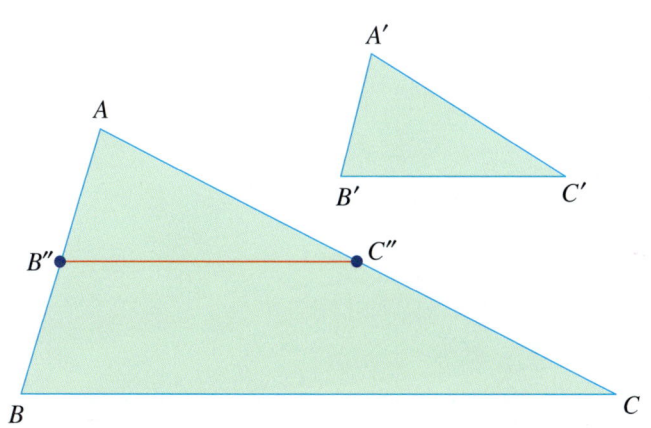

Proof: $\triangle AB''C''$ is congruent to $\triangle A'B'C'$ By SAS.

$\Rightarrow |\triangle AB''C''| = |\triangle ABC|$

$\Rightarrow B''C'' \parallel BC$ By corresponding angles.

Hence, $\dfrac{|AB|}{|AB''|} = \dfrac{|AC|}{|AC''|}$ By Theorem 11.

$\Rightarrow \dfrac{|AB|}{|A'B'|} = \dfrac{|AC|}{|A'C'|}$

Similarly, $\dfrac{|BC|}{|B'C'|} = \dfrac{|AB|}{|A'B'|}$.

Hence $\dfrac{|AB|}{|A'B'|} = \dfrac{|BC|}{|B'C'|} = \dfrac{|CA|}{|C'A'|}$, as required.

Checklist

- ✓ Be familiar with all the axioms and theorems in this chapter.
- ✓ Learn the proofs of Theorems 11, 12 and 13.

Synthetic Geometry 2

5

Learning objectives

In this chapter you will learn how to:
- Solve problems related to Theorems 1 to 21
- Perform the constructions required by the syllabus
- Recognise triangle centres and solve related problems
- Use transformation geometry
- Investigate enlargements and their effect on area, paying attention to
  - Centre of enlargement
  - Scale factor k where $0 < k < 1$ or $k > 1$ and $k \in \mathbb{Q}$
- Solve problems involving enlargements.

Application of Theorems 1 to 21

Refer to Chapter 4 for details of Theorems 1 to 21.

> **Point to note**
> Any synthetic geometry on the exam paper will be based on the geometry set out in the syllabus. There will no longer be a question with internal choice on this topic.

Examples

$[AB]$ and $[CD]$ are chords of a circle that intersect externally at E, as shown.

(a) Name two similar triangles in the diagram and give reasons for your answer.

(b) Prove that $|EA|.|EB| = |EC|.|ED|$.

(c) Given that $|EB| = 6.25$, $|ED| = 5.94$ and $|CB| = 10$, find $|AD|$.

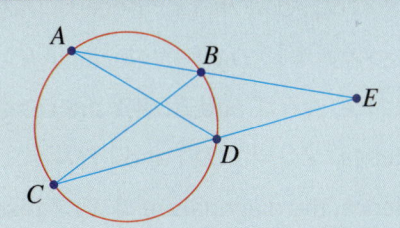

(SEC 2014)

Solutions

(a) $\triangle ADE$ and $\triangle BCE$ are similar.

$	\angle EAD	=	\angle BCE	$	Because they both stand on the arc BD.
$	\angle DEA	=	\angle CEB	$	Because they are the same angle.
$	\angle ADE	=	\angle EBC	$	Because they are the third angles in the triangles.

Therefore, all three angles are the same and the triangles are similar.

(b) $\triangle ADE$ and $\triangle BCE$ are similar.

Hence, $\dfrac{|EA|}{|EC|} = \dfrac{|ED|}{|EB|}$

$\Rightarrow |EA|.|EB| = |EC|.|ED|$.

(c) $\dfrac{|ED|}{|EB|} = \dfrac{|AD|}{|CB|} \Rightarrow \dfrac{5.94}{6.25} = \dfrac{|AD|}{10}$

$\Rightarrow |AD| = \dfrac{5.94 \times 10}{6.25} = 9.504$

Point to note

Other pairs of similar triangles are $\triangle AXB$ and $\triangle DXC$, or $\triangle ACX$ and $\triangle BXD$, where X is the point of intersection of AD and CB.

Example

A quadrilateral (four-sided figure) has two sides which are parallel and equal in length. Prove that the quadrilateral is a parallelogram. *(SEC 2013)*

Solution

Draw a diagram of the quadrilateral and label the vertices W, X, Y and Z.
We are given that $WX \parallel ZY$ and $|WX| = |ZY|$.
We need to prove that $WXYZ$ is a parallelogram.
Join Z to X and Y to W, as in the diagram. 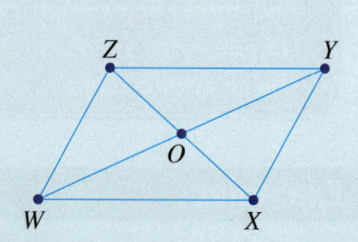
In $\triangle ZOY$ and $\triangle OWX$,
$|ZY| = |WX|$
$|\angle ZYO| = |\angle OWX|$ Because $WX \parallel ZY$.
$|\angle YZO| = |\angle OXW|$ Because $WX \parallel ZY$.
Hence, $\triangle ZOY$ and $\triangle OWX$ are congruent, because of AAS.
Hence, $|ZO| = |OX|$ and $|YO| = |OW|$.
Hence, the diagonals of $WXYZ$ bisect each other, so $WXYZ$ is a parallelogram.

Example

In the diagram, P_1Q_1, P_2Q_2 and P_3Q_3 are parallel, and so are Q_1P_2 and Q_2P_3.

Prove that $|P_1Q_1| \times |P_3Q_3| = |P_2Q_2|^2$. *(SEC 2011)*

Solution

The approach to this proof is to use Theorem 12 and similar triangles to establish relationships between the given segments, then rearrange to the form stated in the question.

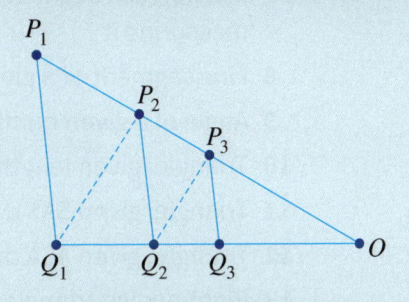

$\dfrac{|OP_3|}{|OP_2|} = \dfrac{|OQ_2|}{|OQ_1|}$ By Theorem 12, because $P_3Q_2 \parallel P_2Q_1$.

$\dfrac{|OP_2|}{|OP_1|} = \dfrac{|OQ_2|}{|OQ_1|}$ By Theorem 12, because $P_2Q_2 \parallel P_1Q_1$.

Therefore, $\dfrac{|OP_3|}{|OP_2|} = \dfrac{|OP_2|}{|OP_1|}$.

$\dfrac{|OP_2|}{|OP_1|} = \dfrac{|P_2Q_2|}{|P_1Q_1|}$ By similar triangles.

$\dfrac{|OP_3|}{|OP_2|} = \dfrac{|P_3Q_3|}{|P_2Q_2|}$ By similar triangles.

Therefore, $\dfrac{|P_2Q_2|}{|P_1Q_1|} = \dfrac{|P_3Q_3|}{|P_2Q_2|}$.   Multiply both sides by $|P_1Q_1|$ and $|P_2Q_2|$ to obtain the equation in the required form.

Therefore, $|P_1Q_1| \times |P_3Q_3| = |P_2Q_2|^2$.

Constructions

There are 22 constructions that you need to be able to carry out using only the instruments listed for each construction:

1. Bisector of a given angle, using only compass and straight edge
2. Perpendicular bisector of a segment, using only compass and straight edge
3. Line perpendicular to a given line l, passing through a given point not on l
4. Line perpendicular to a given line l, passing through a given point on l
5. Line parallel to a given line, through a given point

5. Synthetic Geometry 2

6. Division of a segment into two or three equal segments, without measuring it
7. Division of a segment into any number of equal segments, without measuring it
8. Line segment of a given length on a given ray
9. Angle of a given number of degrees with a given ray as one arm
10. Triangle, given lengths of three sides
11. Triangle, given SAS data
12. Triangle, given ASA data
13. Right-angled triangle, given the length of the hypotenuse and one other side
14. Right-angled triangle, given one side and one of the acute angles (several cases)
15. Rectangle, given side lengths
16. Circumcentre and circumcircle of a given triangle, using only straight edge and compass
17. Incentre and incircle of a given triangle, using only straight edge and compass
18. Angle of 60°, without using a protractor or set-square
19. Tangent to a given circle at a given point on it
20. Parallelogram, given the length of the sides and the measure of the angles
21. Centroid of a triangle
22. Orthocentre of a triangle.

> **Top Tip**
>
> All the required constructions will be covered in your textbook. Useful websites that show how to carry out the constructions are www.projectmaths.ie and www.mathopenref.com.

Examples

(a) Given the points B and C below, construct, without using a protractor or set-square, a point A such that $|\angle ABC| = 60°$.

$B \bullet \text{————————} \bullet C \text{————}$

(b) Hence construct, on the same diagram, using a compass and straight edge only, an angle of 15°.

(SEC 2012)

Solutions

(a) 1. Place the point of the compass on point B and draw a circle passing through point C.

2. Without changing the size of the compass, place the point on point C and draw a circle passing through point B.

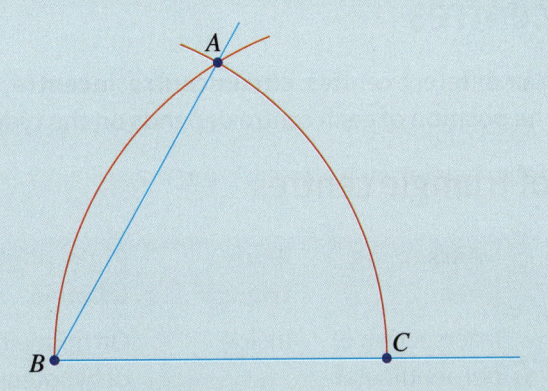

The point where the two circles intersect is point A. Because $|AB| = |AC| = |BC|$, the three points form an equilateral triangle, so $|\angle ABC| = 60°$.

(b) Start by bisecting $|\angle ABC|$ to get a 30° angle, then bisect again to get a 15° angle.

1. Place the point of the compass on point C and draw a small arc roughly halfway between A and C.

2. Without changing the size of the compass, place the point on point A and draw a small arc that intersects the arc from step 1.

3. Draw a line from point B to the point where the arcs intersect.

4. Repeat the steps above, using the point where the line from step 3 intersects the first circle from part (a) in place of point A.

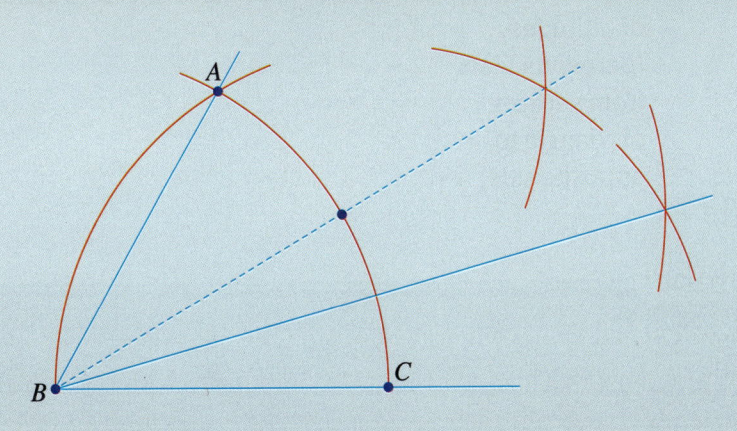

5. Synthetic Geometry 2

> **Top Tip**
>
> If necessary, revise the construction of a perpendicular line through a point from your textbook.

Triangle centres

A triangle has four different centres: **circumcentre**, **incentre**, **centroid** and **orthocentre**. The position of each centre depends on the type of triangle.

Summary of triangle centres

Centre	Intersecting lines	Acute triangle	Right-angled triangle	Obtuse triangle
Circumcentre (equidistant from all three vertices)	Intersection of perpendicular bisectors of the sides	Inside	On midpoint of hypotenuse	Outside
Incentre (equidistant from all three sides)	Intersection of angle bisectors	Inside	Inside	Inside
Centroid (centre of mass or balancing point of triangle)	Intersection of medians (centroid divides each median in ratio 2 : 1)	Inside	Inside	Inside
Orthocentre	Intersection of altitudes (perpendiculars from vertices of triangle to opposite side)	Inside	On right angle	Outside

> **Remember**
>
> An acute triangle has three angles of less than 90°.
> An obtuse triangle has one angle of more than 90°.

Some examples of triangle centres are shown below.

- Circumcentre of a right-angled triangle

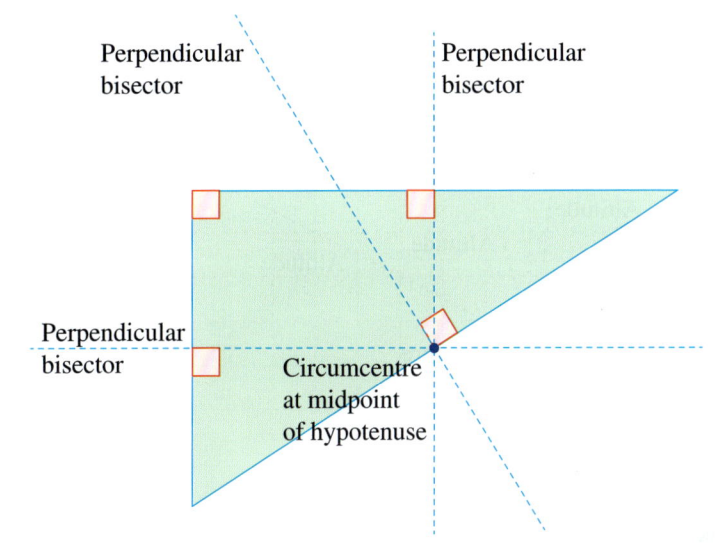

- Incentre of an obtuse triangle

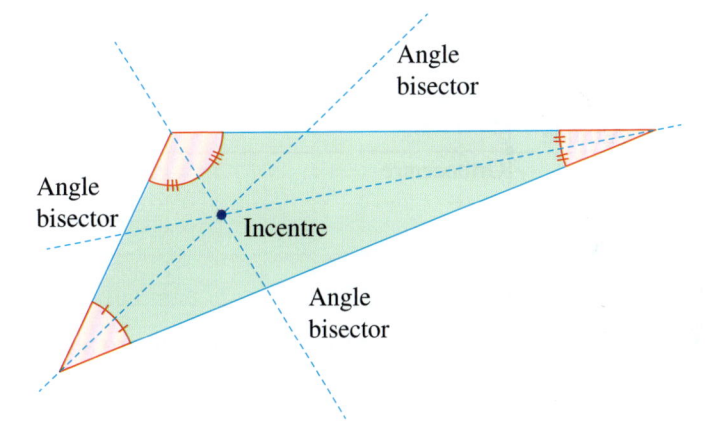

- Centroid of a right-angled triangle

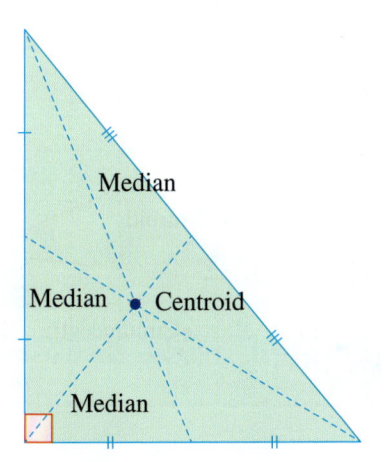

- Orthocentre of an obtuse triangle

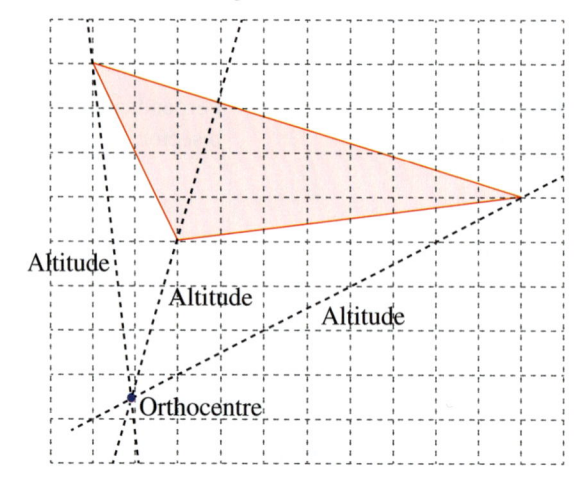

- Orthocentre of a right-angled triangle

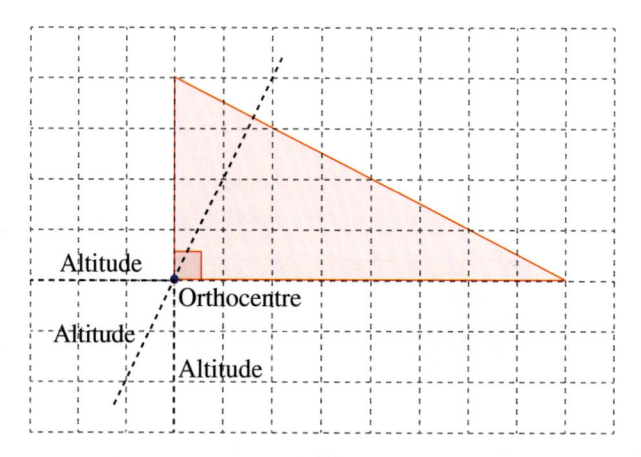

The orthocentre, centroid and circumcentre in any triangle are always in a line, called **Euler's line**.

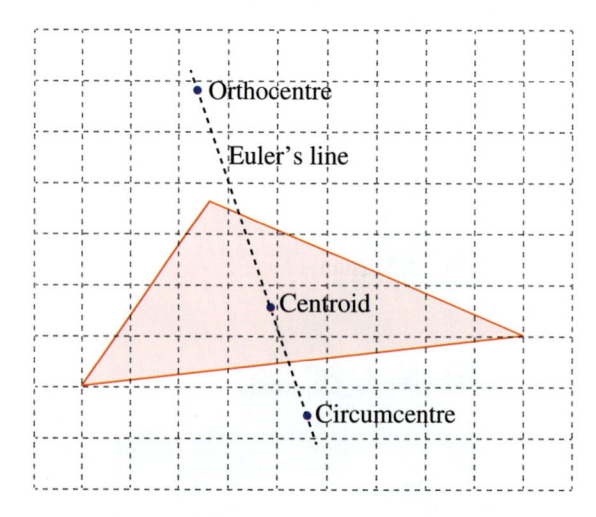

In the case of an equilateral triangle, the orthocentre, centroid, circumcentre and incentre coincide.

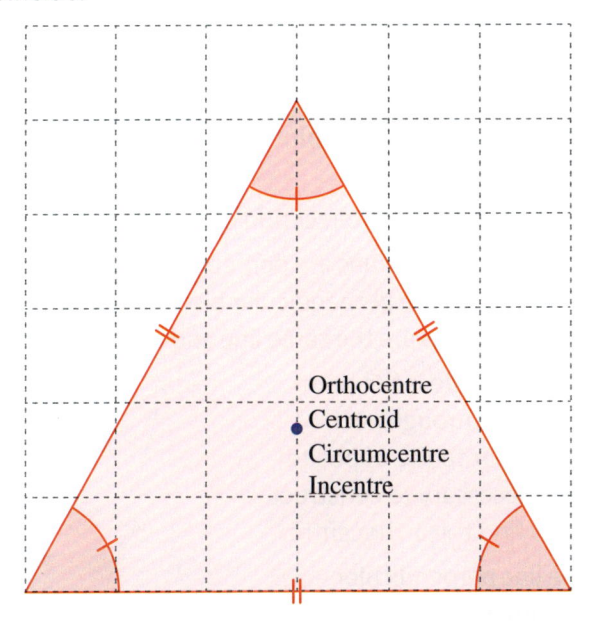

Examples

(a) Complete each of the following statements.

  (i) The circumcentre of a triangle is the point of intersection of …

  (ii) The incentre of a triangle is the point of intersection of …

  (iii) The centroid of a triangle is the point of intersection of …

(b) In an equilateral triangle, the circumcentre, the incentre and the centroid are all in the same place. Explain why this is the case.

(c) Construct the orthocentre of the triangle ABC below. Show all construction lines clearly.

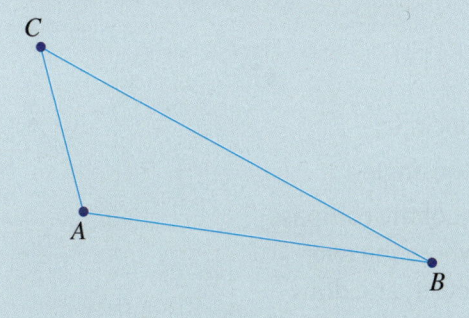

(SEC 2013)

Solutions

(a) **(i)** The circumcentre of a triangle is the point of intersection of … the perpendicular bisectors of the sides of the triangle.

(ii) The incentre of a triangle is the point of intersection of … the bisectors of the angles of the triangle.

(iii) The centroid is the point of intersection of … the medians of the triangle.

(b) In an equilateral triangle the medians are perpendicular to the opposite sides and bisect the angles. Therefore, the perpendicular bisectors of the sides, the bisectors of the angles and the medians are the same line and intersect at one point.

(c) The orthocentre of a triangle is the point where the lines that run through each vertex and perpendicular to the opposite side meet. It is only necessary to construct two of these lines to find the orthocentre.

Start by finding the line perpendicular to AB that passes through point C. Then find the line perpendicular to AC that passes through point B. The point where these lines meet is the orthocentre. In this case, the orthocentre is outside the triangle.

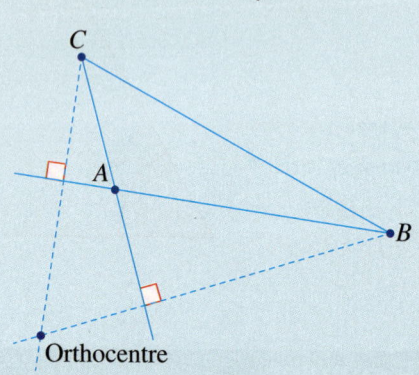

Examples

(a) Construct the incircle of the triangle ABC using only a compass and straight edge. Show all construction lines clearly.

(b) An equilateral triangle has sides of length 2 units. Find the area of its incircle.

(SEC 2010)

Solutions

(a) To construct the incircle:

1. Bisect two of the angles.
2. Place the point of the compass on the place where the two bisectors intersect, and draw a circle that touches all three sides.

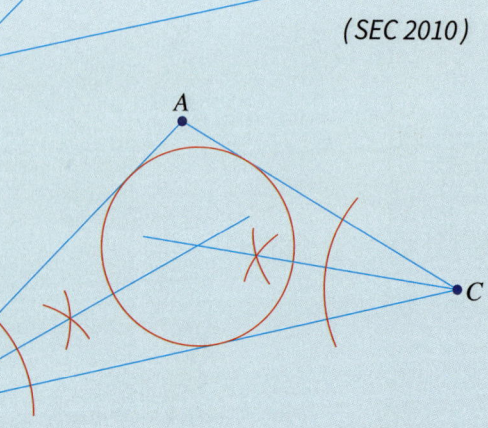

(b) The diagram shows how the radius of the incircle relates to the sides of an equilateral triangle.
We can use trigonometry to find the radius.

$\tan 30° = \dfrac{r}{1}$

$\Rightarrow r = \dfrac{1}{\sqrt{3}}$

Now substitute the value for r into the formula for the area of a circle.

$A = \pi r^2 = \pi \left(\dfrac{1}{\sqrt{3}}\right)^2 = \dfrac{\pi}{3}$ square units

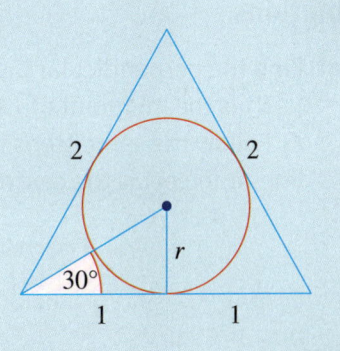

Examples

An interior designer is making a triangular glass table for a customer. The top of the table needs to balance on a single leg, which is at the centroid of the triangle.

(a) Using the diagram on the right construct the centroid of the triangular glass table. Show all construction lines clearly.

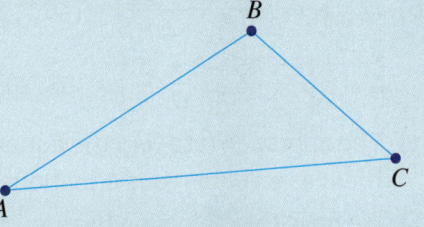

(b) If the vertices of the triangle are given as $A = (16, 16)$, $B = (47, 40)$ and $C = (65, 20)$, find the co-ordinates of the points D and E as shown in the diagram (not graphically).

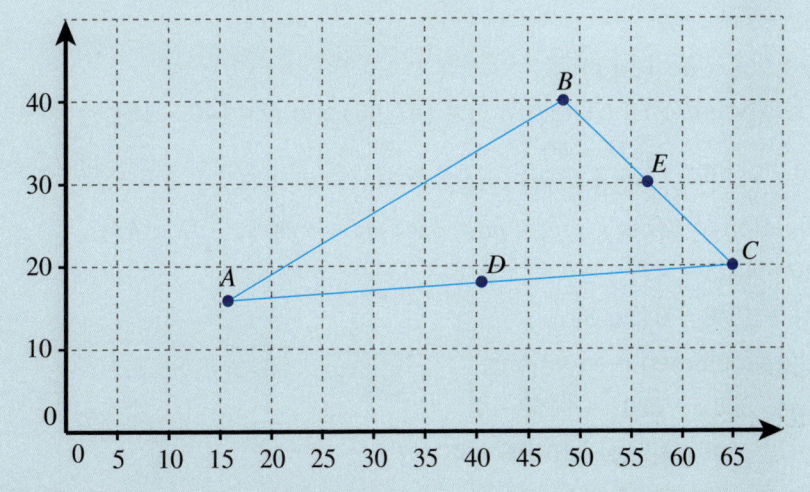

(c) Hence, find the co-ordinates of the centroid O of the triangle ABC.

(d) Verify that the point O divides the median $[BD]$ in the ratio $2:1$.

Solutions

(a) Find the perpendicular bisector of $[AB]$. The point where this line intersects $[AB]$ is the midpoint of $[AB]$. Join this point to C to draw the median through C. Follow the same steps to draw the median through A. The point where these lines intersect is the centroid.

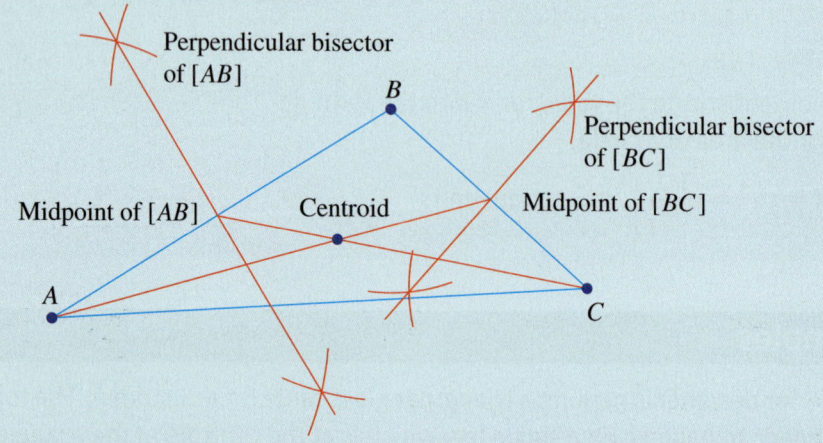

(b) $D = \left(\dfrac{16 + 65}{2}, \dfrac{16 + 20}{2}\right) = (40 \cdot 5, 18)$

$E = \left(\dfrac{47 + 65}{2}, \dfrac{40 + 20}{2}\right) = (56, 30)$

(c) The approach is to find the equations of the medians AE and BD and solve them as simultaneous equations to find the point where they intersect.

We have two points on the line AE: $E = (56, 30)$ and $A = (16, 16)$.

Therefore the slope $= \left|\dfrac{16 - 30}{16 - 56}\right| = \dfrac{7}{20} = m$

So the equation of AE is $y - y_1 = m(x - x_1) \Rightarrow y - 30 = \dfrac{7}{20}(x - 56)$

$20y - 600 = 7x - 392$

$7x - 20y + 208 = 0 \quad \text{(Eq 1)}$

We have two points on the line BD: $B = (47, 40)$ and $D = (40 \cdot 5, 18)$.

Therefore the slope $= \left|\dfrac{18 - 40}{40 \cdot 5 - 47}\right| = \dfrac{44}{13} = m$

So the equation of BD is $y - y_1 = m(x - x_1) \Rightarrow y - 40 = \dfrac{44}{13}(x - 47)$

$13y - 520 = 44(x - 47)$

$44x - 13y - 1548 = 0 \quad \text{(Eq 2)}$

Solving the simultaneous equations:

(Eq 1) × 44: $308x - 880y + 9152 = 0$

(Eq 2) × −7: $-308x + 91y + 10\,836 = 0$

Adding gives: $-789y + 19\,988 = 0$

$\Rightarrow y = \dfrac{76}{3}$

Substitution in (Eq 1) gives $7x - 20\left(\dfrac{76}{3}\right) + 208 = 0$

$\Rightarrow 7x - \dfrac{896}{3} = 0 \Rightarrow 7x = \dfrac{896}{3}$

$\Rightarrow x = \dfrac{128}{3}$

So the centroid O is at $\left(\dfrac{128}{3}, \dfrac{76}{3}\right)$.

We can check this by using the formula for finding the centroid of a triangle:

$O = \left(\dfrac{x_1 + x_2 + x_3}{3}, \dfrac{y_1 + y_2 + y_3}{3}\right) = \left(\dfrac{16 + 47 + 65}{3}, \dfrac{16 + 40 + 20}{3}\right) = \left(\dfrac{128}{3}, \dfrac{76}{3}\right)$

(d) Use the division of a line segment formula: $\left(\dfrac{bx_1 + ax_2}{b + a}, \dfrac{by_1 + ay_2}{b + a}\right)$

$B = (47, 40) = (x_1, y_1)$

$D = (40 \cdot 5, 18) = (x_2, y_2)$

Ratio $2 : 1 = a : b$

$O = \left(\dfrac{1(47) + 2(40 \cdot 5)}{3}, \dfrac{1(40) + 2(18)}{3}\right) = \left(\dfrac{128}{3}, \dfrac{76}{3}\right)$ ✓

Transformations

In geometry, **transformations** involve the movement or mapping of objects in the co-ordinate plane. The shape that is being moved is called the **object**, and the resulting shape after the move or transformation is called the **image**.

There are four main types of transformation:

- **translation**
- **reflection** (in a line or a point)
- **rotation**
- **enlargement**.

Summary of transformations

Transformation	Size of object/image Measure of angle	Position of image	Length of image line segment	Area of object/image
Translation	Same	Depends on distance and direction of given translation	Same	Same

5. Synthetic Geometry 2

Transformation	Size of object/image Measure of angle	Position of image	Length of image line segment	Area of object/image
Reflection in a line	Same	Mirror image on opposite side of line	Same	Same
Reflection in a point	Same	Turned upside down	Same	Same
Rotation	Same	Depends on measure of angle (clockwise or anti-clockwise) and centre of rotation	Same	Same
Enlargement	Size is different Measure of angle remains the same	Depends on centre of enlargement and scale factor	Different	Different

Translation

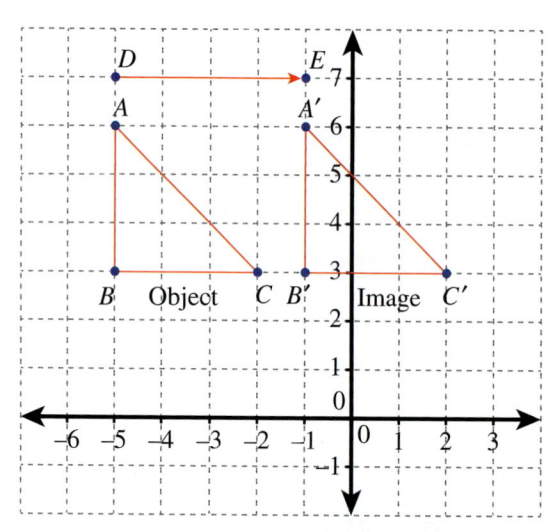

In the above diagram, the triangle ABC has been translated by the vector $\overrightarrow{DE}$. This is a translation of 4 units to the right.

The x co-ordinates of A, B and C are each increased by 4.

$A = (-5, 6) \rightarrow A' = (-1, 6)$

$B = (-5, 3) \rightarrow B' = (-1, 3)$

$C = (-2, 3) \rightarrow C' = (2, 3)$

Triangles ABC and $A'B'C'$ are congruent. The translation has preserved the lengths of the sides and the measures of the angles.

Reflection in axes

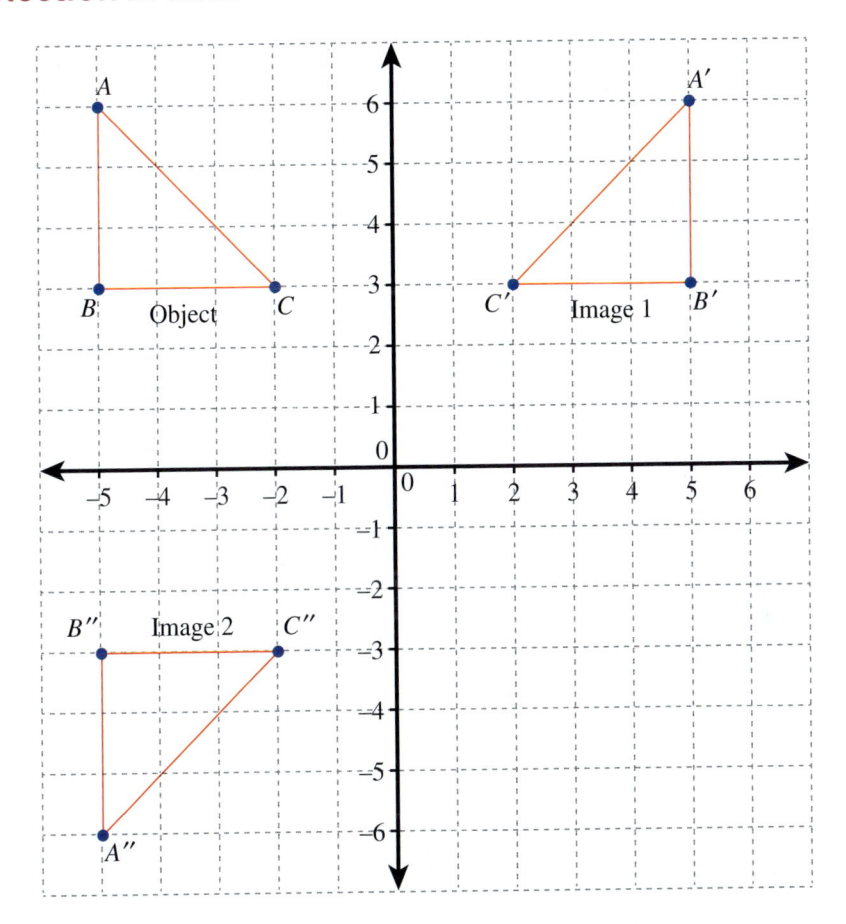

In the above diagram, the triangle ABC has been reflected in the y-axis to give triangle $A'B'C'$, and reflected in the x-axis to give triangle $A''B''C''$.

In the reflection in the y-axis, the x co-ordinates of A, B and C change sign. The y co-ordinates stay the same.

$A = (-5, 6) \rightarrow A' = (5, 6)$

$B = (-5, 3) \rightarrow B' = (5, 3)$

$C = (-2, 3) \rightarrow C' = (2, 3)$

In the reflection in the x-axis, the y co-ordinates of A, B and C change sign. The x co-ordinates stay the same.

$A = (-5, 6) \rightarrow A'' = (-5, -6)$

$B = (-5, 3) \rightarrow B'' = (-5, -3)$

$C = (-2, 3) \rightarrow C'' = (-2, -3)$

Triangles ABC, $A'B'C'$ and $A''B''C''$ are congruent. $A'B'C'$ and $A''B''C''$ are both mirror images of ABC.

Reflection in a point and rotation

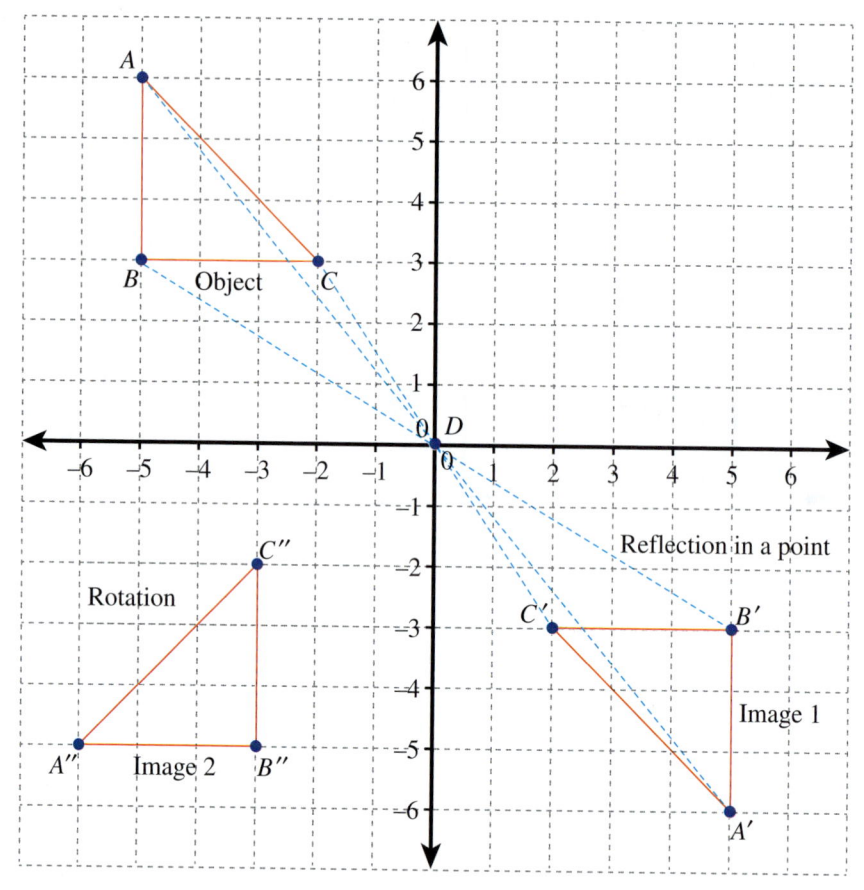

In the above diagram, the triangle ABC has been reflected through the origin to give triangle $A'B'C'$. The triangle ABC has been rotated 90° anti-clockwise about the origin to give triangle $A"B"C"$.

In the reflection through the origin, both the x co-ordinates and the y co-ordinates of A, B and C change sign.

$A = (-5, 6) \to A' = (5, -6)$

$B = (-5, 3) \to B' = (5, -3)$

$C = (-2, 3) \to C' = (2, -3)$

In the rotation of 90° anti-clockwise about the origin, the x co-ordinates and y co-ordinates of A, B and C swap over, and then the y co-ordinates change sign.

$A = (-5, 6) \to A" = (-6, -5)$

$B = (-5, 3) \to B" = (-3, -5)$

$C = (-2, 3) \to C" = (-3, -2)$

Triangles ABC, $A'B'C'$ and $A"B"C"$ are congruent.

Enlargement

Enlargement is the only one of the four transformations which changes the size of the object.

Enlargements can make objects bigger or smaller. To fully describe an enlargement we must have the **centre of enlargement** and the **scale factor** of the enlargement. The distance from the centre of enlargement of each point in the object to be enlarged is increased (or decreased) by the scale factor. The corresponding lengths between the points also increase by the scale factor.

An enlargement can also be called a **dilation**.

> **Point to note**
> The centre of enlargement can be inside, outside or on the figure to be enlarged.

The scale factor of an enlargement is denoted by $k = \dfrac{\text{image length}}{\text{object length}}$.

If $0 < k < 1$, $k \in \mathbb{Q}$ then the object is reduced in size.

If $k > 1$, $k \in \mathbb{Q}$ then the object is increased in size.

> **Point to note**
> $\dfrac{\text{image area}}{\text{object area}} = k^2 \Rightarrow$ image area $= k^2 \times$ object area

Example

Enlarge the rectangle $ABCD$ by a scale factor of 2 from the point shown.

Solution

The point O is the centre of enlargement.

Draw ray lines from O through each of the vertices.

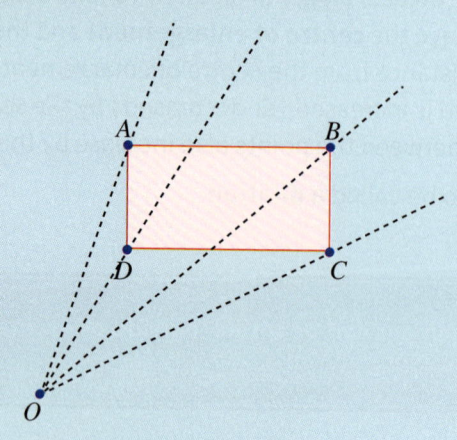

Measure and mark off points A', B', C', D' which are twice as far from O as A, B, C, D.

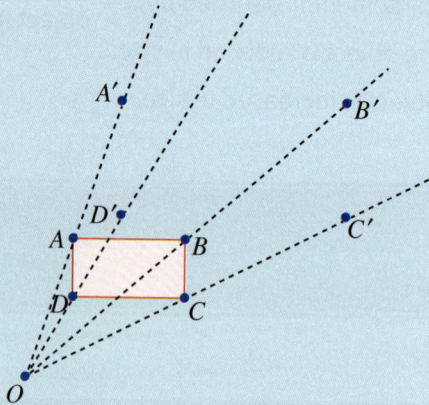

Join the points A', B', C', D' to draw the image of $ABCD$.

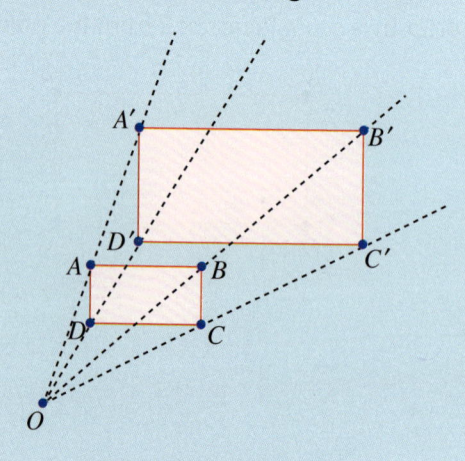

Examples

(a) Find the image of $\triangle BCD$ with C as the centre of enlargement and a scale factor of 3.

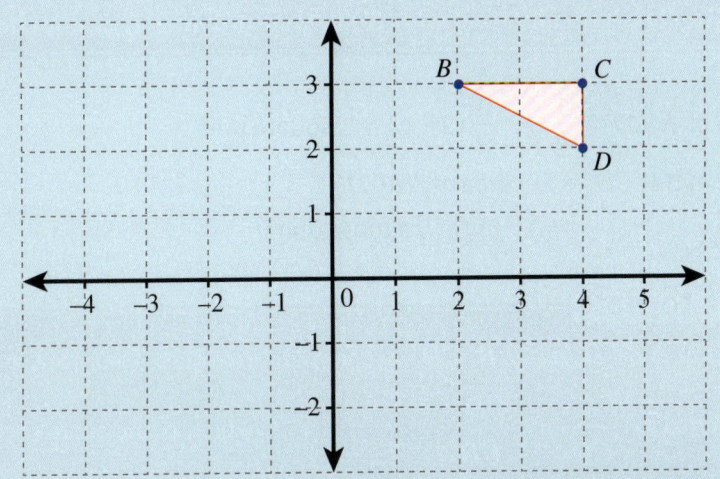

(b) Find the area of $\triangle BCD$ and the area of the image drawn in part (a).

Solutions

(a) Look at each point in turn.

The distance of C from the centre of enlargement is 0, so there is no change in point C ($3 \times 0 = 0$).

Point B is two units to the left of C, so the new point B' should be $3 \times 2 = 6$ units to the left of C. This is a translation of B by 4 units to the left.
$B = (2, 3) \to B' = (2 - 4, 3) = (-2, 3)$.

Point D is one unit below C, so the new point D' should be $3 \times 1 = 3$ units below C. This is a translation of D by 2 units down. $D = (4, 2) \to B' = (4, 2 - 2) = (4, 0)$.

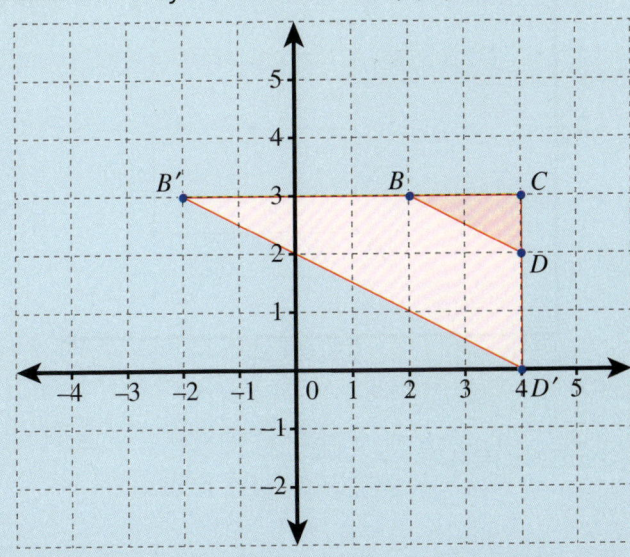

5. Synthetic Geometry 2

Point to note
Because **B** is horizontally level with **C**, its y co-ordinate does not change.
Because **D** is vertically level with **C**, its x co-ordinate does not change.

(b) Area of $\triangle BCD = \frac{1}{2}bh = \frac{1}{2}(2)(1) = 1$ square unit

Area of $\triangle B'CD' = k^2($ area of $\triangle BCD)$
$= (3)^2(1) = 9$ square units

Point to note
Note that $\triangle BCD$ and $\triangle B'CD'$ are similar triangles. Therefore, by Theorem 13, $\dfrac{|CB'|}{|CB|} = \dfrac{|CD'|}{|CD|} = \dfrac{6}{2} = \dfrac{3}{1} = 3$, which is the scale factor.

Example

Find the image of square $ABCD$ with $E = (3, 2)$ as the centre of enlargement, and a scale factor of $k = \dfrac{1}{2}$.

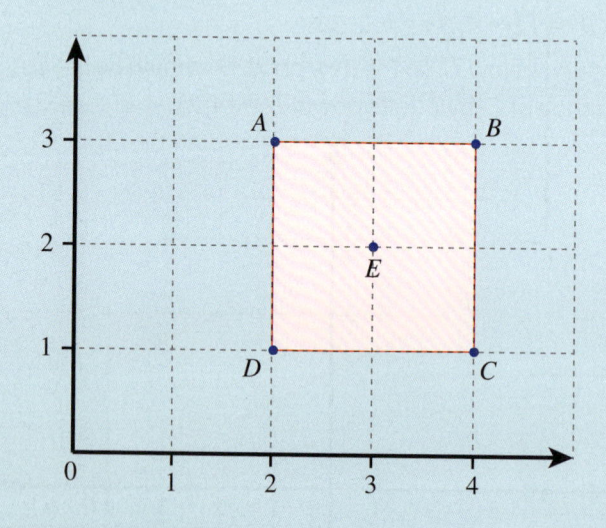

Solution

Draw ray lines from the centre of enlargement through each of the vertices.

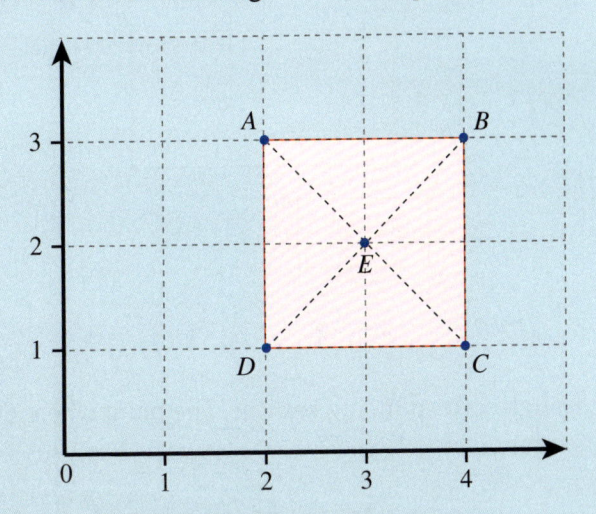

Mark the points halfway between each vertex and the centre of enlargement. Join these points to draw the image.

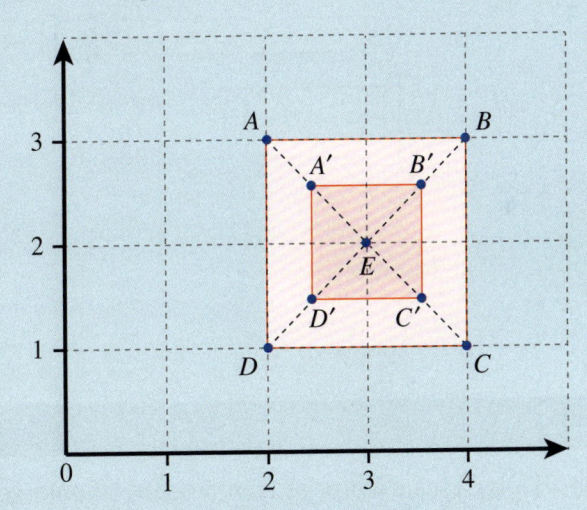

Example

The small rectangle has been enlarged as shown. Find the centre of enlargement.

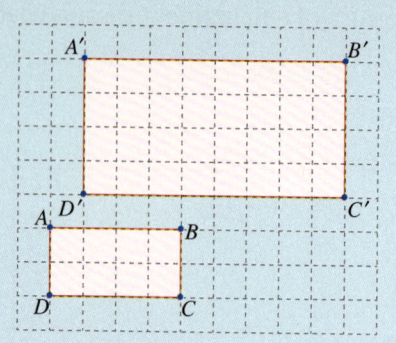

Solution

Draw to ray lines through corresponding vertices. The point where they intersect is the centre of enlargement.

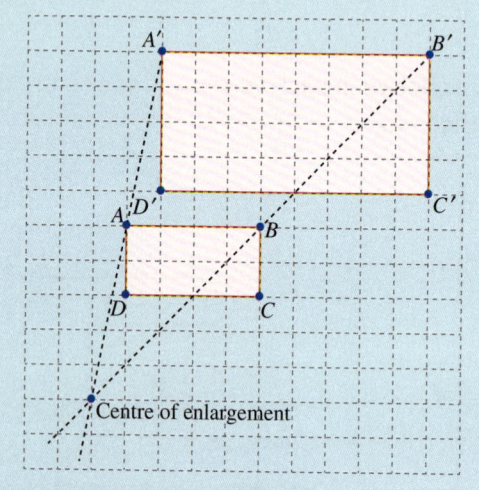

Example

Enlarge the triangle XYZ by a scale factor of 2, with centre of enlargement $(1, 2)$. Find the co-ordinates of the image triangle of XYZ using a scale drawing.

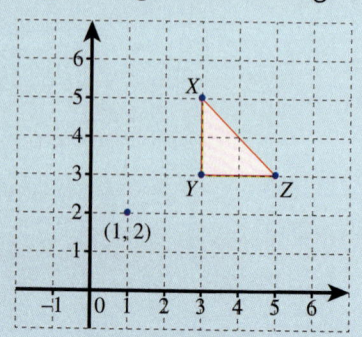

Solution

To get from $(1, 2)$ to $X = (3, 5)$ is a translation of 2 squares right and 3 squares up. Multiply this by 2 to get to the image of $X \Rightarrow X' = (3 + 2, 5 + 3) = (5, 8)$.

To get from $(1, 2)$ to $Y = (3, 3)$ is a translation of 2 squares right and 1 square up. Multiply this by 2 to get to the image of $Y \Rightarrow Y' = (3 + 2, 3 + 1) = (5, 4)$.

To get from $(1, 2)$ to $Z = (5, 3)$ is a translation of 4 squares right and 1 square up. Multiply this by 2 to get to the image of $Z \Rightarrow Z' = (5 + 4, 3 + 1) = (9, 4)$.

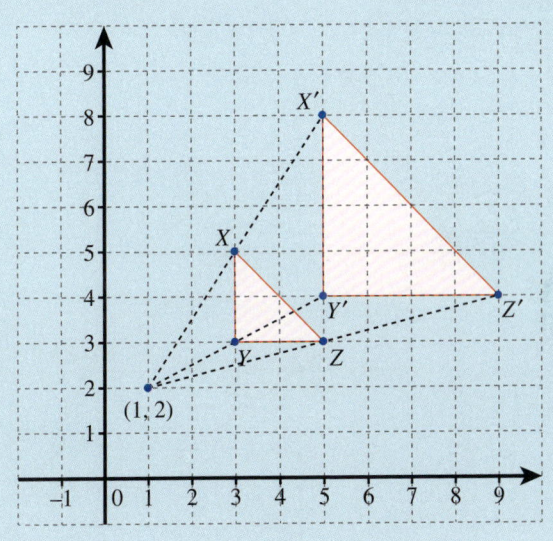

Examples

Two triangles are drawn on a square grid as shown. The points P, Q, R, X and Z are on vertices of the grid, and the point Y lies on $[PR]$. The triangle PQR is an enlargement of the triangle XYZ.

(a) Calculate the scale factor of the enlargement, showing your work.

(b) By construction or otherwise, locate the centre of enlargement on the diagram.

(c) Calculate $|YR|$ in grid units.

(SEC 2011)

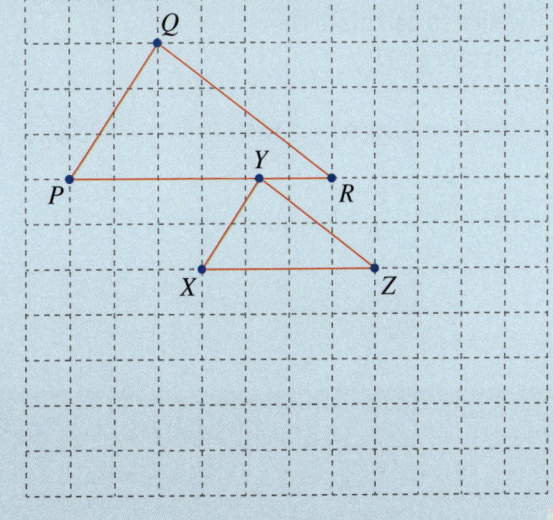

5. Synthetic Geometry 2

Solutions

(a) Use the grid to find the lengths of corresponding sides. Their ratio gives the scale factor.

Scale factor $= \dfrac{|PR|}{|XZ|} = \dfrac{6}{4} = \dfrac{3}{2}$

(b) Draw rays through PX and RZ. The point where they intersect is the centre of enlargement, shown as O in the diagram.

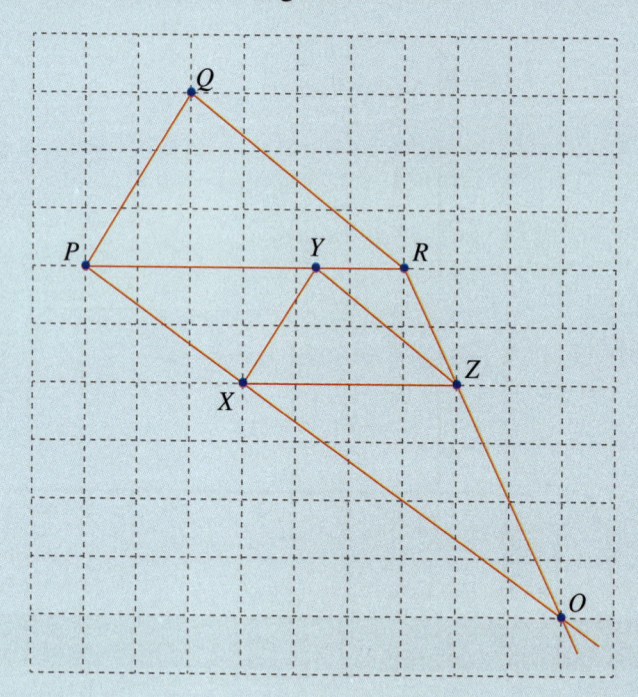

(c) **Method one**

Use points on corresponding sides to calculate the distance $|YR|$.

$|Y'Z| = \dfrac{2}{3}|Q'R| = \dfrac{2}{3}(4) = \dfrac{8}{3}$

$\Rightarrow |YR| = \dfrac{8}{3} - 1 = \dfrac{5}{3}$

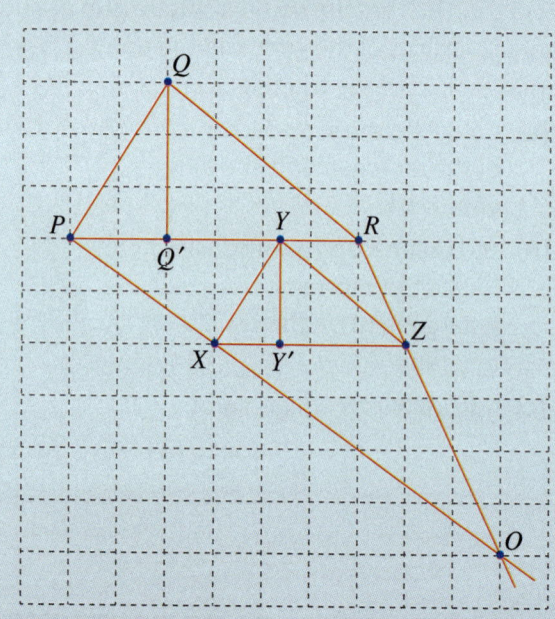

Method two

Use trigonometry.

$\tan \alpha = \dfrac{3}{2}$

$\alpha = \beta$

$\dfrac{2}{|XY'|} = \dfrac{3}{2} \Rightarrow |XY'| = \dfrac{4}{3}$

$\Rightarrow |YR| = 3 - \dfrac{4}{3} = \dfrac{5}{3}$

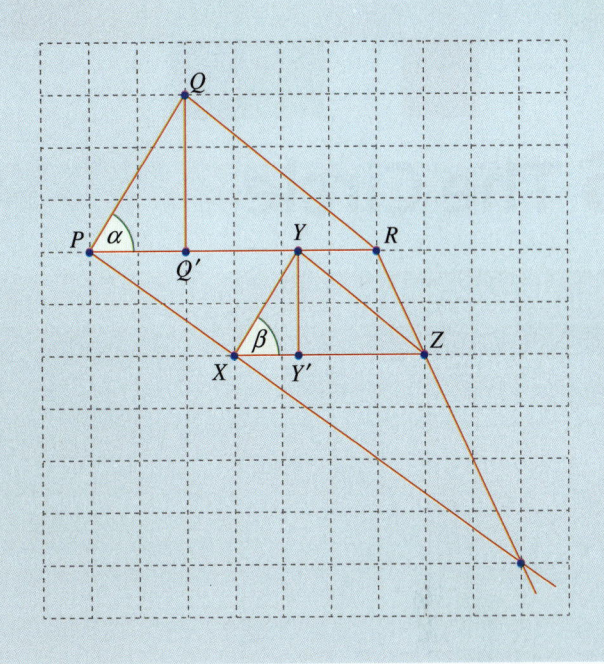

Checklist

- ✓ Practise drawing constructions on a regular basis over the year. Go to the websites www.projectmaths.ie and www.mathopenref.com to see constructions drawn in stages.

- ✓ Revise the theorems in Chapter 4 and use them to try questions on the applications of theorems.

- ✓ Practise drawing enlargements for different shapes. Use GeoGebra to check your answers.

- ✓ Co-ordinate geometry is closely linked to synthetic geometry. Revise the co-ordinate geometry formulae and make sure you know how to apply them in synthetic geometry questions.

- ✓ Learn the summary of triangle centres.

- ✓ Learn the summary of transformations.

6 The Circle

Learning objectives

In this chapter you will learn how to:

- Understand the properties of a circle
- Recognise that $(x - h)^2 + (y - k)^2 = r^2$ represents the relationship between the x and y co-ordinates on a circle with centre (h, k) and radius r
- Recognise that $x^2 + y^2 + 2gx + 2fy + c = 0$ represents the relationship between the x and y co-ordinates of points on a circle with centre $(-g, -f)$ and radius r where $r = \sqrt{g^2 + f^2 - c}$
- Solve problems involving a line and a circle
- Solve problems involving touching circles
- Solve circle problems using algebraic and geometric approaches.

Properties of a circle

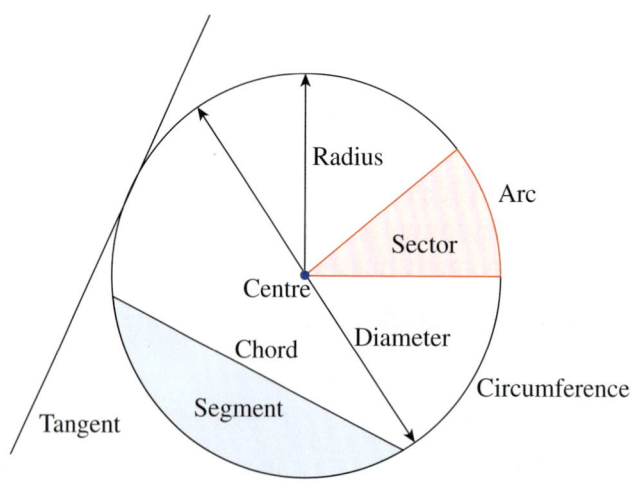

A **circle** is a set of points at a given distance (radius) from a fixed point (centre).
A **radius** is a line segment joining the centre of a circle to a point on the circle.
A **chord** is a line segment joining two points of a circle.

A **diameter** is a chord that passes through the centre of a circle. The diameter of a circle is twice as long as its radius.

The **circumference** of a circle is the length of the whole circle.

An **arc** is a section of the circumference of a circle.

A **sector** is the piece of the plane enclosed by an arc and the two radii to its endpoints.

A **segment** is the area inside a circle enclosed by an arc and a chord.

A **semicircle** is a sector whose radii make a diameter.

Every circle divides the plane into two pieces: the inside and the outside. The piece inside is called a **disc**.

A **tangent** to a circle is a line that touches the circle at one point only. This point is called the **point of contact** or **point of tangency**.

> **Top Tip**
>
> Learn the circle theorems, corollaries, definitions and constructions well!

The equation of a circle

There are three main ways to define the equation of a circle.
1. For a circle of centre $(0, 0)$ and radius r, the equation is $x^2 + y^2 = r^2$.
2. (**Standard form**) For a circle of centre (h, k) and radius r, the equation is $(x - h)^2 + (y - k)^2 = r^2$.
3. (**General form**) For a circle of centre $(-g, -f)$ and radius $\sqrt{g^2 + f^2 - c}$, the equation is $x^2 + y^2 + 2gx + 2fy + c = 0$.

Examples

For each of the following circles, find:
(a) the centre and radius
(b) the x and y intercepts.
(c) Draw each of the circles on the same diagram.
  (i) $x^2 + y^2 = 4$
  (ii) $(x - 4)^2 + (y - 4)^2 = 16$
  (iii) $x^2 + y^2 - 2x + 4y - 5 = 0$

Solutions

(a) (i) The equation is in the form $x^2 + y^2 = r^2$, with centre $(0, 0)$ and radius r.
Centre $= (0, 0)$, radius $= r = \sqrt{4} = 2$

(ii) The equation is in standard form, $(x - h)^2 + (y - k)^2 = r^2$, with centre (h, k) and radius r.

Centre $= (4, 4)$, radius $= r = \sqrt{16} = 4$

(iii) The equation is in general form, $x^2 + y^2 + 2gx + 2fy + c = 0$, with centre $(-g, -f)$ and radius $\sqrt{g^2 + f^2 - c}$.

$2gx = -2x$ so $g = -1$

$2fy = 4y$ so $f = 2$

$c = -5$

Centre $= (1, -2)$, radius $= r = \sqrt{(-1)^2 + (2)^2 - (-5)} = \sqrt{1 + 4 + 5} = \sqrt{10}$

Point to note
To find the x intercept, let $y = 0$ and find the x value.
To find the y intercept, let $x = 0$ and find the y value.

(b) (i) $y = 0 \Rightarrow x^2 + (0)^2 = 4 \Rightarrow x^2 = 4 \Rightarrow x = \pm 2$

$x = 0 \Rightarrow (0)^2 + y^2 = 4 \Rightarrow y^2 = 4 \Rightarrow y = \pm 2$

The x intercepts are $(2, 0), (-2, 0)$ and the y intercepts are $(0, 2), (0, -2)$.

(ii) $y = 0 \Rightarrow (x - 4)^2 + ((0) - 4)^2 = 16$

$\Rightarrow (x - 4)^2 + 16 = 16$

$\Rightarrow (x - 4)^2 = 0$

$\Rightarrow x - 4 = 0 \Rightarrow x = 4$

Similarly, $x = 0 \Rightarrow y = 4$

The x intercept is $(4, 0)$ and the y intercept is $(0, 4)$.

Point to note
There is only one x intercept and one y intercept for this circle, which means that the x- and y-axes are tangents to the circle.

(iii) $y = 0 \Rightarrow x^2 + (0)^2 - 2x + 4(0) - 5 = 0$

$\Rightarrow x^2 - 2x - 5 = 0$

Solve using the formula: $x = 3.45$, $x = -1.45$, correct to 2 decimal places.

$x = 0 \Rightarrow (0)^2 + y^2 - 2(0) + 4y - 5 = 0$

$\Rightarrow y^2 + 4y - 5 = 0$

$\Rightarrow (y + 5)(y - 1) = 0$

$\Rightarrow y = -5, y = 1$

The x intercepts are $(3.45, 0), (-1.45, 0)$ and the y intercepts are $(0, -5), (0, 1)$.

(c) Plot the centres and intercepts of each circle, and use a compass to draw the circles.

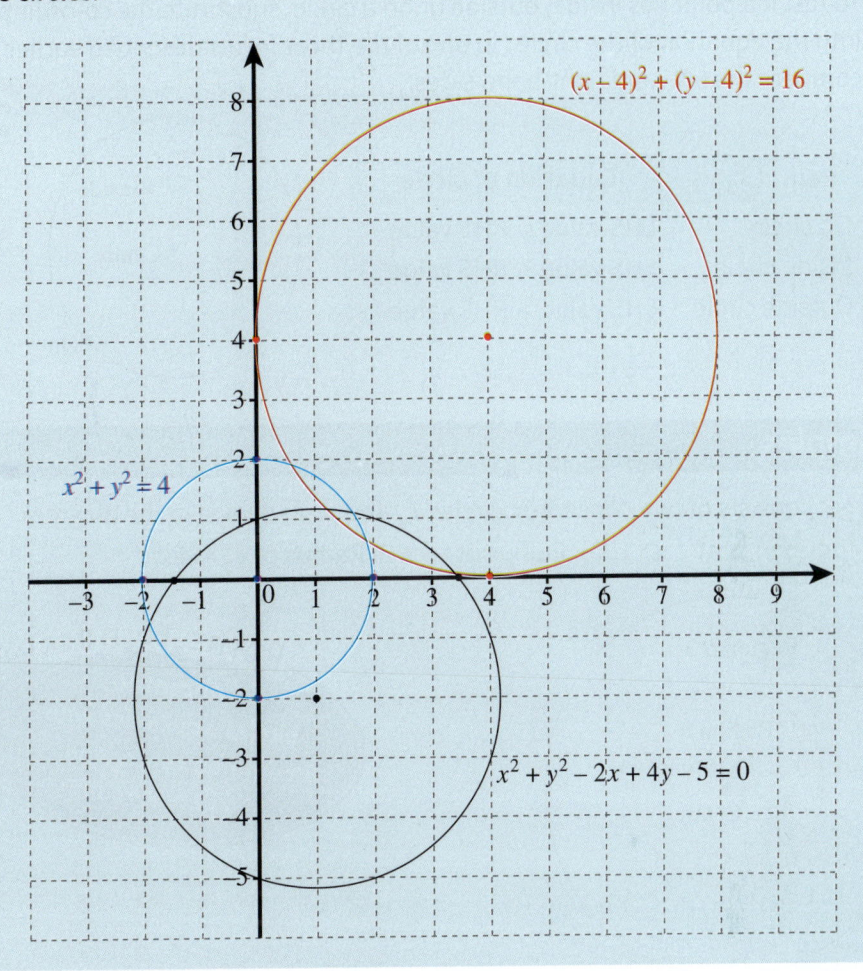

Examples

(a) Find the equation of the circle with centre $(-4, 1)$ and radius 3.

(b) Find the equation of the circle with centre $(1, -3)$ which passes through the point $(0, 1)$.

Solutions

(a) $(h, k) = (-4, 1)$, $r = 3$
$(x - h)^2 + (y - k)^2 = r^2 \Rightarrow (x + 4)^2 + (y - 1)^2 = 9$

(b) $(h, k) = (1, -3)$
radius = distance between centre and point on circle
$r = \sqrt{(1 - 0)^2 + (-3 - 1)^2} = \sqrt{1 + 16} = \sqrt{17}$
$(x - h)^2 + (y - k)^2 = r^2 \Rightarrow (x - 1)^2 + (y + 3)^2 = 17$

6. The Circle

Testing points

To test if a point lies inside, outside or on a circle, substitute the co-ordinates into the equation of the circle (in one of the three forms described earlier) and compare the left- and right-hand sides.

Point (x, y)	Equation of circle
On circle	LHS value = RHS value
Inside circle	LHS value < RHS value
Outside circle	LHS value > RHS value

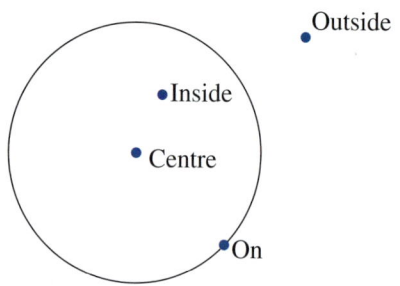

Examples

A target consists of two concentric circles c_1 and c_2 as shown in the diagram. The common centre is $(1, 0)$. Radius of $c_1 = 2$. Radius of $c_2 = 4$.

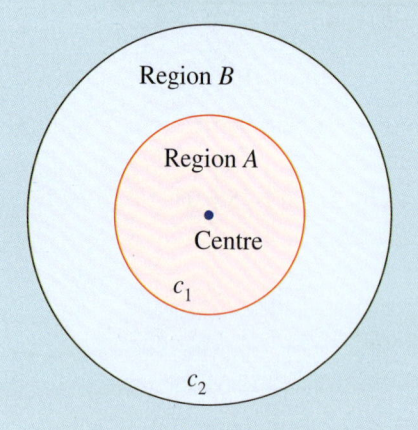

Point to note
Concentric circles are circles with a common centre and different radii.

(a) Test if the following points hit region A, region B or neither.
 (i) $(1, 2)$ (ii) $(3, 3)$ (iii) $(4, 0)$
(b) Find the ratio of the area of region A to the area of region B in its simplest form.

Point to note
Region B is called an **annulus** (the region bounded by two concentric circles).

Solutions

(a) Start by finding the equation of each circle.
c_1: $(h, k) = (1, 0)$, $r = 2$ so $(x - 1)^2 + y^2 = 4$
c_2: $(h, k) = (1, 0)$, $r = 4$ so $(x - 1)^2 + y^2 = 16$

  (i) Testing $(1, 2)$ in c_1 gives $((1) - 1)^2 + (2)^2 = 4 \Rightarrow 4 = 4$. The point lies on c_1 so it is not in either region.

  (ii) Testing $(3, 3)$ in c_1 gives $((3) - 1)^2 + (3)^2 = 13 > 4$, so the point is not in region A.
  Testing $(3, 3)$ in c_2 gives $13 < 16$, so the point is in region B.

  (iii) Testing $(4, 0)$ in c_1 gives $((4) - 1)^2 + (0)^2 = 9 > 4$, so the point is not in region A.
  Testing $(4, 0)$ in c_2 gives $9 < 13$, so the point is in region B.

(b) Area of region A = area of disc $c_1 = \pi r^2 = 4\pi$
Area of disc $c_2 = \pi r^2 = 16\pi$
Area of region B = area of annulus = area of disc c_2 − area of disc c_1
$= 16\pi - 4\pi = 12\pi$
Ratio of areas $A : B = 4\pi : 12\pi = 1 : 3$

Intersection of a line and a circle

There are three cases for the intersection of a line and a circle. The number of points of intersection depends on the perpendicular distance (d) between the line and the centre of the circle and the radius (r) of the circle.

Case	Algebraic approach	Geometric approach
Tangent (one point of intersection)	Solving gives a quadratic equation with one value for x and one value for y.	$d = r$
Secant (two points of intersection)	Solving gives a quadratic equation with two values for x and two values for y.	$d < r$
No intersection	Solving gives a quadratic equation with no real values for x or y.	$d > r$

6. The Circle

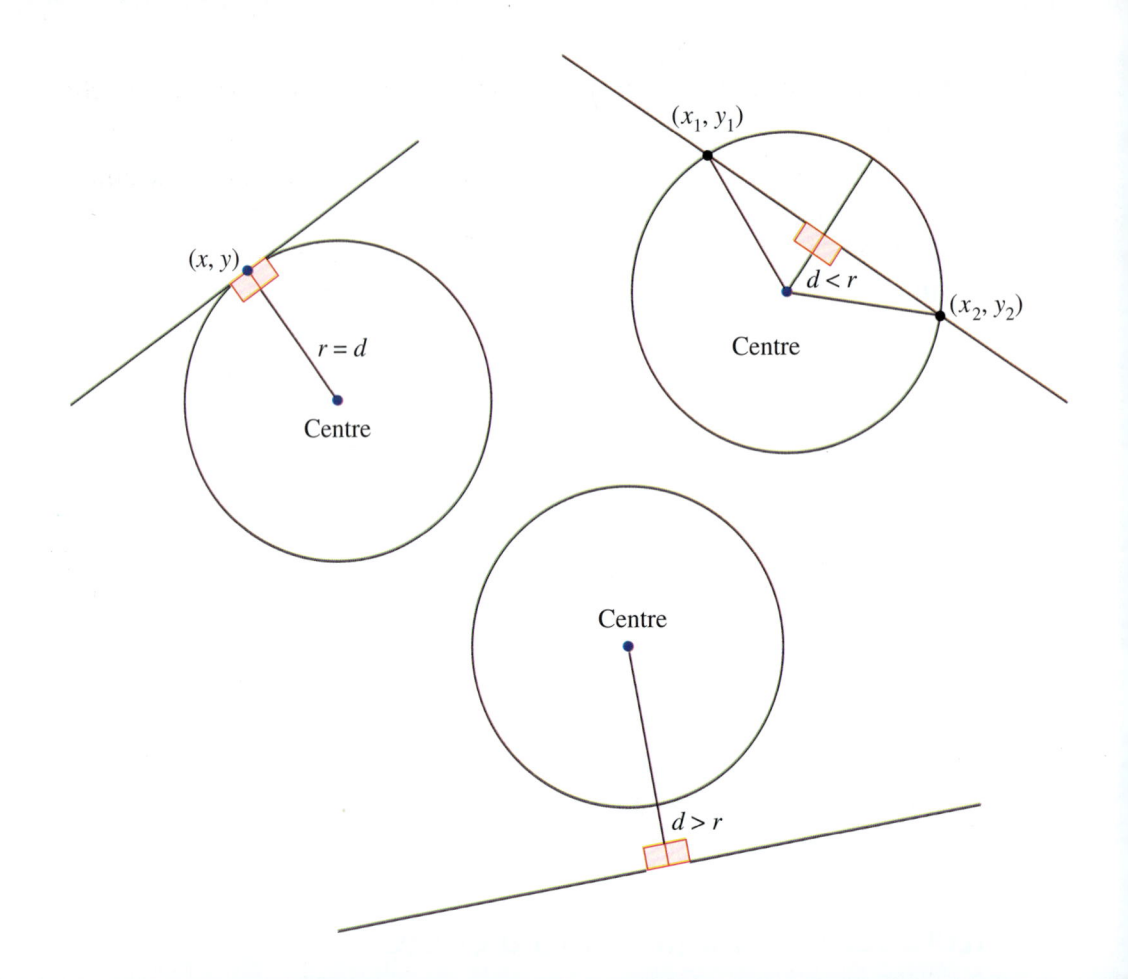

Examples

(a) Using a suitable scale, draw a circle p whose equation is $x^2 + y^2 - 4x - 2y - 5 = 0$.

(b) Use **two** different methods to determine whether the line $l: 3x + y + 3 = 0$ is tangent to the circle p.

Solutions

(a) The equation is in general form, $x^2 + y^2 + 2gx + 2fy + c = 0$, with centre $(-g, -f)$ and radius $\sqrt{g^2 + f^2 - c}$.

$2gx = -4x \Rightarrow g = -2$

$2fy = -2y \Rightarrow f = -1$

$c = -5$

The centre of the circle is $(2, 1)$ and the radius is $\sqrt{(-2)^2 + (-1)^2 - (-5)} = \sqrt{10}$.

Plot the centre of the circle.

As we cannot measure the radius exactly, we now need to find a point on the circle. Consider a right-angled triangle with hypotenuse $\sqrt{10}$. By Pythagoras' theorem, $\left(\sqrt{10}\right)^2 = 10 = a^2 + b^2$, where a and b are the lengths of the other two sides.

9 and 1 are square numbers that sum to 10, giving side lengths of 3 and 1. This means that any point 3 units along and 1 unit up or down from the centre is a point on the circle p. Plot any one of these points, then use a compass to draw the circle.

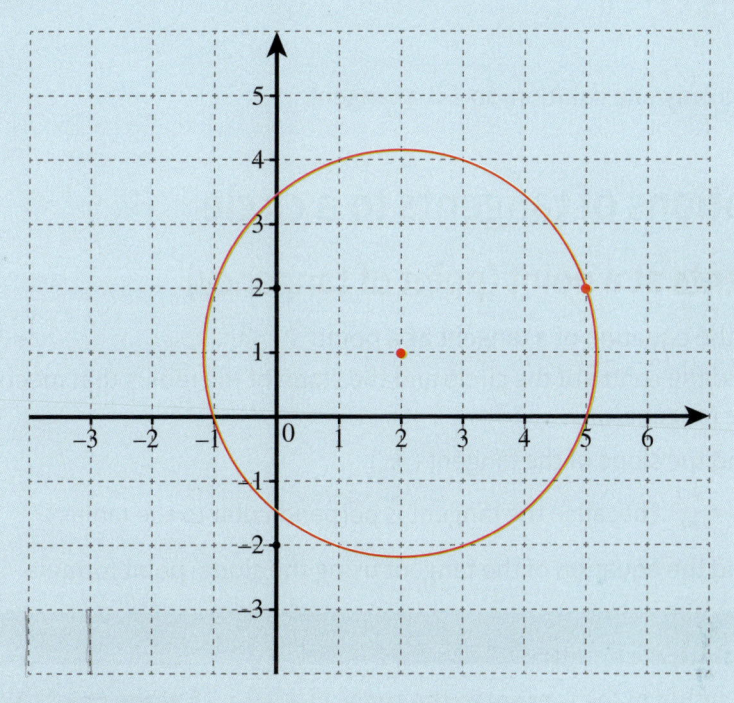

(b) Geometric approach

If l is a tangent to the circle then its perpendicular distance from the centre will be equal to the radius = $\sqrt{10}$.

Use the formula for the perpendicular distance from a line to a point,

$$d = \frac{|ax_1 + by_1 + c|}{\sqrt{a^2 + b^2}}, \text{ where } a = 3, b = 1, c = 3, x_1 = 2, y_1 = 1$$

$$d = \frac{|(3)(2) + (1)(1) + (3)|}{\sqrt{(3)^2 + (1)^2}} = \frac{10}{\sqrt{10}} = \sqrt{10} = r$$

Hence the line is a tangent to the circle.

Algebraic approach

Substitute $y = -3x - 3$ into the equation of the circle. This gives a quadratic equation.

$x^2 + (-3x - 3)^2 - 4x - 2(-3x - 3) - 5 = 0$
$x^2 + 9x^2 + 18x + 9 - 4x + 6x + 6 - 5 = 0$
$10x^2 + 20x + 10 = 0$
$x^2 + 2x + 1 = 0$
$(x + 1)(x + 1) = 0$
$x = -1$

There is only one solution, so l is a tangent.

Equations of tangents to a circle

Tangents at a point (point of tangency)

To find the equation of a tangent **at** a point:
1. Find the centre of the circle and the slope of the radius that meets the tangent (m_r).
2. Find the slope of the tangent (m_t)
   $m_t = \dfrac{-1}{m_r}$ (because the tangent is perpendicular to the radius).
3. Find the equation of the tangent using the slope–point formula.

Example

Find the equation of the tangent to the circle $x^2 + y^2 = 10$ at the point $(3, 1)$.

Solution

Centre $= (0, 0)$, radius $= \sqrt{10}$

Use the centre and the point of tangency to find the slope of the radius at that point:

$m_r = \dfrac{1 - 0}{3 - 0} = \dfrac{1}{3}$

$m_t = \dfrac{-1}{\frac{1}{3}} = -3$

Use the slope–point formula with $(x_1, y_1) = (3, 1)$.

$y - y_1 = m(x - x_1) \Rightarrow y - 1 = -3(x - 3)$

Rearrange to obtain the equation of the tangent: $3x + y = 10$.

Point to note

If the circle has its centre at the origin you can check the equation of the tangent with the formula $xx_1 + yy_1 = r^2$ where (x_1, y_1) is the point of tangency and r is the radius.

If the circle has its centre at (h, k) and radius r you can check the equation of the tangent using the formula
$(x - h)(x_1 - h) + (y - k)(y_1 - k) = r^2$.

If the general form of the circle is given you can check the equation of the tangent using the formula $xx_1 + yy_1 + g(x + x_1) + f(y + y_1) + c = 0$.

These last two formulae are on page 19 of the *Formulae and Tables* booklet.

Example

Find the values of k, where $k \in \mathbb{Z}$, for which $2x - y + k = 0$ is a tangent to the circle $(x + 5)^2 + (y - 5)^2 = 5$.

Solution

The question asks for 'values' of k, so there must be more than one answer. Lines in the form $2x - y + k = 0$ will be parallel to each other, and there can be at most two parallel tangents to a circle, so we are looking for two answers.

It is helpful to draw a quick sketch.

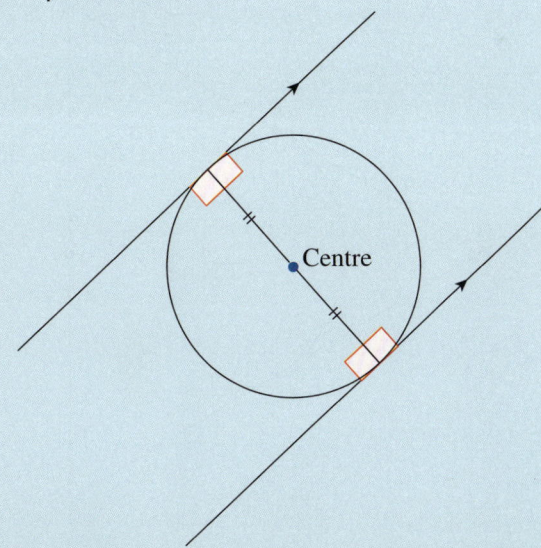

The equation of the circle is in standard form, so we know that the centre is at $(-5, 5)$ and that the radius = $\sqrt{5}$.

We also know that the perpendicular distance of the tangent to the centre = $d = r$.

6. The Circle

Use the formula for the perpendicular distance from a line to a point to find k.

$d = \dfrac{|ax_1 + by_1 + c|}{\sqrt{a^2 + b^2}}$, where $a = 2$, $b = -1$, $c = k$, $(x_1, y_1) = (-5, 5)$.

$d = \dfrac{|(2)(-5) + (-1)(5) + (k)|}{\sqrt{(2)^2 + (-1)^2}} = \dfrac{|-15 + k|}{\sqrt{5}} = \sqrt{5}$

$\Rightarrow |-15 + k| = 5 \Rightarrow -15 + k = \pm 5$

$k - 15 = 5 \Rightarrow k = 20$

or $k - 15 = -5 \Rightarrow k = 10$

Point to note

A line parallel to $ax + by + c = 0$ is of the form $ax + by + k = 0$. The lines have equal slopes.

A line perpendicular to $ax + by + c = 0$ is of the form $bx - ay + k = 0$.

Tangents from a point

Examples

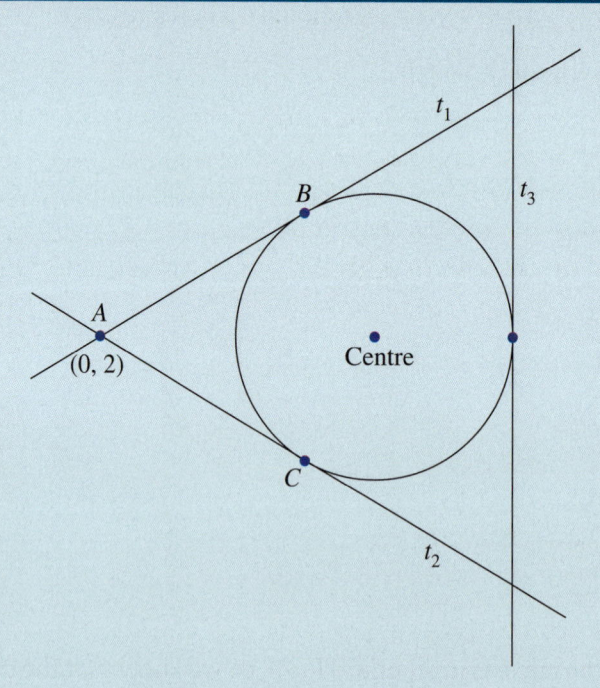

A logo consists of a circle inscribed between three tangents, as shown in the diagram. The equation of the circle c is $x^2 + y^2 - 8x - 4y + 16 = 0$. A is the point $(0, 2)$. B and C are points of tangency for lines t_1 and t_2 respectively.

(a) Find the centre and radius of circle c. What type of circle is c in terms of the triangle formed by t_1, t_2 and t_3?

(b) Find $|AB|$ and $|AC|$. What conclusion can you make from your answer?

(c) Find the equation of tangent t_3.

(d) Find the equations of tangents t_1 and t_2.

Solutions

(a) The equation of c is in general form, $x^2 + y^2 + 2gx + 2fy + c = 0$, with centre $(-g, -f)$ and radius $\sqrt{g^2 + f^2 - c}$.

$2gx = -8x \Rightarrow g = -4$

$2fy = -4y \Rightarrow f = -2$

$c = 16$

Centre of $c = (4, 2)$, radius $= \sqrt{(-4)^2 + (-2)^2 - (16)} = \sqrt{4} = 2$. Circle c is an incircle of the triangle formed by the tangents.

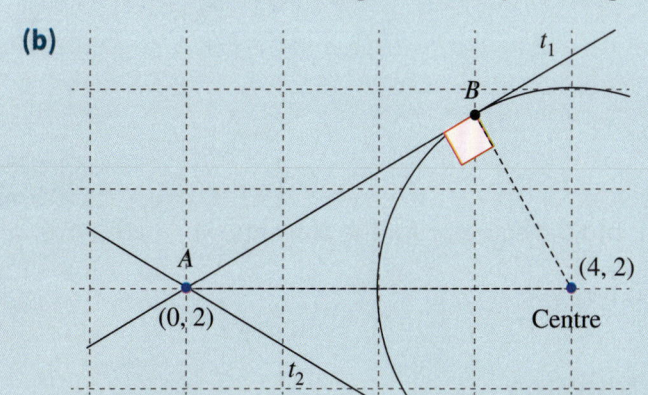

(b)

A, B and the centre of the circle form a right-angled triangle. The hypotenuse is the distance from A to the centre = 4. The length of the radius of the circle is 2 units. By Pythagoras' theorem, $4^2 = |AB|^2 + 2^2 \Rightarrow |AB|^2 = 12 \Rightarrow |AB| = \sqrt{12}$

Similarly, $4^2 = |AC|^2 + 2^2 \Rightarrow |AC|^2 = 12 \Rightarrow |AC| = \sqrt{12}$

Therefore, $|AB| = |AC|$. The lengths of two tangents between a common point and the points of tangency are the same.

(c) The radius of circle c is 2 units, so the point of tangency of t_3 is a translation of 2 units to the right of the centre.

$(4, 2) \rightarrow (6, 2)$

Since the line is parallel to the y-axis, and $(6, 2)$ is on the line, the equation of t_3 is $x = 6$.

(d) Tangents t_1 and t_2 have a common point with different slopes.

$(x_1, y_1) = (0, 2)$, slope $= m$

Perpendicular distance to tangent from centre of circle (d) = radius length (r), so for both tangents $d = r$.

Use the perpendicular distance formula and solve for m. There should be two different values.

First we need the equation for the tangents in the form $ax + by + c = 0$.

$y - y_1 = m(x - x_1)$

$y - (2) = m(x - (0))$

$mx - y + 2 = 0$

So $a = m$, $b = -1$, $c = 2$, $d = r = 2$

We are finding the perpendicular distance relative to the centre, so $(x_1, y_1) = (4, 2)$

$$d = \frac{|ax_1 + by_1 + c|}{\sqrt{a^2 + b^2}} \Rightarrow 2 = \frac{|(m)(4) + (-1)(2) + (2)|}{\sqrt{(m)^2 + (1)}}$$

$\Rightarrow |4m| = 2\sqrt{m^2 + 1}$

$\Rightarrow 16m^2 = 4m^2 + 4$

$\Rightarrow 12m^2 = 4$

$m^2 = \frac{1}{3} \Rightarrow m = \pm \frac{1}{\sqrt{3}}$

Substitute the values for m into the equation for the tangents, $mx - y + 2 = 0$.

$t_1: \frac{1}{\sqrt{3}}x - y + 2 = 0 \qquad m$ is positive

$t_2: \frac{1}{\sqrt{3}}x + y - 2 = 0 \qquad m$ is negative

Touching circles

For external touching circles, the distance between the centres is the sum of the radii.

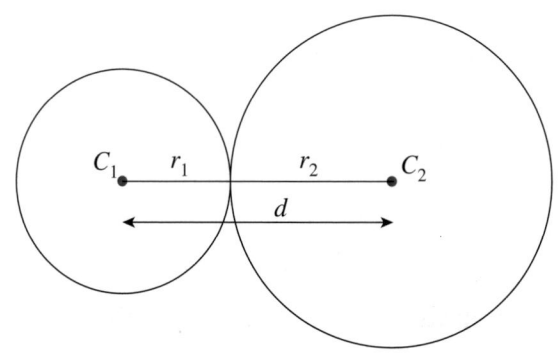

$|C_1C_2| = d = r_1 + r_2$

For internal touching circles, the distance between the centres is the difference of the radii.

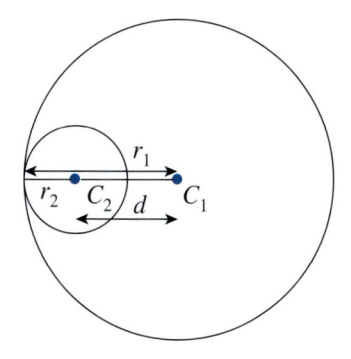

$$|C_1C_2| = d = r_1 - r_2$$

Common chord and tangent

Let the equations of two circles be in the form $s_1 = 0$ and $s_2 = 0$. If the two circles have a common chord (i.e. if the circles overlap), then the equation of the common cord is $s_1 - s_2 = 0$.

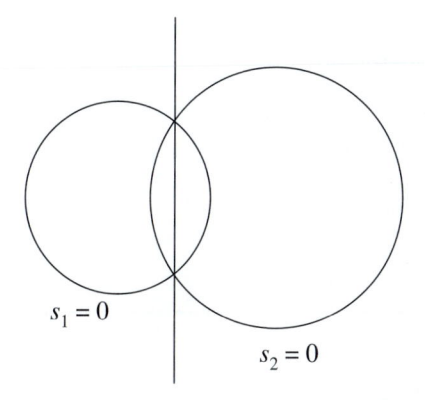

Similarly, if the two circles have a common tangent (i.e. if the circles touch), then the equation of the common tangent is $s_1 - s_2 = 0$.

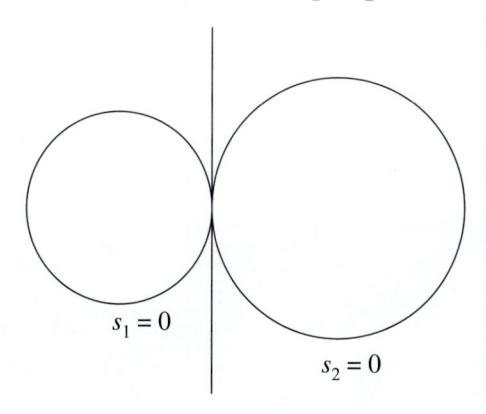

Examples

Given two circles, s_1: $(x - 6)^2 + (y + 3)^2 = 121$ and s_2: $(x + 2)^2 + (y - 3)^2 = 1$:
(a) Find the centres and radii of s_1 and s_2.
(b) Hence sketch circles s_1 and s_2 on the same axes and scale.
(c) Prove that the circles touch internally.
(d) Find the equation of the common tangent.
(e) Using your graph, find the point of intersection of s_1 and s_2.
(f) Use another method to check your answer. Which method is more accurate?

Solutions

(a) The equations are in standard form, $(x - h)^2 + (y - k)^2 = r^2$, with centre (h, k) and radius r.

Centre of s_1 = (6, −3), radius = 11

Centre of s_2 = (−2, 3), radius = 1

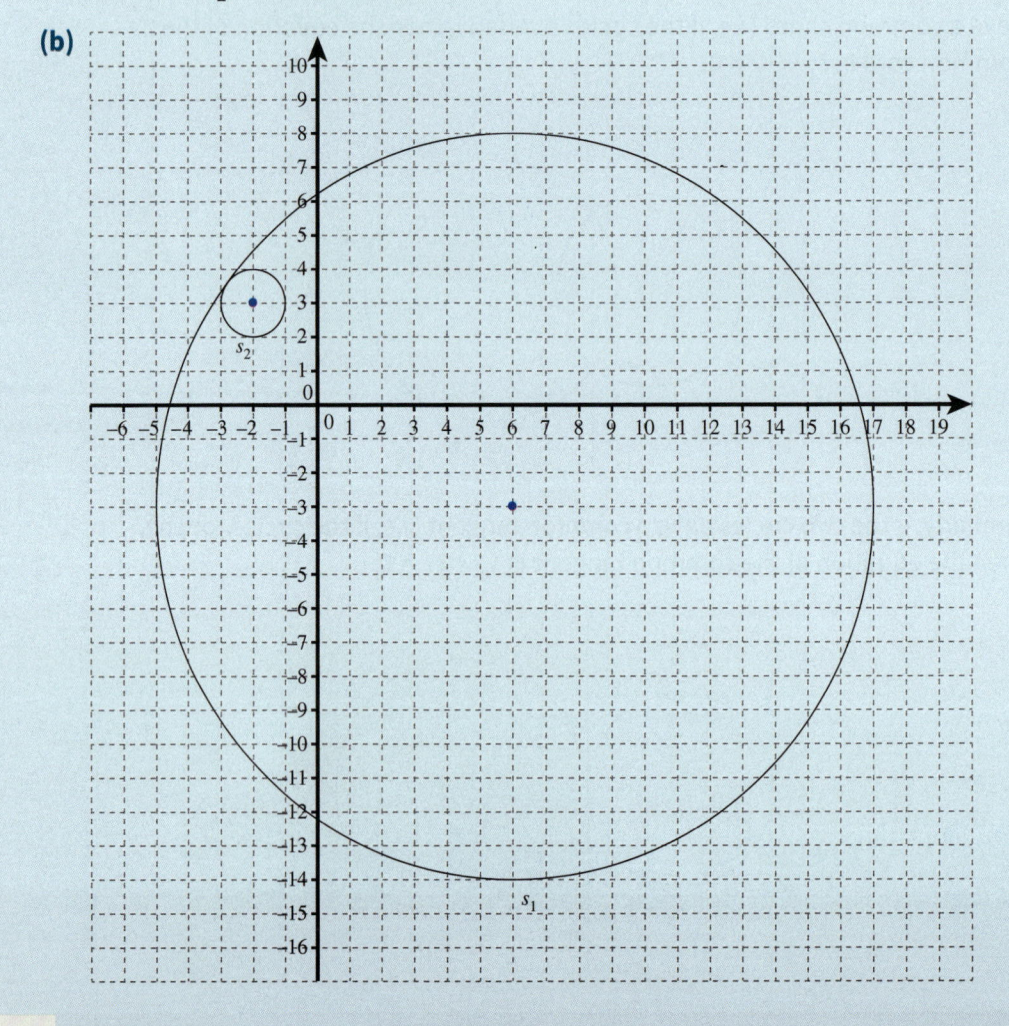

(b)

(c) If two circles touch internally,
the distance between their centres = the difference of their radii.
$|C_1C_2| = \sqrt{((6)-(-2))^2 + ((-3)-(3))^2} = \sqrt{64+36} = 10$
$r_1 = 11, r_2 = 1 \Rightarrow r_1 - r_2 = 11 - 1 = 10$
Hence the circles touch internally.

(d) Equation of common tangent: $s_1 - s_2 = 0$.
$s_1: (x-6)^2 + (y+3)^2 = 121 \Rightarrow x^2 - 12x + 36 + y^2 + 6y + 9 = 121$
$\Rightarrow x^2 + y^2 - 12x + 6y - 76 = 0$
$s_2: (x+2)^2 + (y+3)^2 = 1 \Rightarrow x^2 + 4x + 4 + y^2 - 6y + 9 = 1$
$\Rightarrow x^2 + y^2 + 4x - 6y + 12 = 0$
$s_1 - s_2 = 0 \Rightarrow -16x + 12y - 88 = 0$
Common tangent is $4x - 3y + 22 = 0$

(e) From the graph, the point of intersection is $(-3, 3.5)$.

(f) We can use the division of line segment formula or work with a translation to find the point of intersection.

Let C_1 be the centre of s_1, C_2 be the centre of s_2 and C_3 be the point of intersection of the two circles.

$|C_1C_3| = 11$ and $|C_2C_3| = 1$, so C_2 divides $[C_1C_3]$ in the ratio $a:b = 10:1$.

Let $C_1 = (x_1, y_1) = (6, -3)$ and let $C_3 = (x_2, y_2) = (x, y)$

$(-2, 3) = \left(\dfrac{(1)(6) + (10)(x)}{(1) + (10)}, \dfrac{(1)(-3) + (10)(y)}{(1) + (10)} \right)$

$-2 = \dfrac{6 + 10x}{11} \Rightarrow 6 + 10x = -22 \Rightarrow x = -2.8$

$3 = \dfrac{-3 + 10y}{11} \Rightarrow -3 + 10y = 33 \Rightarrow y = 3.6$

So $C_3 = (-2.8, 3.6)$. This is the exact answer; the answer from the graph is an approximation.

Circles touching axes

> **Remember**
>
> The general form of the equation for a circle of centre $(-g, -f)$ and radius $\sqrt{g^2 + f^2 - c}$ is $x^2 + y^2 + 2gx + 2fy + c = 0$.

Case 1: circle touches the x-axis

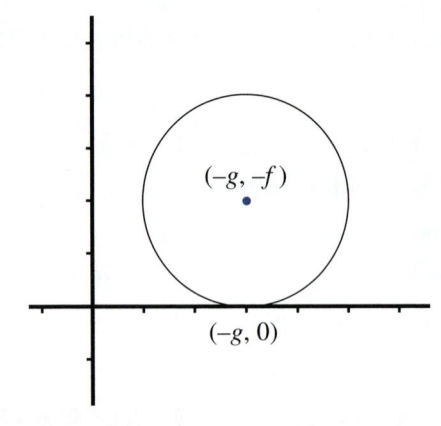

(-g, -f)

(-g, 0)

When the circle touches the x-axis, $r = |-f|$

$\Rightarrow r^2 = f^2 = g^2 + f^2 - c \Rightarrow c = g^2$

Case 2: circle touches the y-axis

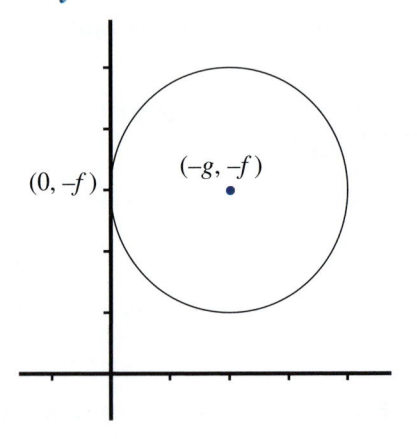

(0, -f)   (-g, -f)

When the circle touches the y-axis, $r = |-g|$

$\Rightarrow r^2 = g^2 = g^2 + f^2 - c \Rightarrow c = f^2$

Case 3: circle touches both axes

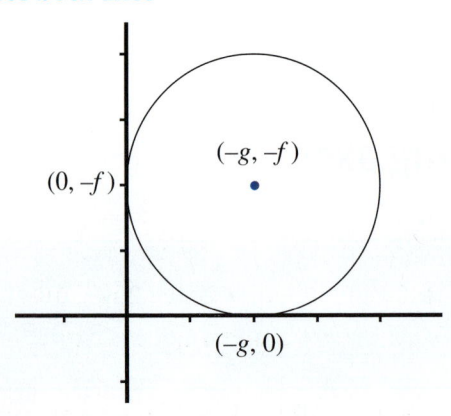

(-g, -f)
(0, -f)

(-g, 0)

When the circle touches both axes, $c = g^2 = f^2$.

Point to note

If the circle touches both axes then $c = g^2 = f^2 \Rightarrow f = \pm g$.

f and g will have the same sign if the circle is in the first or third quadrants. They will have opposite signs if the circle is in the second or fourth quadrants.

Example

Find the equations of the circles touching both axes and passing through the point $(-2, 4)$, and hence find the equation of the common chord of both circles.

Top Tip

Read the question carefully. It mentions equations here, so there will be more than one circle that will satisfy the conditions.

Solution

The circles touch both axes, and all the circles will be in the second quadrant, as $(-2, 4)$ is in the second quadrant.

$c = g^2 = f^2 \Rightarrow f = \pm g$

In the second quadrant, $f = -g$.

Substitute $(-2, 4)$ into $x^2 + y^2 + 2gx + 2fy + c = 0$

$(-2)^2 + (4)^2 + 2g(-2) + 2f(4) + c = 0$

$-4g + 8f + c = -20$

Substitute $f = -g$ and $c = g^2$ into the equation: $-4g + 8(-g) + g^2 = -20$

Simplify the equation and solve for g:

$g^2 - 12g + 20 = 0$

$(g - 10)(g - 2) = 0$

$g = 10$ or $g = 2$

By substitution in $f = -g$, $f = -10$ or $f = -2$

Finally, $c = f^2 = g^2 = 100$ or 4

Link up g, f and c for each circle and substitute into the general equation of a circle.

g	f	c	$x^2 + y^2 + 2gx + 2fy + c = 0$
10	−10	100	$x^2 + y^2 + 20x - 20y + 100 = 0$
2	−2	4	$x^2 + y^2 + 4x - 4y + 4 = 0$

Common chord: $s_1 - s_2 = 0 \Rightarrow 16x - 16y + 96 = 0 \Rightarrow x - y + 6 = 0$

Circle problems

As mentioned earlier, it is important to be familiar with the theorems, corollaries, constructions and definitions on the course, especially those connected with circles and triangles. Refer to your textbook or syllabus.

Example

The following points are on a circle: $B = (2, 0)$, $C = (4, 2)$ and $D = (6, 0)$. Find the equation of the circle.

Solution

We can use different methods to find the equation of the circle.

Approach	Method
Algebraic	Substitute points into the general equation of a circle and solve for the three variables g, f and c. Substitute the values into the general form of a circle.
Geometric	Draw a diagram and find the equations of the two bisectors of sides $[BC]$ and $[CD]$. Solve to find the centre and then find the radius. Substitute the values into the standard form of a circle.
Use Theorem 19, Corollaries 3 and 4	In this example BC is perpendicular to CD, so $[BD]$ is a diameter. The midpoint of $[BD]$ is the centre; use this to find the radius. Substitute the values into the standard form of a circle.

> **Top Tip**
>
> It's always useful to draw a quick diagram to see the different methods of working out a problem.

Slope of $[BC] = \dfrac{2-0}{4-2} = 1$

Slope of $[CD] = \dfrac{0-2}{6-4} = -1$

Product of slopes = -1
$\Rightarrow [BC]$ is perpendicular to $[CD]$.

Using Theorem 19, Corollaries 3 and 4:

Midpoint of $[BD]$ = centre = $(4, 0)$, and radius = 2.

Equation of circle: $(x - 4)^2 + y^2 = 4$

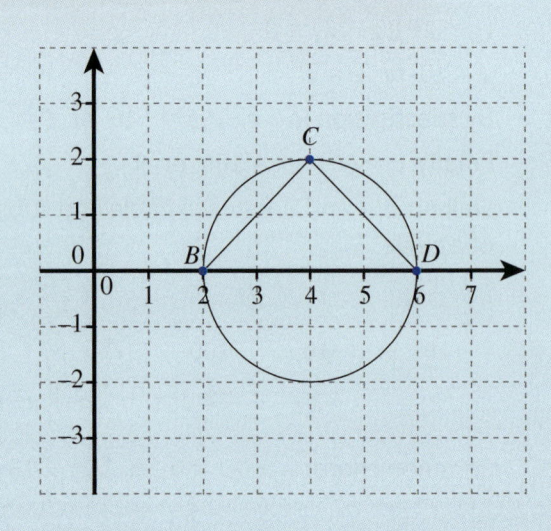

Example

Find the equation of a circle whose centre is on the line $2x - y + 1 = 0$ and which passes through the points $A(1, 3)$ and $B(6, -2)$.

Solution

We can use an algebraic approach or a geometric approach.

Approach	Method
Algebraic	Substitute points into the general equation of a circle. Substitute $(-g, -f)$ into the equation of the given line. Solve equations for the three variables g, f and c. Substitute the values into the general equation of a circle.
Geometric (Theorem 21)	Draw a diagram. Find the midpoint of chord $[AB]$. Find the equation of the bisector of the chord. Find the point of intersection of the given line and the bisector to give the centre of the circle. Find the radius. Substitute the values into the standard form of a circle.

Geometric approach

Draw a diagram. Work out two points on the line $2x - y + 1 = 0$ to plot it, e.g. $x = 0 \Rightarrow y = 1$ and $x = 1 \Rightarrow 2(1) - y + 1 = 0 \Rightarrow y = 3$.

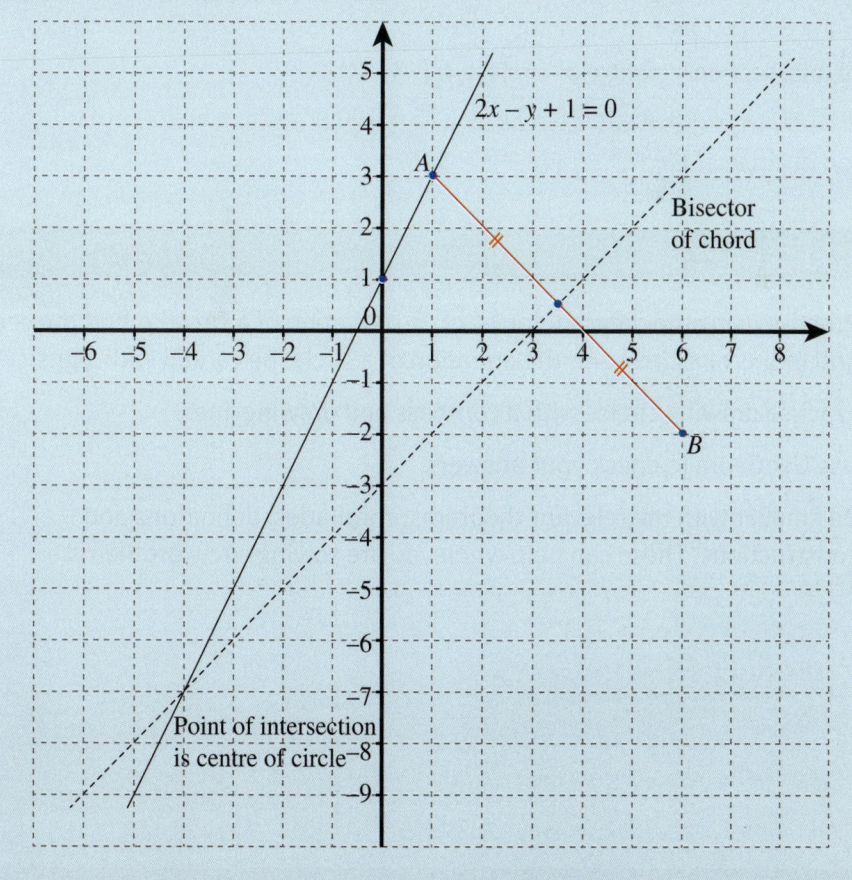

Midpoint of $[AB] = \left(\dfrac{1+6}{2}, \dfrac{3-2}{2}\right) = \left(\dfrac{7}{2}, \dfrac{1}{2}\right)$

Slope of $[AB] = \dfrac{3+2}{1-6} = \dfrac{5}{-5} = -1$

The bisector is perpendicular to $[AB]$, so slope of bisector = 1 (invert and change sign of slope $[AB]$), and the bisector passes through point $\left(\dfrac{7}{2}, \dfrac{1}{2}\right)$.

Equation of bisector: $y - y_1 = m(x - x_1) \Rightarrow y - \dfrac{1}{2} = 1\left(x - \dfrac{7}{2}\right) \Rightarrow 2y - 1 = 2\left(x - \dfrac{7}{2}\right)$

$2y - 1 = 2x - 7$

$2x - 2y - 6 = 0$

$x - y - 3 = 0$

Find the point of intersection of $x - y - 3 = 0$ and $2x - y + 1 = 0$ using algebra.

$x - y - 3 = 0 \Rightarrow x = 3 + y$

Substitute this into the other equation to find y.

$2(3 + y) - y + 1 = 0 \Rightarrow 6 + 2y - y + 1 = 0$

$\Rightarrow y = -7$

Substitute this back into the equation of the bisector to find x.

$x = 3 + y = 3 + (-7) = -4$

Point of intersection = centre of circle = $C(-4, -7)$

Radius = $|AC| = \sqrt{(1+4)^2 + (3+7)^2} = \sqrt{25 + 100} = \sqrt{125} = 5\sqrt{5}$

Equation of circle: $(x + 4)^2 + (y + 7)^2 = 125$.

Checklist

- ✓ Practise using the different forms of the equation of a circle to find the centre and radius of a circle and the equation of a circle. Be careful with signs.
- ✓ Practise drawing circles with a compass and drawing lines.
- ✓ Use GeoGebra to check your answers.
- ✓ Be familiar with the relevant theorems, corollaries, definitions and constructions. These can help when you are solving circle problems.

Statistics 1

Learning objectives

In this chapter you will learn how to:

- Understand the purpose of statistics and the data handling cycle
- Recognise different types of data and different sources of data: primary and secondary
- Discuss different types of studies: sample surveys, observational studies and designed experiments
- Recognise definitions related to statistical enquiries
- Select a sample and define the different types of sample: simple random sample, stratified, cluster, quota
- Recognise the importance of representativeness to avoid biased samples
- Recognise biases, limitations and ethical issues of each type of study
- Design and comment on surveys and questionnaires.

Introduction

Statistics involves using structured methods to collect, analyse, present and interpret data. There are two types of statistics: descriptive and inferential.

Descriptive statistics use graphs (pie charts, histograms, etc.) to analyse data.

Inferential statistics make predictions (infer) based on the data obtained.

The diagram below shows the data handling cycle.

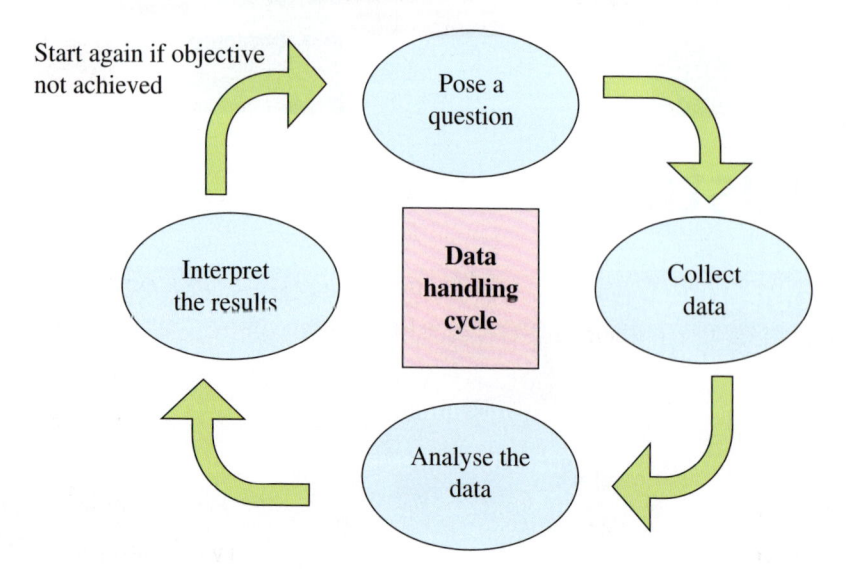

```
            Start again if objective
            not achieved                    Pose a
                                           question


                                Data
                Interpret      handling            Collect
               the results      cycle               data


                                Analyse the
                                   data
```

Types of data

```
                        Types of data

            Categorical                    Numerical
            (qualitative)                 (quantitative)

        Nominal    Ordinal      Continuous        Discrete
        (name)     (order)    (involves scale)  (specific values)
```

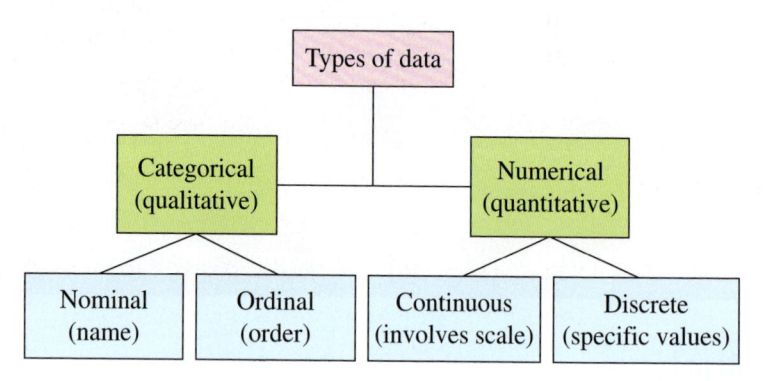

Categorical data is **qualitative**, which means that it is descriptive and cannot be measured.

Categorical data can be further divided into nominal and ordinal. **Nominal data** involves a name or classification, with no specific order. **Ordinal data** is categorical data that can be put in order, for example from low to high.

Numerical data is **quantitative**, which means that it can be measured. For example, number of people unemployed, height, weight, or number of students.

Numerical data can be further divided into continuous and discrete. **Continuous data** is measured on a scale that is meaningful at all points. Height is an example of continuous data, because you can have any value on the scale: 1 m, 1·5 m, 1·25 m, etc. **Discrete data** has specific values and there is no meaning to the points between the data values. Number of students is an example of discrete data, because you can have 3 students or 4 students but nothing in-between.

The tables below give some examples of different types of data.

Categorical	Numerical
Colour of eyes, car, hair	Unemployment figures
Exam grade	Emigrants in 2014
Gender	Height, weight, arm span, etc.
Favourite soccer team	Temperature
Social class	Number of students in your school
Pain level (e.g. low, medium, high)	Percentage mark in exam
County of birth	Time taken to complete a marathon
Blood type	Average rainfall in Dublin in a certain month

Ordinal categorical	Nominal categorical
Exam grade	Favourite TV programme
Pain level (e.g. low, medium, high)	Colour of hair
Opinion scales (e.g. strongly agree, agree, disagree, strongly disagree)	Country of residence

Continuous numerical	Discrete numerical
Time spent on the internet	Shoe size
Height and weight	Mark in an exam
Speed of Formula One cars	Number of students doing Higher Level maths
Time taken to complete 100 m	Number of times a six occurs when tossing a die

Univariate data is data that has **one value**, e.g. height of student, favourite soccer team, cost of membership to a gym.

Bivariate data is data that has **two paired values**, e.g. height and weight of athletes, time spent on study and exam results, number of years working and salary.

Collecting data

Primary data is data collected first-hand by the student, class or researcher.

Types of studies that generate primary data include:

Observational studies, where the researcher collects information but does not influence events, e.g. traffic surveys, television viewing habits, eating behaviour of elderly people in nursing homes.

Experimental studies (also called **designed experiments**), where the researcher influences events or the subjects' environment and then investigates the effects of this intervention, e.g. clinical trials, research intervention.

> **Point to note**
>
> A **control group** is often used in both observational studies and designed experiments.
>
> An observational study might compare two groups, where the members of one group (the cases) have a certain disease and the members of the other group (the control) don't have the disease. A famous case–control study done by Austin Hill and Richard Doll in 1950 established the link between lung cancer and smoking.
>
> In designed experiments, a researcher will apply some treatment to a group and then observe the effects the treatment has on the group. The effects will be compared with a control group, who did not receive the treatment. Pharmaceutical companies carry out designed experiments when testing a new drug. The drug is called an **explanatory variable** and the effect caused by the drug is called the **response variable**.

Secondary data is data collected from another source, for example the internet, published databases, newspapers and magazines, CensusAtSchool.

Types of graph

There are many different types of graph that can be used to represent data. Which is the most suitable type of graph depends on the data type. The table below suggests appropriate graphs for different types of data.

Univariate/ bivariate	Type of data (example)	Bar chart	Frequency table	Histogram	Line of best fit	Pie chart	Scatter plot	Stem and leaf plot	Line plot
Univariate (single variable)	Categorical (colours)	✓	✓			✓			✓
	Discrete (number of students)	✓	✓			✓		✓	✓
	Continuous (height)		✓	✓				✓	
Bivariate (paired variable)	Discrete (number of students and marks in exam)		✓		✓		✓		
	Continuous (height and weight)		✓		✓		✓		

Key definitions relating to statistical enquiries

Population – the entire group of subjects about which information is required.

Data – set of facts or values.

Sampling frame – list of every item in the population, e.g. a list of all customers for a mobile phone company.

Census – survey of whole population.

Sample – any subset of a population.

Random sample – a sample in which every member of the population has an equal chance of being selected.

Sample survey – investigation that collects data from a sample of the population.

Unit – individual member of a population.

Variable – a characteristic being recorded or a particular element of interest from a sample or population, e.g. rating of customer service from 1 to 10.

Explanatory variable (also called **independent variable**) – the variable whose effect on the response we want to study.

Response variable (also called **dependent variable**) – the variable whose changes we wish to study.

Parameter – a number that describes a population characteristic, e.g. average gross income of workers in Ireland.

Statistic – a number that describes a sample characteristic, e.g. gross income of workers in Cork.

Bias – something that might distort data so that there will not be a correct representation from the sample, e.g. misleading questions on a questionnaire, sample size too small, failure to respond to survey, incorrect identification of population. Samples that are not representative are called biased samples. Bias can be eliminated by taking a random sample, where everyone has an equal chance of being included in the sample.

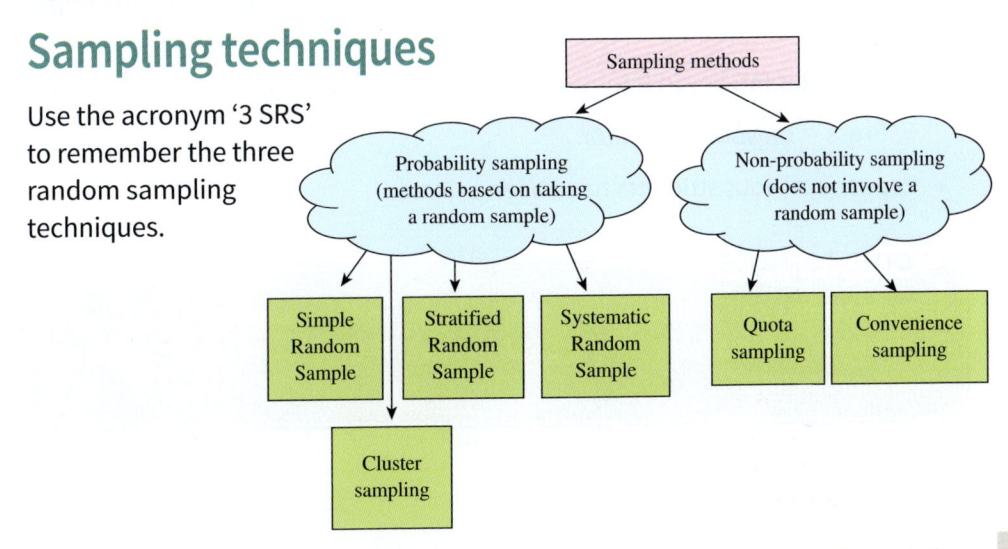

Sampling techniques

Use the acronym '3 SRS' to remember the three random sampling techniques.

Sampling methods:

- Probability sampling (methods based on taking a random sample)
  - Simple Random Sample
  - Stratified Random Sample
  - Systematic Random Sample
  - Cluster sampling
- Non-probability sampling (does not involve a random sample)
  - Quota sampling
  - Convenience sampling

Simple random sampling

- Probability sampling method.
- Each member of the population has an equal chance of being selected.
- Techniques include:
  - identify each member of the population with a number, and use the random number generator on a calculator to select the sample
  - put the name of each member of the population in a hat and pick out the number required to form the sample (this is called the **lottery method**).

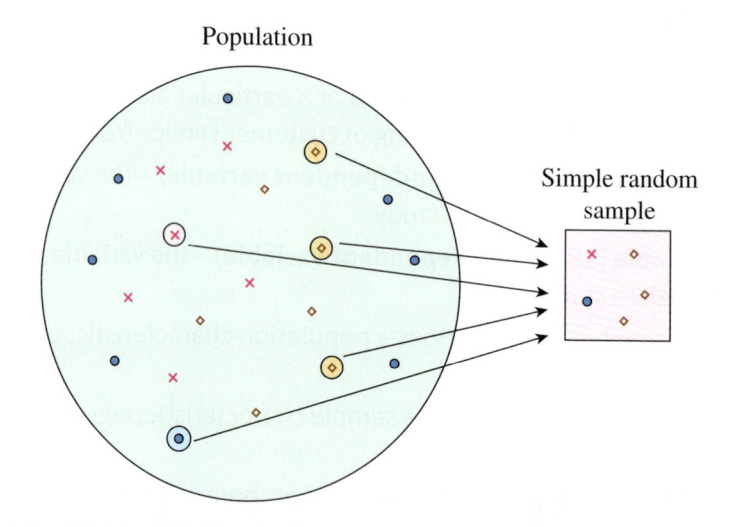

For example, to select a random sample of four students in a class of 30 to represent the class at a student debate:

- Assign each student in the class with a number from 1 to 30.
- Use the random number generator on your calculator to generate an integer between 1 and 30.
  - Using RanInt, key in RanInt#(1,30).
  - Press = on your calculator.
- Repeat until four students have been selected.

Point to note

Presentations showing you how to generate random numbers on a calculator are available on the Student Area of the Project Maths website, www.projectmaths.ie.

Stratified random sampling

- Probability sampling method based on a random sample.
- Population is divided into two or more groups (**strata**). These might be geographic location, age, gender, income, etc.
- Members of your sample belonging to each stratum are identified.
- A simple random sample is collected from each stratum. The number taken from each stratum is proportional to size of the stratum relative to the whole population.

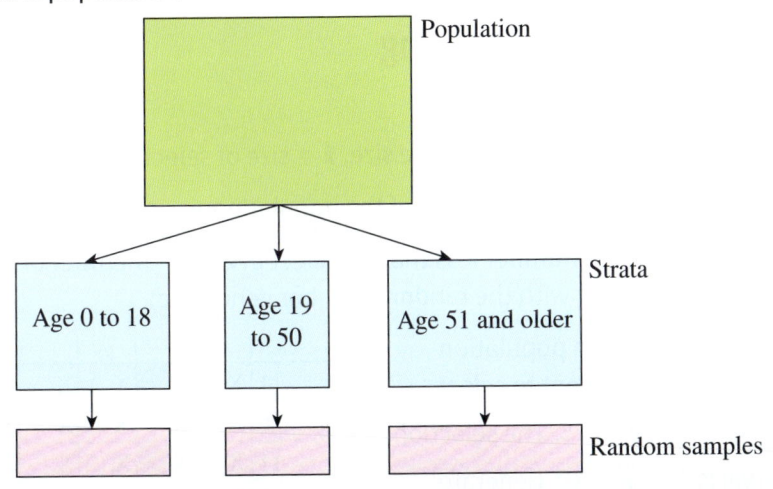

Example

A company employs a total of 360 people in different categories:

Managers = 36

Drivers = 48

Administration staff = 96

Production staff = 180

The company decides to interview staff about possible redundancies in the next year. How many from each category should be included in a stratified random sample of size 90?

Solution

$\frac{90}{360} = \frac{1}{4}$ of the employees to be interviewed.

Take $\frac{1}{4}$ from each category for the stratified random sample.

Category	Total number	Number for sample
Managers	36	$36 \times \frac{1}{4} = 9$
Drivers	48	$48 \times \frac{1}{4} = 12$
Administration staff	96	$96 \times \frac{1}{4} = 24$
Production staff	180	$180 \times \frac{1}{4} = 45$

Systematic random sampling

- Probability sampling method.
- N = size of population, n = sample size, k = size of selection interval = $\frac{N}{n}$.
- Assign a number to each member of the population.
- Generate a random number less than k. Select every k^{th} member of the population, starting with the random number generated.
- For example, given a population of size $N = 50$, we want to select a sample of size $n = 5$. The selection interval is $k = \frac{50}{5} = 10$. Generate a random number between 1 and 10, e.g. 2. We need to select every 10th unit, starting with the 2nd. That is, we select units 2, 12, 22, 32 and 42.

Cluster sampling

- Probability sampling method.
- Population is divided into **clusters** (subgroups).
- A simple random sample of clusters is selected.
- All members of each chosen cluster are surveyed.

For example, a survey is carried out to check how many Leaving Certificate students use the resources for students on the Project Maths website. A cluster sample could be taken by using the different counties in Ireland as clusters. A sample of these counties (clusters) would be chosen at random, and all Leaving Certificate students in each of the chosen counties would be included in the sample. It is much easier to visit several schools in the same county than to travel to each school in a random sample.

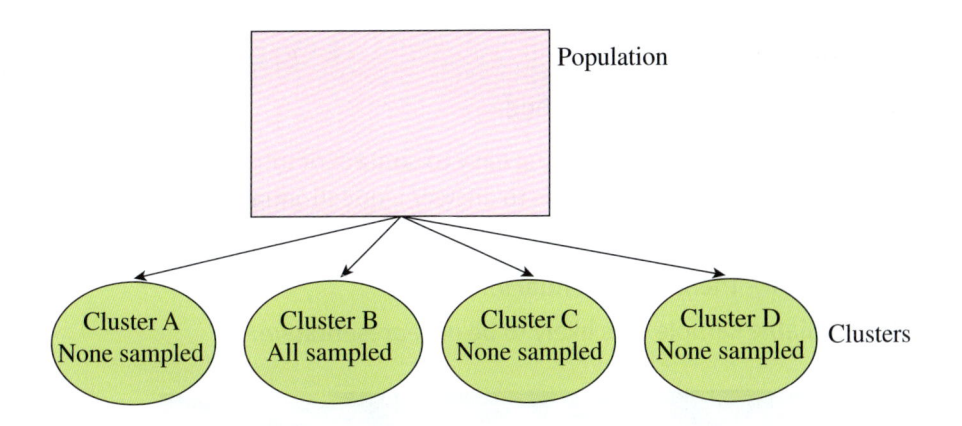

Quota sampling

- Non-probability sampling method.
- Similar to stratified sampling.
- Widely used in opinion polls and market research.
- Population divided into groups based on certain criteria, e.g. age, social class, gender.
- A quota of subjects are interviewed in each group.
- Interviewer chooses subjects – it is not random. There is a potential for bias.
- There might be sampling errors.
- No sampling frame required.

For example, an interviewer requires a sample of 1000 from a population. He knows from census data that approximately 30% of the population are aged under 20; 45% are between 20 and 49; and 25% are 50 or older. He would generate a quota for each age group based on these percentages, then sample each age group until his quota is achieved. Quota sampling achieves a representative age distribution, but it is not a random sample because the sampling frame is not known. The sample may not be representative.

Age group	Population distribution	Quota ($n = 1000$)
<20	30%	300
20–49	45%	450
50+	25%	250

Convenience sampling

- Non-probability sampling method.
- Sample chosen by virtue of being easy to contact or interview, e.g. choosing family and friends to answer a questionnaire, interviewing people in a supermarket.
- Not random – there is a potential for bias.
- Not a reliable sample. It is likely to be unrepresentative.

Point to note

A reliable sample should be large enough to accurately represent the population without risk of bias.

For a small population, you need a large percentage of members to be surveyed to achieve accurate results.

For a large population, it is possible to achieve accurate results by surveying a smaller percentage of members.

Examples

A company wanted to find out how its customers rated the customer service offered. A list of all customers was obtained and 800 customers were randomly selected from this list. These 800 customers were posted a questionnaire asking them to rate customer service on a scale from 1 to 10. Customers who responded were given a discount on their account. 300 customers responded, and gave an average rating of 6 for customer service.

(a) Identify the population, the sampling frame, the sample and the variable measured.
(b) What is the parameter of interest in this example?
(c) Identify the statistic in the example.
(d) Identify the potential bias in this example and suggest a way of eliminating the bias.

Solutions

(a) Population = all customers
Sampling frame = list of all customers
Sample = the 800 randomly-selected customers
Variable = customer service rating on a scale from 1 to 10

(b) The parameter of interest is the average customer service rating.

(c) The statistic is the value found for the average customer service rating = 6.

(d) There was a low response rate, so the sample might not be large enough to achieve accurate results. The incentive to respond might have an effect on the customer service rating.
Eliminate potential bias by increasing the sample size and eliminating the discount.

Example

Explain what is meant by stratified sampling and cluster sampling. Your explanation should include

- a clear indication of the two methods
- one reason why each method might be chosen instead of simple random sampling.

(SEC Sample 2014)

Solution

Stratified sampling: A probability sampling method based on random sampling. Population is divided into groups (strata), e.g. age, gender. Simple random samples are collected from each group, proportional to the size of the group.
Advantage: Selecting from different groups ensures a more representative sample.

Cluster sampling: A probability sample method. Population is divided into subgroups (clusters) that have something in common, e.g. Irish teachers in a certain school. A simple random sample of clusters is selected and all members of each chosen cluster are surveyed.
Advantage: If clusters are based on location then the cost of sampling could be reduced.

Surveys and questionnaires

Data can be collected in many different ways. Most surveys involve a questionnaire. There are advantages and disadvantages to each method.

Method	Advantages	Disadvantages
Face-to-face interviews	Accurate screening by gender, age, etc. Opportunity to explain questions that are not understood.	Not random. Can be expensive. Potential for bias from interviewer.
Telephone interviews	High response rate.	Potential for bias from interviewer.
Postal questionnaire	Inexpensive.	Response rate can be low. Potential for bias.
Online questionnaire	Inexpensive.	Not representative of population.
Observation	Accurate screening by gender, age, etc. Access to situations where questionnaires are not possible.	Reseacher has no control of sample. Subject to bias.

Questionnaire design

A good questionnaire:

- gives an example of how to answer the questions (e.g. circle an answer from a list of answers)
- covers different types of data
- can be answered quickly
- starts with simple questions
- has questions ordered carefully
- has been tested on a small sample group first
- has a specific time frame for responses
- has been checked for errors.

A good question:
- is relevant to the topic of the survey
- uses clear, precise language
- is multi-choice
- avoids bias.

Snapshots at jasonlove.com

"Of students surveyed, 64% prefer English and 32% prefer math. The fact that these numbers do not add up to 100 may help explain why."

Checklist

- ✓ Know the different types of data and suitable representations for each type.
- ✓ Recognise the definitions for statistical enquiries.
- ✓ Learn the different types of sampling and which sampling method or methods would be suitable for a particular example. Revise the possible advantages and disadvantages of each type.
- ✓ Be able to suggest how data could be collected and comment on the design of a questionnaire.

8 Probability 1

Learning objectives

In this chapter you will learn how to:
- Understand key terms in probability
- Use the fundamental principle of counting, arrangements and combinations
- Use set theory to discuss experiments, outcomes and sample spaces
- Discuss the basic rules of probability (AND/OR, mutually exclusive) through the use of Venn diagrams
- Extend your understanding of the basic rules of probability through the use of formulae:
  - Addition rule: $P(A \cup B) = P(A) + P(B) - P(A \cap B)$
  - Multiplication rule (independent events): $P(A \cap B) = P(A) \times P(B)$
  - Multiplication rule (general case): $P(A \cap B) = P(A) \times P(B|A)$
- Solve problems involving sampling, with or without replacement
- Appreciate that in general $P(A|B) \neq P(B|A)$
- Use tree diagrams in probability
- Use the counting method (combinations) to evaluate probabilities.

Introduction and key words

Probability is a numerical measure of the chance of an event happening. It can be expressed as a fraction, decimal or percentage.

Key words

Trial	The experiment being carried out – throwing a die, etc.
Permutation	An arrangement of a number of objects in a certain order, where the order is important.
Factorial	Number of permutations of n different objects, written as $n!$.
Combination	A selection of objects selected from a given set, where order is not important.
Outcome	Any possible result of a trial, e.g. throwing a die and getting a 1.
Event	Desired or successful outcome, e.g. selecting a king from a deck of cards.
Sample space	List or set of all possible outcomes.
Two-way table	Representation of an experiment on a table showing all possible outcomes. This is useful when there is a small number of outcomes.
Equally likely events	Two or more events which have an equal chance of happening, e.g. getting a head or tail when tossing a coin.
Experimental probability	The chance of an event happening based on the results of an experiment after a large number of trials, e.g. a coin is tossed a 100 times and head occurred 45 times so the experimental probability is $P(E) = \dfrac{\text{number of times a head occurred}}{\text{total number of trials}} = \dfrac{45}{100}$.
Theoretical probability	The chance of an event happening based on the possible outcomes assuming equally likely events. $P(E) = \dfrac{\text{number of successful outcomes}}{\text{number of possible outcomes}}$.

Fundamental principle of counting

If one event has m possible outcomes and a second event has n possible outcomes, then the total number of possible outcomes is $m \times n$.

This can be extended to more events. We simply multiply the outcomes.

Example

A car manufacturer makes four models of car: a mini, a saloon, a jeep and an estate. These cars are all available in a choice of six colours: red, blue, grey, green, black and white. How many different cars are available?

Solution

m = number of models = 4
n = number of colours = 6
Number of different cars = $m \times n$ = 24

Example

Complete the table by writing down the number of outcomes for each series of events. Assume no restrictions for parts (f) and (g); letters or digits can be repeated.

	Event 1	Event 2	Event 3	No. of outcomes
(a)	4 main courses	3 desserts	Tea or coffee	$4 \times 3 \times 2 = 24$
(b)	Tossing a coin	Tossing a coin	Tossing a coin	
(c)	Throwing a die	Throwing a die	-	
(d)	Throwing a die	Tossing a coin	-	
(e)	Spinner with numbers 1–3 inclusive	Spinner with numbers 4–9 inclusive	-	
(f)	Digit 0–9	Digit 0–9	Digit 0–9	
(g)	Letter in the alphabet	Letter in the alphabet	Digit 0–9	
(h)	Even digit 2–10 inclusive	Odd digit 3 or 5 or 7	Letter Z	

Solution

	Event 1	Event 2	Event 3	No. of outcomes
(a)	4 main courses	3 desserts	Tea or coffee	$4 \times 3 \times 2 = 24$
(b)	Tossing a coin	Tossing a coin	Tossing a coin	$2 \times 2 \times 2 = 8$
(c)	Throwing a die	Throwing a die	-	$6 \times 6 = 36$
(d)	Throwing a die	Tossing a coin	-	$6 \times 2 = 12$
(e)	Spinner with numbers 1–3 inclusive	Spinner with numbers 4–9 inclusive	-	$3 \times 6 = 18$
(f)	Digits 0–9	Digits 0–9	Digits 0–9	$10 \times 10 \times 10 = 1000$
(g)	Letter in the alphabet	Letter in the alphabet	Digit 0–9	$26 \times 26 \times 10 = 6760$
(h)	Even digit 2–10 inclusive	Odd digit 3 or 5 or 7	Letter Z	$5 \times 3 \times 1 = 15$

Permutations

A **permutation** is an arrangement of objects in a certain order.

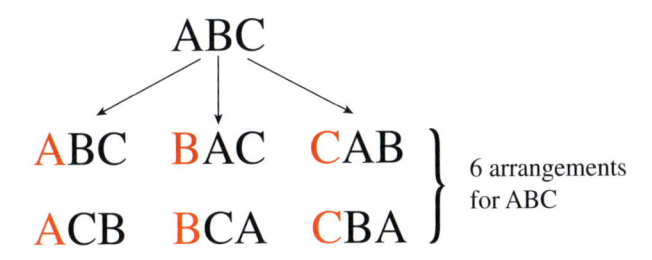

ABC

ABC BAC CAB
ACB BCA CBA } 6 arrangements for ABC

> **Top Tip**
> Look out for the key word 'arrange' or 'arrangement'. This usually indicates a question about permutations.

Example

Write down the number of arrangements for each word.

Word	Arrangements	Number of arrangements
AT	AT TA	
CAR	CAR ARC RAC CRA ACR RCA	
FAST	FAST FATS FSAT…	
MATHS	MATHS MATSH MASHT…	

Solution

To answer this question, notice that the number of options for the first letter of each arrangement is the same as the number of letters in the word.

The number of options for the second letter of each arrangement is one less than the number of letters in each word, because one letter has already been used. The pattern continues for the remaining letters.

By the fundamental principle of counting, this means that a word with n letters has $n(n-1)(n-2)...(2)(1)$ different arrangements.

Word	Arrangements	Number of arrangements
AT	AT TA	$2 \times 1 = 2$
CAR	CAR ARC RAC CRA ACR RCA	$3 \times 2 \times 1 = 6$
FAST	FAST FATS FSAT…	$4 \times 3 \times 2 \times 1 = 24$
MATHS	MATHS MATSH MASHT…	$5 \times 4 \times 3 \times 2 \times 1 = 120$

8. Probability 1

> **Point to note**
> The multiplication $n(n-1)(n-2)...(2)(1)$ is called n factorial, denoted by $n!$. It is a formula for the number of permutations of n different objects when all the objects are included in each arrangement.

> **Top Tip**
> Your calculator should have a button to calculate the factorial.

Examples

There are six students sitting in a row in a classroom. Peter and John are two of the students.

(a) In how many ways can the six students be arranged in a row?

(b) In how many ways can the students be arranged if Peter is always sitting on the extreme right?

(c) In how many ways can the students be arranged if Peter and John must sit together?

(d) In how many ways can the two named students be apart?

Solutions

> **Top Tip**
> Draw a diagram and write in the relevant information to help understand the question.

(a) The students can be arranged in $6! = 720$ different ways.

(b) ☐ ☐ ☐ ☐ ☐ Peter

Fixing Peter on the far right leaves five other students to be seated. These can be arranged in $5! = 120$ different ways.

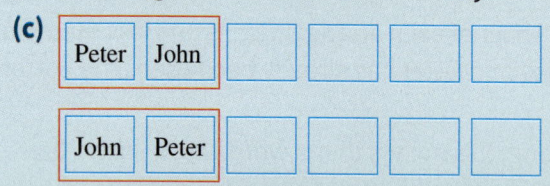

(c) Peter John ☐ ☐ ☐ ☐

John Peter ☐ ☐ ☐ ☐

Considering John and Peter as one block, along with each of the four remaining students, there are $5! = 120$ arrangements.

Within the John and Peter block, there are $2! = 2$ ways in which they can be seated.

Therefore there are $120 \times 2 = 240$ ways in which John and Peter can be seated together.

(d) Number of arrangements apart = total number of arrangements − number of arrangements together = $720 - 240 = 480$

The $n!$ formula calculates the number of permutations when we are using *all* the available objects in the arrangements. If we don't want to arrange all the objects, we need a different formula.

$nPr = \dfrac{n!}{(n-r)!}$, where r is the number of objects to be arranged and n is the total number of objects.

If there are no restrictions in the arrangements, we can use this formula as it is.

If there are restrictions, we can use boxes to take these out and work out the number of objects remaining after the restrictions.

> **Top Tip**
> Use the nPr button on your calculator to find the number of permutations. Enter the total number of objects, followed by the nPr button, followed by the number of objects to be arranged.

Examples

(a) How many different arrangements can be formed from the letters of the word CHEMISTRY?

(b) How many different ways can the letters be arranged if:
  (i) the first letter is a vowel and the last letter is Y
  (ii) the letters C and H must be together
  (iii) the letters C and H must not be together?

Solutions

(a) $nPr = \dfrac{9!}{(9-9)!} = 9! = 362\,880$

> **Top Tip**
> 0! is defined to equal 1.

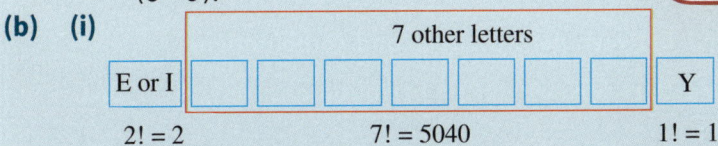

(b) (i)

E or I			7 other letters				Y
2! = 2			7! = 5040				1! = 1

There are $2! \times 7! \times 1! = 2 \times 5040 \times 1 = 10\,080$ different arrangements.

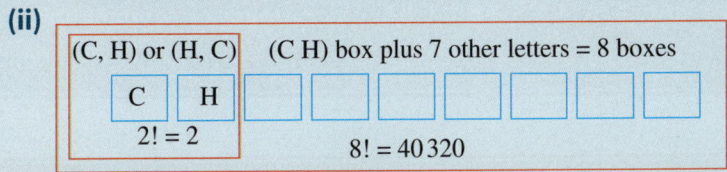

(ii)

(C, H) or (H, C) (C H) box plus 7 other letters = 8 boxes

C	H
2! = 2	

8! = 40 320

There are $2! \times 8! = 2 \times 40\,320 = 80\,640$ different arrangements.

(iii) Use the subtraction method.

Number of arrangements with C and H apart = total number of arrangements − number of arrangements with C and H together
= 362 880 − 80 640 = 282 240

Examples

A three-digit number is to be formed from the digits 0, 1, 4, 5, 7 and 9.

(a) How many of these numbers are greater than 500?

(b) How many of the numbers are odd?

Solutions

(a) There are three options for the first digit: 5, 7 or 9.

There are five options for the second digit: 0, 1, 4 and the two from 5, 7 or 9 that aren't used for the first digit.

There are four options for the third digit: the four options from the second digit that weren't used.

Therefore there are 3 × 5 × 4 = 60 numbers that are greater than 500.

(b) There are four options for the third digit: 1, 5, 7 or 9.

As a three-digit number is formed, the first digit can't be 0. Therefore, there are four options for the first digit: 4, and the three from 1, 5, 7 or 9 that aren't used for the third digit.

The second digit can then be chosen from the remaining four options.

There are 4 × 4 × 4 = 64 odd numbers.

Combinations

A **combination** is a selection of objects chosen from a given set. The order of the objects is not important.

> **Point to note**
>
> Note the difference between permutations and combinations.
>
> If we arrange the letters ABC we get six permutations: ABC, ACB, BAC, BCA, CAB, CBA.
>
> With combinations the order isn't important, so ABC = ACB = BAC = BCA = CAB = CBA. The number of combinations is just 1.

> **Top Tip**
>
> Watch out for the words 'choose', 'selected' or 'selection'. This usually indicates a question about combinations.

To calculate the number of combinations of r objects from a total set of n objects, we use the formula

$nCr = \binom{n}{r} = \dfrac{n!}{r!(n-r)!}.$

This formula is on page 20 of the *Formulae and Tables* booklet.

> **Top Tip**
>
> Use the nCr button on your calculator to find the number of permutations. Enter the total number of objects, followed by the nCr button, followed by the number of objects to be selected.

For example, the number of ways of selecting 3 objects from a total of 8 is

$\binom{8}{3} = \dfrac{8!}{3!(8-3)!} = \dfrac{8!}{3!(5!)} = \dfrac{8 \times 7 \times 6 \times 5 \times 4 \times 3 \times 2 \times 1}{3 \times 2 \times 1 \times 5 \times 4 \times 3 \times 2 \times 1} = \dfrac{8 \times 7 \times 6}{3 \times 2 \times 1} = 56.$

If $r = 1$ then $\binom{n}{r} = \binom{n}{1} = \dfrac{n!}{1!(n-1)!} = \dfrac{n!}{(n-1)!} = n.$

The **twin rule** states that $\binom{n}{r} = \binom{n}{n-r}$. For example, $\binom{5}{3} = \binom{5}{2} = 10.$

By the twin rule, if $n = r$ then $\binom{n}{r} = \binom{n}{n} = \binom{n}{n-n} = \binom{n}{0} = 1.$

Combinations from one set

Examples

(a) In how many ways can 6 numbers be chosen from 42?

(b) In a 20 team league, how many matches can be organised if:
   (i) each team plays each other exactly once
   (ii) each team plays each other home and away?

Solutions

(a) In this question, $n = 42$ and $r = 6$. $nCr = \binom{42}{6} = 5\,245\,786.$

(b) (i) We are selecting 2 teams from a set of 20, so $n = 20$ and $r = 2$.

$\binom{20}{2} = 190$

(ii) The teams being selected are the same as in part (i), only now each pairing occurs twice.

$\binom{20}{2} \times 2 = 190 \times 2 = 380$

8. Probability 1

Combinations from two sets

Examples

Five men (Andrew, Billy, Chris, Dave and Eugene) and three women (Fiona, Grace and Helen) are standing for election to a local committee.

Four people will serve on the committee for one year.

How many ways can the committee be formed if:

(a) there are no restrictions
(b) Andrew must be on the committee as he was chairperson last year
(c) Grace cannot go forward for election
(d) there must be an equal number of men and women on the committee
(e) there must be at least one woman on the committee?

Solutions

(a) If there are no restrictions, then it is a simple matter of choosing four people from the eight candidates.

$$\binom{8}{4} = 70$$

(b)

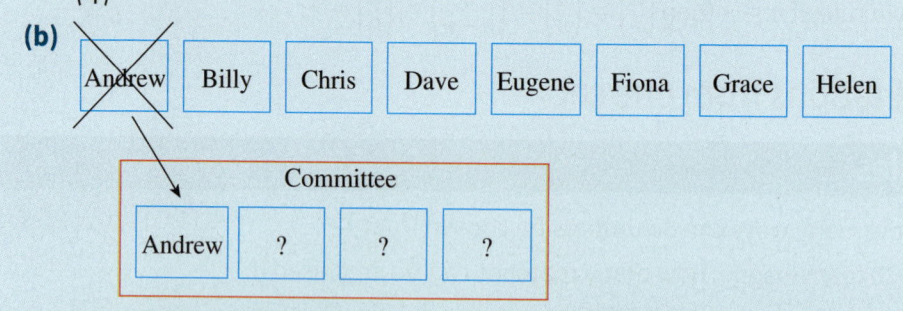

| ~~Andrew~~ | Billy | Chris | Dave | Eugene | Fiona | Grace | Helen |

Committee: | Andrew | ? | ? | ? |

If Andrew must be on the committee, then there are three places left to fill from seven candidates.

$$\binom{7}{3} = 35$$

(c)

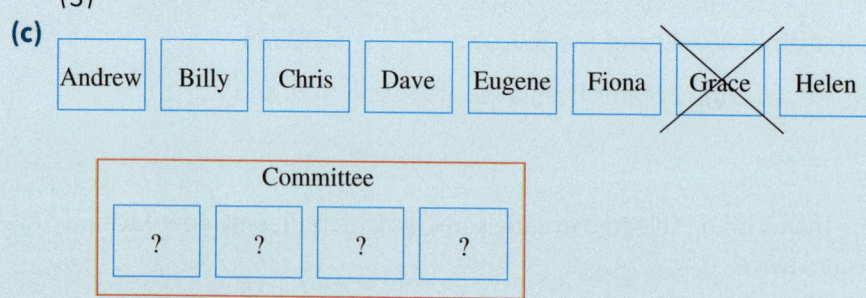

| Andrew | Billy | Chris | Dave | Eugene | Fiona | ~~Grace~~ | Helen |

Committee: | ? | ? | ? | ? |

If Grace cannot go forward for election, then there are still four places left, but only seven candidates.

$$\binom{7}{4} = 35$$

(d) To have an equal number of men and women, there must be two men and two women. Therefore, we are choosing two men from a set of five, and two women from a set of three.

The number of combinations is $\binom{5}{2} \times \binom{3}{2} = 10 \times 3 = 30$.

(e) 'At least one woman' means one, two or three women, so there are three different situations to calculate. It is easier to calculate the number of combinations with no women, and subtract the answer from the total number of combinations.

To find the number of combinations with no women, we are choosing four men from a set of five, and no women from a set of three.

The number of combinations is $\binom{5}{4} \times \binom{3}{0} = 5 \times 1 = 5$.

The number of combinations with at least one woman is 70 − 5 = 65.

Examples

Two parallel lines a and b are drawn.

Five points are chosen at random on line a and six points are chosen at random on line b.

(a) Find the maximum number of triangles that can be formed by joining points between the parallel lines a and b.
(b) If two points X and Y are used in line a, how many triangles can now be formed?

Solutions

(a) Three points are needed to form a triangle. This could be two points from line a and one point from line b **or** one point from line a and two points from line b.

$$\binom{5}{1} \times \binom{6}{2} + \binom{5}{2} \times \binom{6}{1} = 75 + 60 = 135 \text{ triangles}$$

(b) If two points are already fixed on line a then we just need one point from line b.

$$\binom{6}{1} = 6 \text{ triangles}$$

Probability rules

Notation

$P(A)$ means the probability that event A occurs.

$P(A \cap B)$ means the probability that both event A and event B occur.

$P(A \cup B)$ means the probability that either event A or event B occurs.

$P(A|B)$ means the probability that event A occurs, given that event B has occurred.

Point to note

Events A and B are **mutually exclusive events** if they have no outcomes in common (no **intersection**). For example, when picking a card from a pack of cards, 'picking a diamond' and 'picking a heart' are mutually exclusive events. If you are picking one card, it is not possible for it to be both a heart and a diamond.

If events A and B are not mutually exclusive then they have outcomes in common. For example, 'picking a diamond' and 'picking a four' are not mutually exclusive events. It is possible for one card to be both a diamond and a four.

Point to note

Two events are **independent** if the outcome of one does not depend on the outcome of the other.

If event A is throwing an odd number with a blue die and event B is throwing an even number with a red die, then the probability of event A happening is $\frac{3}{6} = \frac{1}{2}$, regardless of whether or not event B occurs.

If two events A and B are independent then $P(A \cap B) = P(A) \times P(B)$. Also, $P(A|B) = P(A)$ and $P(B|A) = P(B)$. If you are given these probabilities then you can use them to prove that the events are independent.

If A and B are not independent then $P(A \cap B) \neq P(A) \times P(B)$.

Summary of probability rules

Rule	Formula/Diagram
The probability of any event E is a number between 0 and 1 (fraction or decimal).	$0 \leq P(E) \leq 1$ 0 — Impossible, 0.5 — Unlikely / Even / Likely, 1 — Certain
The sum of the probabilities of all outcomes in the sample space is 1.	$P(S) = 1$ For example, tossing two coins. |	H	T
---	---	---
H	$P(H, H) = 0.25$	$P(H, T) = 0.25$
T	$P(T, H) = 0.25$	$P(T, T) = 0.25$	 The sum of all the probabilities is 1.
Complementary events $P(E)$ = probability of event E occurring $P(E')$ = probability of event E not occurring	$P(E) + P(E') = 1$ $P(E) = 1 - P(E')$ $P(E') = 1 - P(E)$
Addition rule 1 Gives the probability that A or B occurs for two mutually exclusive events A and B.	$P(A \text{ or } B) = P(A) + P(B)$ OR $\Rightarrow$ ADD $P(A \cup B) = P(A) + P(B)$
Addition rule 2 Gives the probability that A or B occurs for two events A and B that are not mutually exclusive.	$P(A \text{ or } B) =$ $P(A) + P(B) - P(A \text{ and } B)$ $P(A \cup B) =$ $P(A) + P(B) - P(A \cap B)$

8. Probability 1

Rule	Formula/Diagram
Multiplication rule 1 (independent events) **Gives the probability of both events occurring for two independent events.**	$P(A \text{ and } B) = P(A) \times P(B)$ $P(A \cap B) = P(A) \times P(B)$
Multiplication rule 2 (general case)	$P(A \text{ and } B) = P(A) \times P(B\|A)$ $P(A \cap B) = P(A) \times P(B\|A)$
Conditional probability **The probability the second event B occurs given that the first event A has occurred.**	$P(B\|A) = \dfrac{P(A \text{ and } B)}{P(A)}$ $P(B\|A) = \dfrac{P(A \cap B)}{P(A)}$
'At least one' means one or more.	$P(E \text{ occurs at least once}) = 1 - P(E \text{ does not occur at all})$

Examples

A bag contains 3 white beads, 4 blue beads and 3 black beads.

Two beads are chosen at random and not replaced.

(a) Find the probability that the beads chosen are:
  (i) both black
  (ii) black and blue in that order
  (iii) black and blue in any order.
(b) Find the probability that at least one of the beads is white.

Solutions

It is useful to draw a diagram to visualise the problem.

3 white + 4 blue + 3 black = 10 beads in total

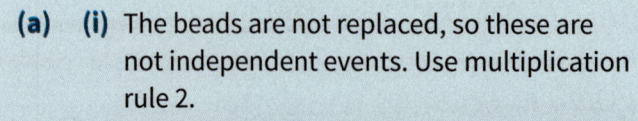

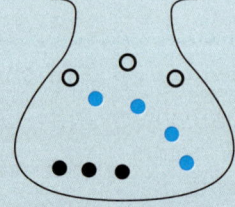

(a) (i) The beads are not replaced, so these are not independent events. Use multiplication rule 2.

$P(\text{black}_1 \text{ and } \text{black}_2) = P(\text{black}_1) \times P(\text{black}_2 | \text{black}_1)$

$= \dfrac{3}{10} \times \dfrac{2}{9} = \dfrac{6}{90} = \dfrac{1}{15}$

(ii) $P(\text{black and blue}) = P(\text{black}) \times P(\text{blue}|\text{black})$
$$= \frac{3}{10} \times \frac{4}{9} = \frac{12}{90} = \frac{2}{15}$$

(iii) The events [black and blue] and [blue and black] are mutually exclusive, so use addition rule 1.
$$P([\text{black and blue}] \text{ or } [\text{blue and black}]) = \frac{3}{10} \times \frac{4}{9} + \frac{4}{10} \times \frac{3}{9}$$
$$= \frac{2}{15} + \frac{2}{15} = \frac{4}{15}$$

(b) 'At least one white bead' means one white bead or more.

It is easier to use $P(\text{at least one white}) = 1 - P(\text{no white})$ than to calculate all the probabilities of more than one white bead.

$P(\text{no white}) = \frac{7}{10} \times \frac{6}{9} = \frac{42}{90} = \frac{7}{15}$

$P(\text{at least one white}) = 1 - P(\text{no white}) = 1 - \frac{7}{15} = \frac{8}{15}$

Examples

(a) Explain each of the following terms:

(i) Sample space (ii) Mutually exclusive events

(iii) Independent events.

(b) In a class of 30 students, 20 study Physics, 6 study Biology and 4 study both Physics and Biology.

(i) Represent the information on the Venn diagram.

A student is selected at random from this class.

The events E and F are:

E: The student studies Physics

F: The student studies Biology.

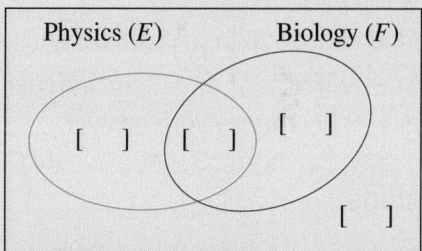

(ii) By calculating probabilities, investigate if the events E and F are independent.

(SEC 2013)

Solutions

(a) (i) A sample space is the set of all possible outcomes of an experiment.

(ii) Events E and F are mutually exclusive if they have no outcomes in common, i.e. $P(E \cup F) = P(E) + P(F)$.

(iii) Two events are independent if the outcome of one does not depend on the outcome of the other, i.e. $P(E \cap F) = P(E) \times P(F)$
or $P(E|F) = P(E)$ or $P(F|E) = P(F)$.

8. Probability 1   147

(b) (i) Work out the intersection first. There are 4 students studying both subjects.

This means that there are 20 − 4 = 16 studying Physics, and 6 − 4 = 2 studying Biology.

There are 30 students altogether, so the number studying neither subject is 30 − (16 + 4 + 2) = 8.

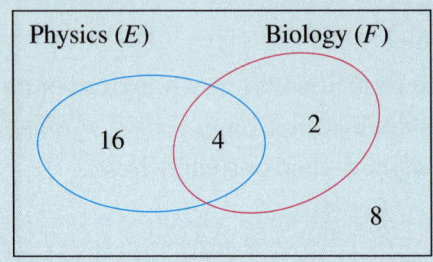

Physics (E)   Biology (F)

16   4   2

8

(ii) From the diagram, $P(E \cap F) = \frac{4}{30}$.

$P(E) \times P(F) = \frac{20}{30} \times \frac{6}{30} = \frac{4}{30}$

$P(E \cap F) = P(E) \times P(F)$, so E and F are independent.

Examples

Two events A and B are such that $P(A) = 0{\cdot}2$, $P(A \cap B) = 0{\cdot}15$ and $P(A' \cap B) = 0{\cdot}6$.

(a) Complete this Venn diagram.
(b) Find the probability that neither A nor B happens.
(c) Find the conditional probability $P(A|B)$.
(d) State whether A and B are independent events and justify your answer.

(SEC 2010)

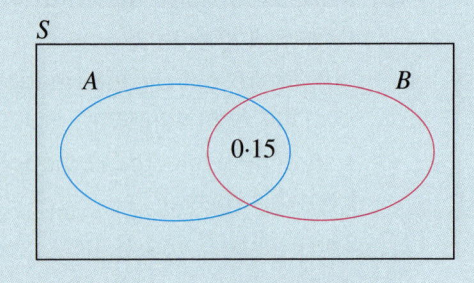

S

A   B

0·15

Solutions

(a) $P(A \cap B') = 0{\cdot}2 - 0{\cdot}15 = 0{\cdot}05$

$P(A' \cap B') = 1 - (0{\cdot}05 + 0{\cdot}15 + 0{\cdot}6) = 0{\cdot}2$

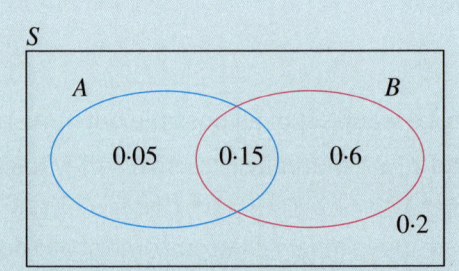

S

A   B

0·05   0·15   0·6

0·2

(b) From part (a), $P(A' \cap B') = 0.2$.

(c) $P(A|B) = \dfrac{P(A \cap B)}{P(B)} = \dfrac{0.15}{(0.15 + 0.6)} = 0.2$

(d) A and B are independent events because $P(A|B) = P(A) = 0.2$.

Sample space

The **sample space** is the set of all possible outcomes of an experiment.

We can use a sample space to work out the probabilities of events happening, e.g. tossing coins, throwing a pair of dice, tossing a coin and spinning a spinner.

Sample space for throwing a pair of dice

	1	2	3	4	5	6
1	1, 1	1, 2	1, 3	1, 4	1, 5	1, 6
2	2, 1	2, 2	2, 3	2, 4	2, 5	2, 6
3	3, 1	3, 2	3, 3	3, 4	3, 5	3, 6
4	4, 1	4, 2	4, 3	4, 4	4, 5	4, 6
5	5, 1	5, 2	5, 3	5, 4	5, 5	5, 6
6	6, 1	6, 2	6, 3	6, 4	6, 5	6, 6

Sample space for a deck of cards

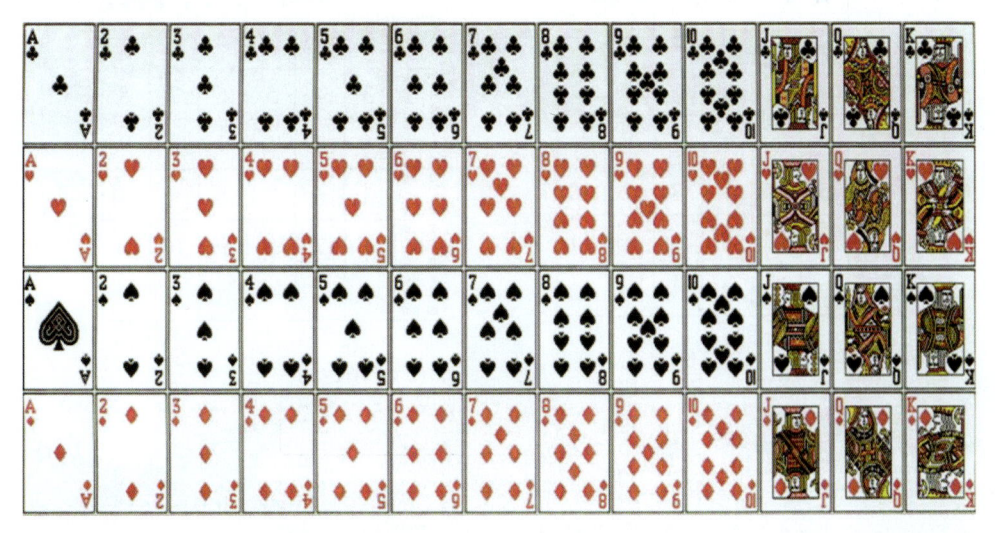

8. Probability 1

Examples

A pair of dice is thrown.
  (a) Find the probability of:
      (i) scoring 7   (ii) scoring 5   (iii) scoring less than 5
      (iv) scoring 9 or more   (v) getting a double.
  (b) If A is the event 'total score is 7', B is the event 'second die score is 6' and C is the event 'total score is 9 or more', show that A and B are independent, but B and C are not independent.

Solutions

There are 36 possibilities in the sample space, so every answer will be a fraction with a denominator of 36.

(a) (i)

	1	2	3	4	5	6
1	2	3	4	5	6	⑦
2	3	4	5	6	⑦	8
3	4	5	6	⑦	8	9
4	5	6	⑦	8	9	10
5	6	⑦	8	9	10	11
6	⑦	8	9	10	11	12

$P(7) = \dfrac{6}{36} = \dfrac{1}{6}$

(ii)

	1	2	3	4	5	6
1	2	3	4	⑤	6	7
2	3	4	⑤	6	7	8
3	4	⑤	6	7	8	9
4	⑤	6	7	8	9	10
5	6	7	8	9	10	11
6	7	8	9	10	11	12

$P(5) = \dfrac{4}{36} = \dfrac{1}{9}$

(iii)

	1	2	3	4	5	6
1	②	③	④	5	6	7
2	③	④	5	6	7	8
3	④	5	6	7	8	9
4	5	6	7	8	9	10
5	6	7	8	9	10	11
6	7	8	9	10	11	12

$P(\text{less than 5}) = \dfrac{6}{36} = \dfrac{1}{6}$

(iv)

	1	2	3	4	5	6
1	2	3	4	5	6	7
2	3	4	5	6	7	8
3	4	5	6	7	8	⑨
4	5	6	7	8	⑨	⑩
5	6	7	8	⑨	⑩	⑪
6	7	8	⑨	⑩	⑪	⑫

$P(9 \text{ or more}) = \dfrac{10}{36} = \dfrac{5}{18}$

(v)

	Second die					
First die	1,1	1,2	1,3	1,4	1,5	1,6
	2,1	2,2	2,3	2,4	2,5	2,6
	3,1	3,2	3,3	3,4	3,5	3,6
	4,1	4,2	4,3	4,4	4,5	4,6
	5,1	5,2	5,3	5,4	5,5	5,6
	6,1	6,2	6,3	6,4	6,5	6,6

$P(\text{double}) = \dfrac{6}{36} = \dfrac{1}{6}$

(b)

	Second die					
First die	1,1	1,2	1,3	1,4	1,5	1,6
	2,1	2,2	2,3	2,4	2,5	2,6
	3,1	3,2	3,3	3,4	3,5	3,6
	4,1	4,2	4,3	4,4	4,5	4,6
	5,1	5,2	5,3	5,4	5,5	5,6
	6,1	6,2	6,3	6,4	6,5	6,6

Event A
Event B
Event C

$P(A) = \dfrac{6}{36} = \dfrac{1}{6}, P(B) = \dfrac{6}{36} = \dfrac{1}{6}, P(C) = \dfrac{10}{36} = \dfrac{5}{18}$

From the sample space, $P(A \cap B) = \dfrac{1}{36}, P(B \cap C) = \dfrac{4}{36} = \dfrac{1}{9}$

$P(A) \times P(B) = \dfrac{1}{6} \times \dfrac{1}{6} = \dfrac{1}{36} = P(A \cap B) \Rightarrow A$ and B are independent.

$P(B) \times P(C) = \dfrac{1}{6} \times \dfrac{5}{18} = \dfrac{5}{108} \neq P(B \cap C) \Rightarrow B$ and C are not independent.

Tree diagrams

We use a **tree diagram** to work out the possible outcomes of two or more events. It consists of a branching diagram that shows all the possible outcomes. Each branch represents a possible outcome of one event.

> **Point to note**
>
> In a tree diagram:
> - **multiply** probabilities going **across**
> - **add** probabilities **going down.**
>
> To check that all the probabilities are correct, add them together. The sum of all probabilities = 1.

Examples

John travels to work in his car. He has to go through two sets of traffic lights on his way. At the first set of lights, the probability that they will be green is $\frac{6}{10}$. At the second set the probability that they will be green is $\frac{2}{5}$.

(a) What is that probability that both sets will be green?

(b) What is the probability that John will have to stop once and only once at a set of lights?

Solutions

Draw a tree diagram to show the probability of each outcome.

First set → Second set

- $\frac{6}{10}$ Green
  - $\frac{2}{5}$ Green: $P(\text{both green}) = \frac{6}{10} \times \frac{2}{5} = \frac{12}{50}$
  - $\frac{3}{5}$ Not green: $P(\text{green, not green}) = \frac{6}{10} \times \frac{3}{5} = \frac{18}{50}$
- $\frac{4}{10}$ Not green
  - $\frac{2}{5}$ Green: $P(\text{not green, green}) = \frac{4}{10} \times \frac{2}{5} = \frac{8}{50}$
  - $\frac{3}{5}$ Not green: $P(\text{both not green}) = \frac{4}{10} \times \frac{3}{5} = \frac{12}{50}$

Sum of all probabilities = 1

(a) $P(\text{both green}) = \frac{12}{50} = \frac{6}{25}$

(b) $P(\text{only stopping once}) = P(\text{green, not green}) + P(\text{not green, green})$
$$= \frac{18}{50} + \frac{8}{50} = \frac{26}{50} = \frac{13}{25}$$

Examples

Blood tests are sometimes used to indicate if a person has a particular disease. Sometimes such tests give an incorrect result, either indicating the person has the disease when they do not (called a false positive) or indicating that they do not have the disease when they do (called a false negative). It is estimated that 0·3% of a large population have a particular disease. A test developed to detect the disease gives a false positive in 4% of tests and a false negative in 1% of tests. A person picked at random is tested for the disease.

(a) Write the probability associated with each branch of the tree diagram in the blank boxes provided.

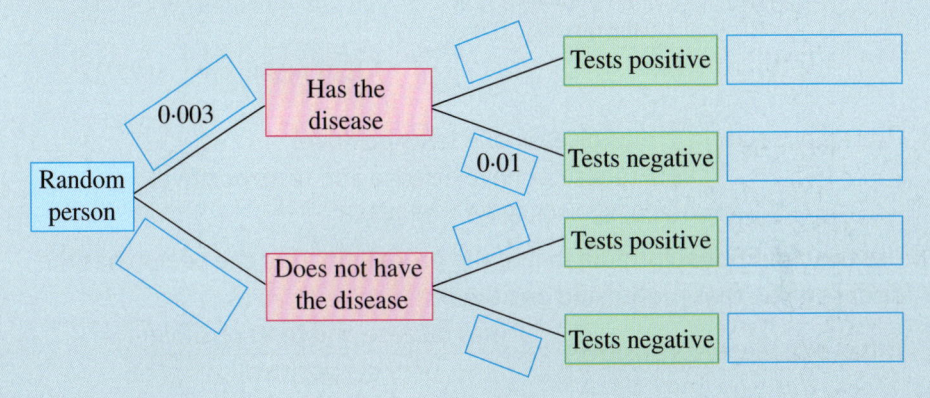

```
                              ┌── Tests positive ──[  ]
              ┌── Has the ────┤
      0·003   │   disease     │
              │               └── Tests negative ──[  ]
Random ───────┤                   0·01
person        │               ┌── Tests positive ──[  ]
              └── Does not ───┤
         [  ]    have the     │
                 disease      └── Tests negative ──[  ]
                         [  ]
```

(b) Hence, or otherwise, calculate the probability that a person selected at random from the population tests positive for the disease.

(c) A person tests positive for the disease. What is the probability that the person actually has the disease? Give your answer correct to three significant figures.

(d) The health authority is considering using a test on the general population with a view to treatment of the disease. Based on your results, do you think that the above test would be an effective way to do this? Give a reason for your answer.

(SEC 2014)

Solutions

(a) Each pair of branches must add to 1, so the probability of the random person not having the disease is 1 − 0·003 = 0·997.

If the person has the disease, the probability that they will test positive is 1 − the probability of a false negative = 1 − 0·01 = 0·99.

If the person does not have the disease, the probability that they will test negative is 1 – the probability of a false positive = 1 – 0·04 = 0·96.

Multiply along the branches to fill in the boxes on the right-hand side.

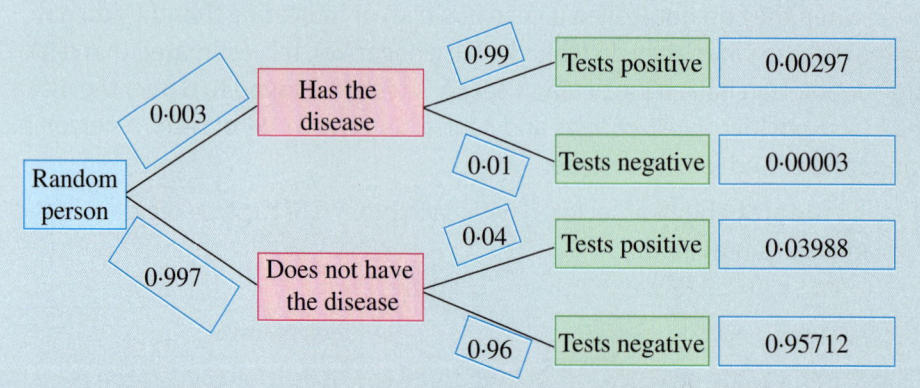

```
                         0·99  Tests positive    0·00297
              Has the
      0·003   disease
                         0·01  Tests negative    0·00003
Random
person
                         0·04  Tests positive    0·03988
      0·997  Does not have
             the disease
                         0·96  Tests negative    0·95712
```

(b) $P(\text{tests positive}) = P(\text{has disease and tests positive})$
$\qquad\qquad\qquad\qquad\; + P(\text{does not have disease and tests positive})$
$\qquad\qquad\qquad = 0\cdot00297 + 0\cdot03988 = 0\cdot04285$

(c) Use the conditional formula to find the probability that the person has the disease given that they tested positive.

$$P(\text{has disease} \,|\, \text{tests positive}) = \frac{P(\text{has disease and tests positive})}{P(\text{tests positive})}$$

$$= \frac{0\cdot00297}{0\cdot04285} = 0\cdot0693$$

(d) The test is not very useful. A person who tests positive has the disease only 7% of the time.

Probabilities involving the counting method (combinations)

We can use combinations to solve more difficult probability questions which involve ordering of outcomes, e.g. selecting three kings from a deck of cards can be done in 3! ways before we calculate any probability.

We know that order doesn't matter with combinations, so we can use the counting method without worrying about the order of the outcomes.

> **Point to note**
> Combinations only work for situations where objects are not replaced.

Examples

Three cards are drawn at random from a pack of 52 cards without replacement. Find the probability that:

(a) the three cards are three kings
(b) two cards are black and the other card is a diamond
(c) the three cards are of the same suit.

Solutions

(a) The number of ways of selecting three cards from a set of 52 is $\binom{52}{3} = 22\,100$.

The number of ways of selecting three kings from a set of four kings is $\binom{4}{3} = 4$.

So there are 22 100 ways of selecting three cards, and four of those ways will result in three kings. Therefore the probability of selecting three kings is $\frac{4}{22\,100} = \frac{1}{5525}$.

(b) The number of ways of selecting two black cards from a set of 26 is $\binom{26}{2}$.

The number of ways of selecting one diamond from a set of 13 is $\binom{13}{1}$.

Multiply these to find the probability of two black cards *and* a diamond.

$$P(\text{two black cards and one diamond}) = \frac{\binom{26}{2} \times \binom{13}{1}}{\binom{52}{3}} = \frac{325 \times 13}{22\,100} = \frac{4225}{22\,100} = \frac{13}{68}$$

(c) $P(\text{three cards of the same suit})$

$= P(\text{three clubs or three spades or three hearts or three diamonds})$

$$= \frac{\binom{13}{3} + \binom{13}{3} + \binom{13}{3} + \binom{13}{3}}{\binom{52}{3}} = \frac{4\binom{13}{3}}{\binom{52}{3}} = \frac{4 \times 286}{22\,100} = \frac{1144}{22\,100} = \frac{22}{425}$$

Checklist

✓ Learn the key words for probability and the summary of probability rules.

✓ Know the difference between permutations and combinations. Read the question carefully and look out for the key words 'arrange' and 'choose'.

✓ Practise probability questions involving sample spaces, tree diagrams and Venn diagrams.

9 Statistics 2

Learning objectives

In this chapter you will learn how to:

- Select and use appropriate methods to describe the distribution of data in terms of mean, median and mode, and the advantages and disadvantages of each
- Recognise the relative positions of mean, mode and median in symmetric and skewed data
- Select and use appropriate methods to describe the data in terms of spread (range, interquartile range and standard deviation)
- Use a calculator to calculate standard deviation
- Analyse and compare data sets to explain differences in measures of centre and spread
- Use percentiles to assign relative standing
- Compare data sets using appropriate displays including back-to-back stem-and-leaf plots
- Interpret a histogram in terms of distribution of data
- Determine the relationship between variables using scatter plots
- Recognise that correlation is a value from -1 to $+1$ and that it measures the extent of the linear relationship between two variables
- Match correlation coefficient values to appropriate scatter plots
- Draw the line of best fit by eye
- Make predictions based on the line of best fit
- Calculate the correlation coefficient by calculator
- Recognise the effect of outliers
- Understand that correlation does not imply causality.

Measures of location (central tendency)

When analysing data it is often useful to know the average value in order to compare it with other data. We have three measures of central tendency: **mean**, **mode** and **median** (the three Ms).

The mean is the most commonly used measure of location. When people say 'the average' of a list of numbers they are often referring to the mean.

The formula to calculate the mean is on page 33 of the *Formulae and Tables* booklet.

For a list of numbers, mean = $\mu = \frac{\sum x}{n}$, where $\sum x$ is the sum of the values in the data set and n is the number of values in the data set.

> **Point to note**
> The mean is denoted by μ or $\bar{x}$. Later on we will see that $\bar{x}$ is used for the sample mean and μ is used for the population mean.

For a frequency table, mean = $\mu = \frac{\sum fx}{\sum f}$, where $\sum fx$ is the sum of each value multiplied by its respective frequency and $\sum f$ is the sum of the frequencies.

Example

Find the mean of the following list of data: 2, 3, 6, 2, 5, 9, 3, 8, 7, 2.

Solution

$\sum x = 2 + 3 + 6 + 2 + 5 + 9 + 3 + 8 + 7 + 2 = 47$

$n = 10$ (there are 10 numbers in the list)

$\mu = \frac{47}{10} = 4 \cdot 7$

> **Point to note**
> Note the effect on the mean of adding or subtracting a common constant to each number in the data set.
>
> In the example above, if 3 was added to each number the mean would be 4·7 + 3 = 7·7.
>
> If 4 was subtracted from each number the mean would be 4·7 − 4 = 0·4.
>
> If you multiply each number in the data set by a common constant then the mean is also multiplied by that constant.

In the example above, if each number was multiplied by 2 then the mean would be 2 × 4·7 = 9·4.

If an extra item, with a value of zero, is added to the data set then the value of the mean is decreased.

In the example above the mean would be $\frac{47}{11} = 4\cdot27$.

Example

The number of goals scored by 20 soccer teams in their most recent matches is shown in the table.

Calculate the mean number of goals scored by these soccer teams in their most recent matches.

Number of goals (x)	0	1	2	3	4
Number of matches (f)	5	7	4	2	2
Total goals scored (fx)	0	7	8	6	8

Solution

Mean = $\dfrac{\sum fx}{\sum f} = \dfrac{0+7+8+6+8}{5+7+4+2+2} = \dfrac{29}{20} = 1\cdot45$

The **mode** is the most frequently occurring data value (the most common value).

Sometimes a data set has more than one mode. If there are two modes then the data set is **bimodal**. If there are more than two modes then the data set is **multimodal**.

Sometimes a data set has no mode.

For a frequency distribution we talk about the **modal class**, which is the interval with the highest frequency.

Examples

Find the modes of the following data sets.
(a) 2, 3, 5, 6, 8, 5
(b) 4, 3, 4, 6, 9, 0, 6
(c) 1, 4, 5, 8, 9, 0.
Use a line plot to check your answer.

Solutions

(a) 5 appears twice, and the other numbers appear only once. The mode is 5.

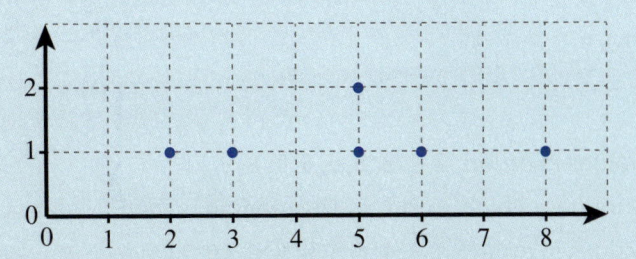

(b) 4 and 6 both appear twice, and the other numbers appear only once. The data set is bimodal, and the modes are 4 and 6.

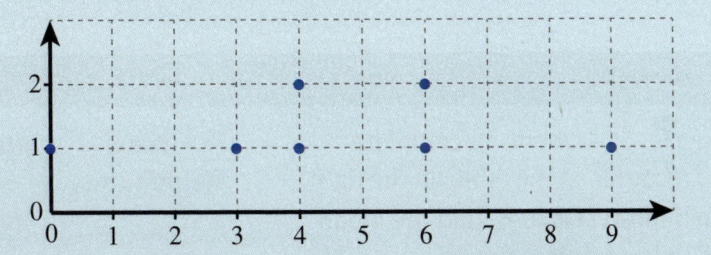

(c) Each value appears only once. The data set has no mode.

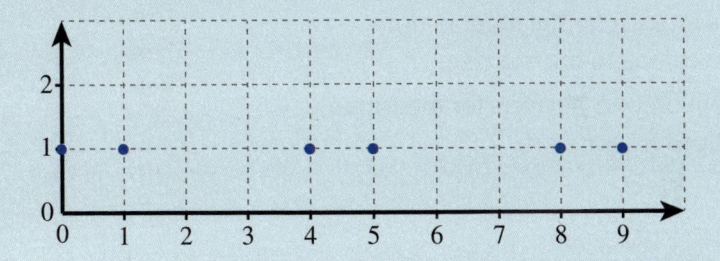

The **median** is the middle value when the data set is placed in order.

If the number of values is even then the median is the mean of the two middle values.

If the number of values is odd then the median is the middle value.

Examples

Find the median of:
(a) 2, 3, 6, 2, 6, 9, 3, 8, 7
(b) 4, 3, 11, 4, 10, 9, 3, 8, 7, 8.

Solutions

(a) Place the values in order: 2, 2, 3, 3, 6, 6, 7, 8, 9
There are 9 values, which is odd, so the median is the 5th value = 6.

(b) Place the values in order: 3, 3, 4, 4, 7, 8, 8, 9, 10, 11
There are 10 values, which is even, so the median is the mean of the 5th and 6th values = $\frac{7 + 8}{2}$ = 7·5.

Examples

The time taken for 60 students to complete an exercise is recorded in the table on the right.

(a) Using mid-interval values, find the mean time taken to complete the exercise.
(b) State the modal class.
(c) Find the interval for the median time taken to complete the exercise.
(d) Comment on your answers for measures of location for each part.

Time (t minutes)	Number of students (frequency)
3–4	7
4–5	14
5–6	24
6–7	10
7–8	5

Solutions

(a)

Time (t minutes)	Frequency (f)	Mid-interval value (x)	fx
3–4	7	3·5	24·5
4–5	14	4·5	63
5–6	24	5·5	132
6–7	10	6·5	65
7–8	5	7·5	37·5

Mean = $\frac{\Sigma fx}{\Sigma f}$ = $\frac{24·5 + 63 + 132 + 65 + 37·5}{60}$

= 5·37 minutes (to 2 decimal places)

(b) Modal class is 5–6 minutes (5 ≤ t < 6).
(c) Total frequency = 60 (even) so the median is the mean of the 30th and 31st values, which is in the interval 5 ≤ t < 6.
(d) The answers are all in the same interval.

Uses, advantages and disadvantages of mode, mean and median

Average	Use	Advantages	Disadvantages
Mean	Numerical data	Easy to find All data used Useful for comparing sets of data	Affected by extreme values (outliers) Not always in data set
Mode	Numerical data or nominal categorical data	Easy to find (can be obtained from graph) Not affected by extreme values Mode exists in data set	Not always a mode (small samples) Several modes might exist (bimodal or multimodal)
Median	Numerical data or ordinal categorical data	Easier to calculate than mean (can be obtained from graph) Not affected by extreme values Useful for comparing sets of data	Not always in data set Need to arrange data in order

Measures of variability

Range and interquartile range

The **range** of a data set is the highest (maximum) value minus the lowest (minimum) value.

It is easy to find, and useful when comparing two sets of data, but it can be a poor measure of spread if the data set contains outliers.

Remember: An outlier is an extreme value that is not typical of the set.

The **interquartile range** (**IQR**) is a better measure of the spread of a dataset.

To find the interquartile range, the data is arranged in ascending order and divided into quarters (**quartiles**).

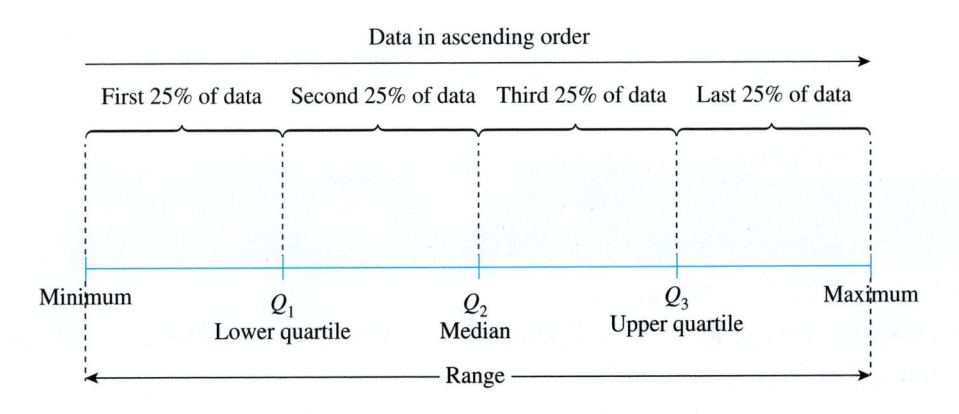

Data in ascending order

First 25% of data | Second 25% of data | Third 25% of data | Last 25% of data

Minimum — Q_1 Lower quartile — Q_2 Median — Q_3 Upper quartile — Maximum

Range

9. Statistics 2   161

- The lower quartile = Q_1 is the point that cuts off the first 25% of the data.
- The middle quartile (the median) = Q_2 is the point that cuts off the second 25% of the data.
- The upper quartile = Q_3 is the point that cuts off the third 25% of the data.

Interquartile range = upper quartile − lower quartile = $Q_3 - Q_1$

How to find quartiles from a list of numbers

This is one method for finding quartiles. It assumes that the data is arranged in ascending order.

This method can also be used for finding percentiles.

Lower quartile	Q_1	$k = \dfrac{n}{4}$
Middle quartile	Q_2	$k = \dfrac{n}{2}$
Upper quartile	Q_3	$k = \dfrac{3n}{4}$

n is the number of items in the list. k is the position of a quartile.

If k is an integer, the quartile is the mean of the kth and the $(k+1)^{th}$ numbers in the list.

If k is not an integer, round up to the next integer; the quartile is the number with that position in the list.

Example

Find the interquartile range for the following list of numbers:

11, 13, 17, 25, 33, 34, 42, 43, 50, 52.

Solution

First check if the list is in ascending order. In this example, it is.

$n = 10$

Lower quartile: $k = \dfrac{n}{4} = \dfrac{10}{4} = 2.5$. This is not an integer, so round up to the 3rd number in the list = 17.

Point to note

If $k = \dfrac{n}{4}$ was equal to 2.25 we still round up to the 3rd number in the list.

Upper quartile: $k = \dfrac{3n}{4} = \dfrac{3(10)}{4} = 7.5$. This is not an integer, so round up to the 8th number in the list = 43.

Interquartile range = 43 − 17 = 26

Example

The cholesterol level of 20 adults is recorded in a laboratory. The results are as follows.

3·2, 4·3, 5·5, 5·7, 8·9, 5·7, 4·7, 5·3, 4·3, 3·7

3·5, 4·6, 5·0, 6·0, 4·7, 5·9, 5·7, 4·9, 5·9, 7·9

(a) Find the range of the data.
(b) Find the lower and upper quartiles.
(c) Hence, find the interquartile range of the data.
(d) To test for outliers the score must be within a certain range.

$x < Q_1 - (1·5 \times IQR)$, $x > Q_3 + (1·5 \times IQR)$

Check if any of the cholesterol levels are outliers, and comment on which measure of variability gives the best measure of spread of the data.

Solutions

Arrange the data in ascending order:

3·2, 3·5, 3·7, 4·3, 4·3, 4·6, 4·7, 4·7, 4·9, 5·0

5·3, 5·5, 5·7, 5·7, 5·7, 5·9, 5·9, 6·0, 7·9, 8·9

(a) Range = 8·9 − 3·2 = 5·7

(b) Lower quartile: $k = \dfrac{n}{4} = \dfrac{20}{4} = 5$. This is an integer, so find the mean of the 5th and 6th values from the data set = $\dfrac{4·3 + 4·6}{2}$ = 4·45.

Upper quartile: $k = \dfrac{3n}{4} = \dfrac{3}{4}(20) = 15$. This is an integer, so find the mean of the 15th and 16th values from the data set = $\dfrac{5·7 + 5·9}{2}$ = 5·8.

(c) $IQR = Q_3 - Q_1$ = 5·8 − 4·45 = 1·35

(d) $Q_1 - (1·5 \times IQR)$ = 4·45 − (1·5 × 1·35) = 4·45 − 2·025 = 2·425

$Q_3 + (1·5 \times IQR)$ = 5·8 + (1·5 × 1·35) = 5·8 + 2·025 = 7·825

There are no scores under 2·425 but there are two scores above 7·825. The outliers are 7·9 and 8·9.

The best measure of variability is IQR = 1·35, because the range = 5·7 (which is quite large compared to the IQR) is affected by the outliers.

Standard deviation

The **standard deviation** shows the scale of variation there is from the average. It gives the average difference of the data points from the mean. A low standard deviation means that the data points tend to be very near to the mean. A high standard deviation means that the data points are more spread out from the mean.

The standard deviation of a set of data is the measure of dispersal about the mean.

Consider the two sets $A = \{4, 6, 10, 12, 18\}$, $B = \{2, 4, 6, 18, 20\}$.

The mean of each set is 10.

If we plot each set we can see clearly that the data points are closer to the mean in set A compared to set B.

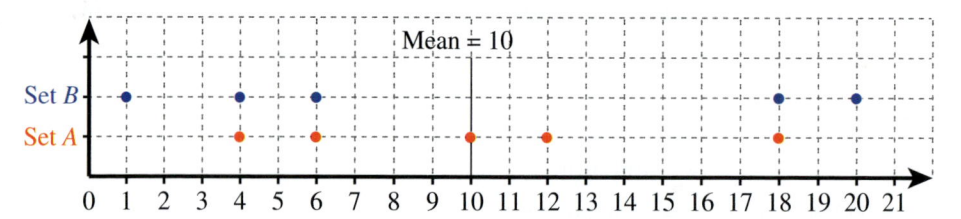

In set B the data points are more spread out from the mean. The standard deviation for set B will be higher than the standard deviation for set A.

We can find the standard deviation for a list of numbers by using a formula or we can use a calculator.

The formula for the standard deviation for a list of numbers is on page 33 of the *Formulae and Tables booklet*.

Standard deviation $= \sigma = \sqrt{\dfrac{\Sigma(x - \mu)^2}{n}}$

where μ = the mean

$x - \mu$ = the difference or deviation of each value from the mean (can be positive or negative)

n = the number of values.

Example

Find the standard deviation for set A and set B correct to 1 decimal place.

$A = \{4, 6, 10, 12, 18\}$, $B = \{2, 4, 6, 18, 20\}$

Solution

The mean of each set = μ = 10.

We will use the formula for set A and a calculator for set B.

Set A:

x	$x - \mu$	$(x - \mu)^2$
4	4 − 10 = −6	36
6	6 − 10 = −4	16
10	10 − 10 = 0	0
12	12 − 10 = 2	4
18	18 − 10 = 8	64

$$\sigma = \sqrt{\frac{\Sigma(x-\mu)^2}{n}} = \sqrt{\frac{36 + 16 + 0 + 4 + 64}{5}} = \sqrt{\frac{120}{5}} = 4\cdot 9, \text{ correct to 1 decimal place}$$

Set B:

Using a calculator, $\sigma = 7\cdot 5$ for set B.

Top Tip

Look at the 'Learn to use calculators' section of the Project Maths website to see how to calculate the standard deviation and other statistical measures.

We can see now that set B has a higher standard deviation than set A.

The formula for the standard deviation for a frequency distribution is on page 33 of the *Formulae and Tables* booklet.

$$\text{Standard deviation} = \sigma = \sqrt{\frac{\Sigma f(x-\mu)^2}{\Sigma f}}$$

where f = frequency, $x - \mu$ = the difference or deviation of each value from the mean (can be positive or negative).

Point to note

If the frequency distribution is a grouped frequency distribution, find the mid-interval values first and then use the formula or a calculator.

Point to note

If you are using the formula to find the standard deviation, include a column in your table for the frequency and a column for the frequency × deviation².

x	f	$x - \mu$	$(x - \mu)^2$	$f(x - \mu)^2$

9. Statistics 2

Examples

A die was thrown 100 times. The scores are summarised in the following table.

Find:

(a) the mean of the scores

(b) the standard deviation of the scores.

Give your answers correct to 1 decimal place.

Score	1	2	3	4	5	6
Frequency	19	12	13	20	17	19

Solutions

(a)

x	f	fx
1	19	19
2	12	24
3	13	39
4	20	80
5	17	85
6	19	114
Total	100	361

Mean = $\dfrac{\Sigma fx}{\Sigma f} = \dfrac{361}{100} = 3.61 = 3.6$ to 1 decimal place

(b)

x	f	$x - \mu$	$(x-\mu)^2$	$f(x-\mu)^2$
1	19	1 − 3·61 = −2·61	6·8121	129·4299
2	12	2 − 3·61 = −1·61	2·5921	31·1052
3	13	3 − 3·61 = −0·61	0·3721	4·8373
4	20	4 − 3·61 = 0·39	0·1521	3·042
5	17	5 − 3·61 = 1·39	1·9321	32·8457
6	19	6 − 3·61 = 2·39	5·7121	108·5299
Total	100	−0·66	17·5726	309·79

Standard deviation = $\sigma = \sqrt{\dfrac{\Sigma f(x-\mu)^2}{\Sigma f}} = \sqrt{\dfrac{309\cdot79}{100}}$

= 1·760085 = 1·8 to 1 decimal place.

Example

Complete the table, with justification for your answers.

Data	Mean	Standard deviation
A: 1, 4, 5, 6, 10	5·2	2·9
B: 11, 14, 15, 16, 20		
C: 100, 400, 500, 600, 1000		
D: 0, 3, 4, 5, 9		

Solution

Data	Mean	Standard deviation
A: 1, 4, 5, 6, 10	5·2	2·9
B: 11, 14, 15, 16, 20	5·2 + 10 = 15·2	2·9 (unchanged)
C: 100, 400, 500, 600, 1000	5·2 × 100 = 520	2·9 × 100 = 290
D: 0, 3, 4, 5, 9	5·2 − 1 = 4·2	2·9 (unchanged)

In set B each element of set A has been increased by 10, so the mean is also increased by 10.

In set C each element of set A has been multiplied by 100, so both the mean and standard deviation are multiplied by 100.

In set D each element of set A has been decreased by 1, so the mean is also decreased by 1.

Percentiles

Percentiles are comparison scores. The data is divided into 100 equal parts, and the nth percentile is the cut-off point for the nth part of the data.

Percentiles are not the same as percentages. They are used for IQ scores, exam results, etc. to compare scores in a data set. If a student is in the 80th percentile on an IQ test then this means that 80% of the other students had a score lower than this student, and 20% had a score equal to or higher than this student.

We find percentiles in the same way as we find quartiles. The lower quartile is the same as the 25th percentile and the upper quartile is the same as the 75th percentile.

Examples

12 students scored the following in a class test:
35, 45, 67, 78, 54, 80, 56, 67, 66, 77, 89, 54

(a) Find P_{70} (the 70th percentile).
(b) John scored 80 in the test. In what percentile does his mark lie?
(c) Calculate the median.

Solutions

(a) $P_{70} = \dfrac{70}{100} \times 12 = 8 \cdot 4$

This not an integer, so round up to the next whole number, which is 9.
Put the data set in ascending order and find the 9th value.
35, 45, 54, 54, 56, 66, 67, 67, 77, 78, 80, 89
The 9th value is 77, so $P_{70} = 77$.

9. Statistics 2   167

(b) If John scored 80 then 10 students scored less than him.

Percentile $= \dfrac{10}{12} \times 100 = 83\cdot\dot{3}$

His score lies in the 83rd percentile.

(c) As there are 12 values, the median is the mean of the 6th and 7th values.

Median $= \dfrac{66 + 67}{2} = 66\cdot 5$

Statistical diagrams

Stem-and-leaf plots

In a **stem-and-leaf plot**, each data value is split into a stem and a leaf. The stem shows the leftmost digit (or digits) and the leaf shows the last digit.

The stem-and-leaf plot for the following data is shown below:

28, 38, 42, 5, 13, 23, 14, 38, 56, 20, 32, 47, 58, 3, 18, 18, 19, 42, 48, 29, 14, 24, 28, 50, 31, 35.

Tens	Stem	Leaf
0–9	0	3 5
10–19	1	3 4 4 8 9
20–29	2	0 3 4 8 8 9
30–39	3	1 2 5 8 8
40–49	4	2 2 7 8
50–59	5	0 6 8

Units

Key: 2 | 3 = 23

Examples

The back-to-back stem-and-leaf diagram shows the daily sales of two competing newsagents.

```
       Newsagent 1      Newsagent 2
                   5 | 3 4 9
                 8 6 | 1 2
         8 6 5 2 1 1 7 | 0 7
         9 7 5 4 4 4 2 8 | 6 6 7
                   9 | 0 5
                  10 | 8
                  11 | 8
```

Key: 8 | 6 = €68 of sales for Newsagent 1
5 | 3 = €53 of sales for Newsagent 2

(a) Calculate the mean and median sales for each newsagent.

Use your answers to compare the measures of location of the two data sets and the average daily sales for both newsagents.

(b) Calculate the standard deviation for each newsagent's sales.

Use your answers to compare the dispersion of the two data sets.

(c) Comment on the shape and spread of distribution for both data sets.

Solutions

(a) Mean for Newsagent 1 = €79 (using a calculator)

Median for Newsagent 1 = average of 7th and 8th values = $\frac{78 + 82}{2}$ = €80

Mean for Newsagent 2 = €79 (using a calculator)

Median for Newsagent 2 = average of 7th and 8th values = $\frac{77 + 86}{2}$ = €81·50

The mean sales are the same for both data sets and the medians are very close, so overall the average daily sales in both newsagents are very similar.

(b) Standard deviation for Newsagent 1 = €6·59 (using a calculator)

Standard deviation for Newsagent 2 = €19·46 (using a calculator)

The standard deviation is a lot higher for Newsagent 2, so the sales are more varied compared to Newsagent 1.

The sales are more consistent in Newsagent 1 since the standard deviation is smaller.

(c) Both sets have very similar measures of location.

The shape of the distribution peaks in the middle for Newsagent 1 since the data points are more tightly packed about the mean.

The shape of the distribution is more spread out for Newsagent 2 since the data points are more dispersed about the mean.

Histograms

A **histogram** is used to display a frequency distribution. Histograms look like bar charts, but have no gaps between the bars.

Histograms can be used to display discrete or continuous data. Data is grouped into intervals. For the purposes of the Leaving Certificate exam, the class intervals will always have equal width.

When the class intervals have equal width, the height of the bars can be used to represent the frequency.

If the class intervals do not have equal width, the height of each bar represents the frequency density, and the area of each bar represents the frequency.

Examples

The histogram below shows the maximum daily temperature as recorded over a period of time by a student.

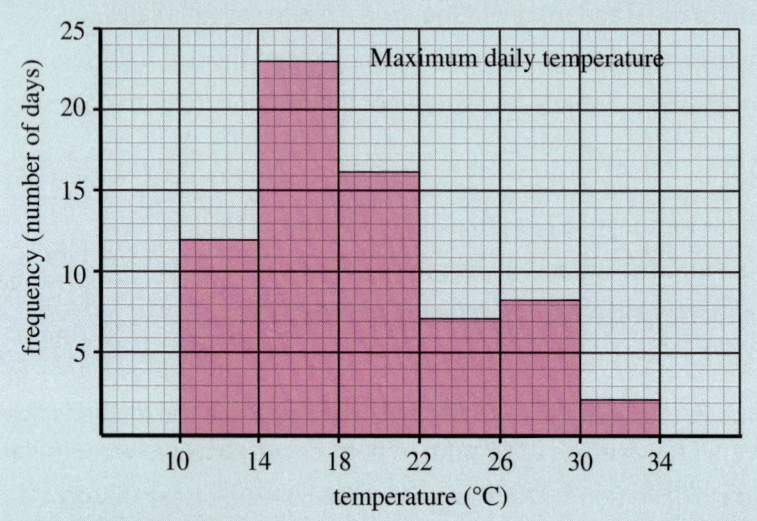

Maximum daily temperature

(a) Write down the modal class.
(b) In which interval does the median lie?
(c) Using mid-interval values, calculate the mean temperature μ over the period of time. Comment on the shape of the distribution using your answers for median and mean.
(d) Calculate the standard deviation σ of the temperature over the period of time.
(e) Hence find the number of days that were within one standard deviation of the mean. Show this on the histogram.
(f) Calculate the percentage of days that were within one standard deviation of the mean.

Solutions

(a) The modal class is the one with the largest area.

In this case the intervals are all the same width, so the modal class is the tallest, which is 14–18 °C.

(b) Check the total number of days recorded by adding the heights of the bars.

Total frequency = 12 + 23 + 16 + 7 + 8 + 2 = 68 days

The median is therefore the mean of the 34th and 35th data values when the data is put in ascending order.

The histogram is already in ascending order, so sum the frequencies starting from the left until you find the class containing the 34th and 35th data values.

> **Point to note**
> The sum of the frequencies of all class intervals up to a given interval is called the **cumulative frequency**.

10–14 °C: cumulative frequency = 12 days

14–18 °C: cumulative frequency = 12 + 23 = 35 days

Both the 34th and the 35th values lie in the interval 14–18 °C, so the median lies in the interval 14–18 °C.

(c) The mid-interval values are 12, 16, 20, 24, 28 and 32 °C.

$$\text{Mean} = \mu = \frac{(12 \times 12) + (23 \times 16) + (16 \times 20) + (7 \times 24) + (8 \times 28) + (2 \times 32)}{68}$$

= 18·94 °C

The mean value is greater than the median and modal class. The shape of the distribution has a tail to the right, as can be seen from histogram. We can say that the graph is positively skewed.

(d)

x	f	$x - \mu$	$(x - \mu)^2$	$f(x - \mu)^2$
12	12	12 – 18·94 = –6·94	48·18	578·16
16	23	16 – 18·94 = –2·94	8·65	198·96
20	16	20 – 18·94 = 1·06	1·12	17·94
24	7	24 – 18·94 = 5·06	25·59	179·14
28	8	28 – 18·94 = 9·06	82·06	656·50
32	2	32 – 18·94 = 13·06	170·53	341·07
Total	68		18·35	336·14	1971·76

$$\text{Standard deviation} = \sigma = \sqrt{\frac{\Sigma f(x - \mu)^2}{\Sigma f}} = \sqrt{\frac{1971 \cdot 76}{68}} = 5 \cdot 38 \text{ °C}$$

(e) $\mu - \sigma = 18 \cdot 94 - 5 \cdot 38 = 13 \cdot 56$ °C. This lies in the interval 10–14 °C.

Estimate the number of days between 13·56 °C and 14 °C by calculating the difference as a proportion of the interval size and multiplying the result by the frequency.

Number of days = $\left(\dfrac{14 - 13 \cdot 56}{4}\right)(12) = 1 \cdot 32$ days

$\mu + \sigma = 18 \cdot 94 + 5 \cdot 38 = 24 \cdot 32$ °C. This lies in the interval 22–26 °C.

Estimate the number of days between 22 °C and 24·32 °C by calculating the difference as a proportion of the interval size and multiplying the result by the frequency.

Number of days = $\left(\dfrac{24 \cdot 32 - 22}{4}\right)(7) = 4 \cdot 06$ days

The shaded region shows the days within one standard deviation of the mean.

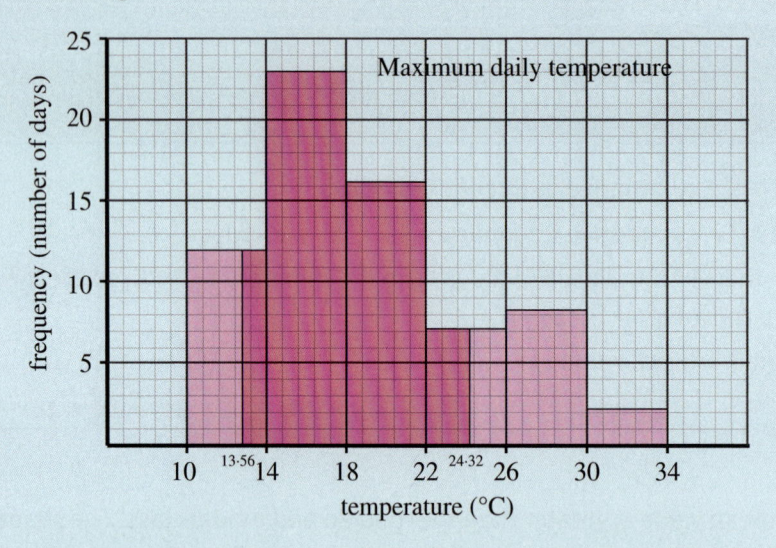

Maximum daily temperature

(f) Percentage of days:

$$\frac{1\cdot32 + 23 + 16 + 4\cdot06}{68} \times 100 = \frac{44\cdot38}{68} \times 100$$

$$= 65\cdot3\% \text{ correct to 1 decimal place}$$

Examples

The table below gives details of the number of males (M) and females (F) aged 15 years and over at work, unemployed, or not in the labour force for each year in the period 2004 to 2013.

Labour Force Statistics 2004 to 2013 – Persons aged 15 years and over (000s)

Year	At work M	F	Total	Unemployed M	F	Total	Not in labour force M	F	Total	Total
2004	1045·9	738·9	1784·8	79·6	31·6	111·2	457·1	854·2	1311·3	3207·3
2005	1087·3	779·7	1867·0	81·3	33·5	114·8	459·5	846·6	1306·1	3287·9
2006	1139·8	815·1	1954·9	80·6	38·1	118·7	457·6	844·9	1302·5	3376·1
2007	1184·0	865·6	2049·6	84·3	39·2	123·5	472·4	852·7	1325·1	3498·2
2008	1170·9	889·5	2060·4	106·3	41·0	147·3	494·8	872·5	1367·3	3575·0
2009	1039·8	863·5	1903·3	234·0	82·4	316·4	505·6	874·9	1380·5	3600·2
2010	985·1	843·5	1828·6	257·6	98·2	355·8	529·2	884·6	1413·8	3598·2
2011	970·2	843·2	1813·4	260·7	103·4	364·1	540·1	881·5	1421·6	3599·1
2012	949·6	823·8	1773·4	265·2	108·0	373·2	546·5	896·9	1443·4	3590·0
2013	974·4	829·0	1803·4	227·7	102·3	330·0	557·8	895·0	1452·8	3586·2

(Source: Central Statistics Office http://www.cso.ie)

(a) Suggest two categories of people, aged 15 years and over, who might not be in the labour force.

(b) Find the median and the interquartile range of the total persons at work over the period.

(c) The following data was obtained from the table. The percentages of persons aged 15 years and over at work, unemployed, or not in the labour force for the year 2006 are given below.

	Year	At work	Unemployed	Not in the labour force
Persons aged 15 years and over	2006	57·9%	3·5%	38·6%
	2011			

(i) Complete the table for the year 2011. Give your answers correct to 1 decimal place.

(ii) A census in 2006 showed that there were 864 449 persons in the population aged under 15 years of age. The corresponding number in the 2011 census was 979 590. Assuming that none of these persons are in the labour force, complete the table below to give the percentages of the total population at work, unemployed, or not in the labour force for the year 2011.

	Year	At work	Unemployed	Not in the labour force
Total population	2006	46·1%	2·8%	51·1%
	2011			

(iii) A commentator states that 'The changes reflected in the data from 2006 to 2011 make it more difficult to balance the Government's income and expenditure.' Do you agree with this statement? Give two reasons for your answer based on your calculations above.

(d) Liam and Niamh are analysing the number of males and the number of females at work over the period 2004 to 2013.

Liam draws the following chart, using data from the table.

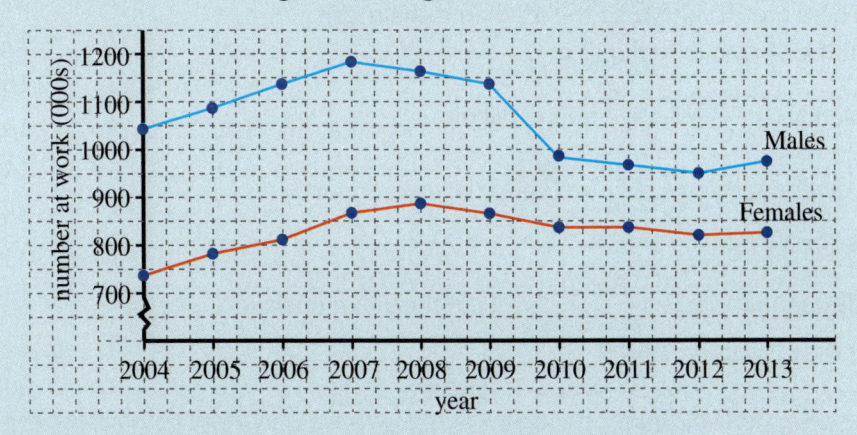

9. Statistics 2   173

Niamh uses the same data and calculates the number of females at work as a percentage of the total number of persons at work and then draws the following chart.

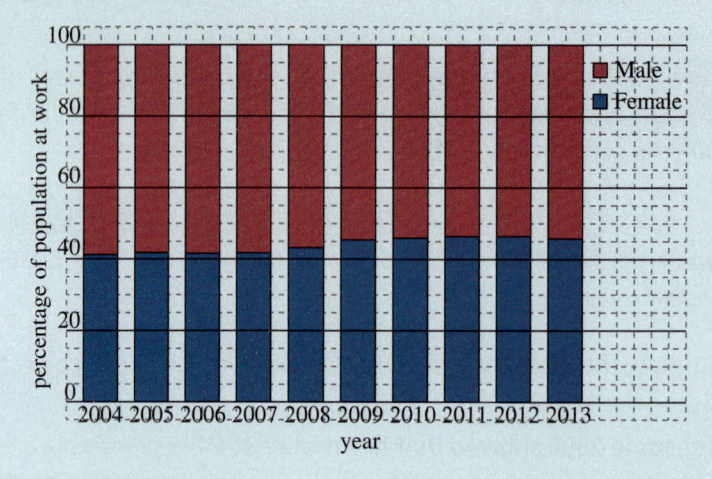

(i) Having examined both charts, a commentator states 'Females were affected as much as males by the downturn in employment.' Do you agree or disagree with this statement? Give a reason for your conclusion.

(ii) Which, if any, of the two charts did you find most useful in reaching your conclusion above? Give a reason for your answer.

(iii) Use the data in the table, for the years 2012 and 2013 only, to predict the percentage of persons, aged 15 years and over, who will be at work in 2014.

(SEC 2014)

Solutions

(a) Choose from students, retired, stay-at-home parents, disabled. You might think of other categories.

(b) To find the median and quartiles, put the data from the 'At work – Total' column in ascending order.

There are 10 values, so the median is the mean of the 5th and 6th values.

$$\text{Median} = \frac{1828 \cdot 6 + 1867 \cdot 0}{2} = 1847 \cdot 8$$

Lower quartile: $k = \frac{10}{4} = 2 \cdot 5$, so the lower quartile is the 3rd value = 1803·4.

Upper quartile: $k = \frac{3 \times 10}{4} = 7 \cdot 5$, so the upper quartile is the 8th value = 1954·9.

Interquartile range = 1954·9 − 1803·4 = 151·5

Position	Value
1	1784·8
2	1773·4
3	1803·4
4	1813·4
5	1828·6
6	1867·0
7	1903·3
8	1954·9
9	2049·6
10	2060·4

(c) (i) Percentage at work = $\dfrac{\text{number at work}}{\text{total}} \times 100 = \dfrac{1813\cdot 4}{3599\cdot 1} \times 100 = 50\cdot 4\%$

The percentages unemployed and not in the labour force can be calculated similarly.

	Year	At work	Unemployed	Not in the labour force
Persons aged 15	2006	57·9%	3·5%	38·6%
years and over	2011	50·4%	10·1%	39·5%

(ii) Total population in 2011 (in thousands) = 3599·1 + 979·59 = 4578·69.

Percentage at work = $\dfrac{1813\cdot 4}{4578\cdot 69} \times 100 = 39\cdot 6\%$

Percentage unemployed = $\dfrac{364\cdot 1}{4578\cdot 69} \times 100 = 8\cdot 0\%$

Percentage not in the labour force = $\dfrac{1421\cdot 6 + 979\cdot 59}{4578\cdot 69} \times 100 = 52\cdot 4\%$

	Year	At work	Unemployed	Not in the labour force
Total	2006	46·1%	2·8%	51·1%
population	2011	39·6%	8·0%	52·4%

(iii) Yes. Percentage in work is down, so reduced taxes collected, so Government income reduced.

Percentage not in work is up, so increased Government expenditure on support, pensions, etc.

(d) (i) I disagree.

Male employment declined from 2007, female from 2008.

There was a greater decline in the number of males employed.

(ii) Liam's graph shows the trend over time as well as the numbers.

Niamh's graph only shows the percentage in the workforce and gives no information about actual numbers.

(iii) In 2012 the percentage of persons in work was $\dfrac{1773\cdot 4}{3590\cdot 0} \times 100 = 49\cdot 4\%$.

In 2013 the percentage of persons in work was $\dfrac{1803\cdot 4}{3586\cdot 2} \times 100 = 50\cdot 3\%$.

This is an increase of 0·9% so a sensible prediction for 2014 is 50·3 + 0·9 = 51·2% of persons in work.

Shape of distributions

We have seen in previous examples how the shape of a distribution varies depending on the measures of location and variability. The most common shapes that we deal with are:

- symmetrical distribution
- negatively skewed distribution
- positively skewed distribution.

A symmetrical distribution has an axis of symmetry in the middle of the distribution, so there is no skew. Mean = median = mode. A normal distribution has this shape.

Examples: weights of students in a year group, IQ of a population.

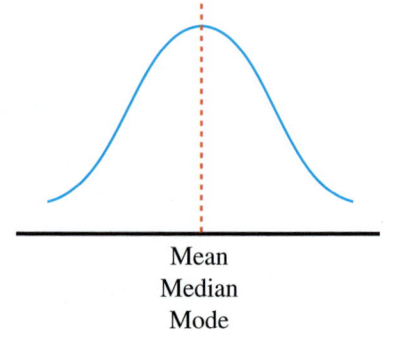

Mean
Median
Mode

A negatively skewed distribution has a 'tail' on the left (skewed to the left). Most data values are relatively high but there are some extreme low values. Mean < median < mode.

Examples: weights of competitors in weight-lifting competition, ages at which people retire.

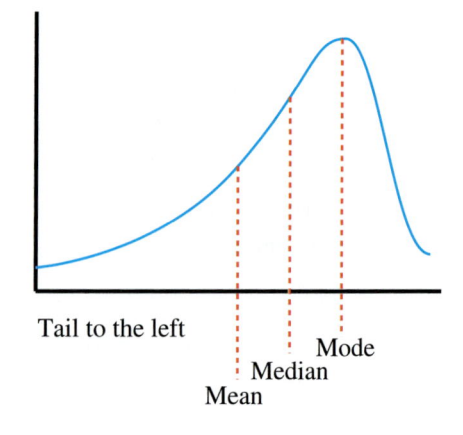

Tail to the left
Mode
Median
Mean

A positively skewed distribution has a 'tail' on the right (skewed to the right). Most data values are relatively low but there are some extreme high values. Mode < median < mean.

Examples: income distribution, number of children in a family.

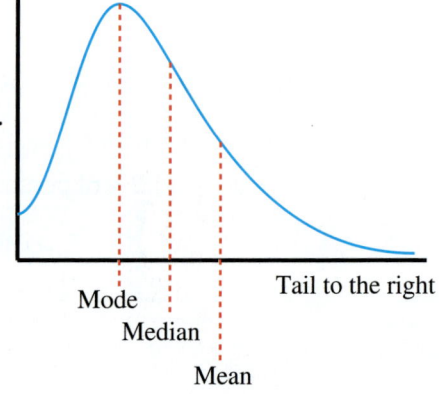

Mode
Median
Mean
Tail to the right

Example

This histogram shows a data set with equal class intervals. The mode, mean and median have the same value (6) and the standard deviation σ is small (2·02). This distribution is symmetric.

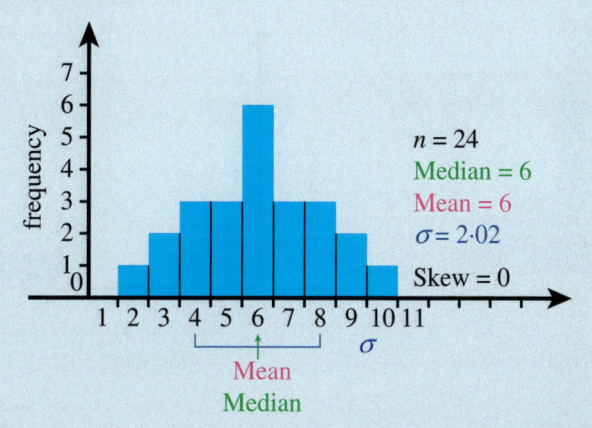

$n = 24$
Median = 6
Mean = 6
σ = 2·02
Skew = 0

In this data set the modes (9 and 10) are bigger than the median (8), which is bigger than the mean (7·54). We can see that there is a tail to the left, so the distribution is negatively skewed; most data values are relatively high.

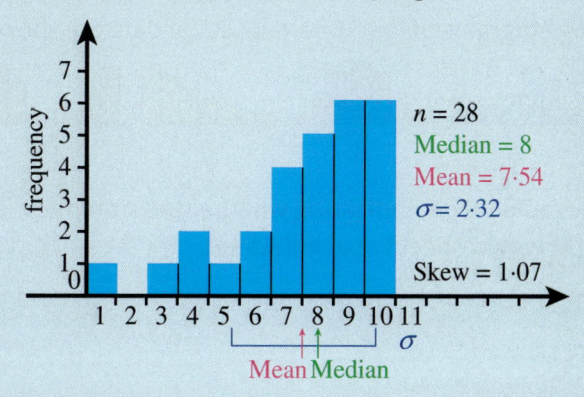

$n = 28$
Median = 8
Mean = 7·54
σ = 2·32
Skew = 1·07

In this data set the mean (3·42) is bigger than the median (3), which is bigger than the mode (2). We can see that there is a tail to the right so the distribution is positively skewed; most data values are relatively low.

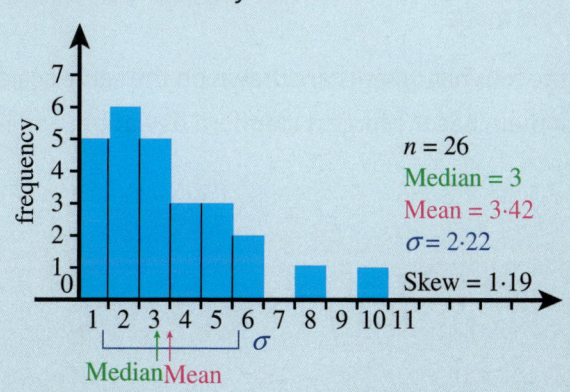

$n = 26$
Median = 3
Mean = 3·42
σ = 2·22
Skew = 1·19

9. Statistics 2

These two data sets have similar means and medians, but look very different. In the diagram on the left, most of the data is close to the mean, so the standard deviation is low. In the diagram on the right, the data is more widely dispersed away from the mean, so the standard deviation is much higher.

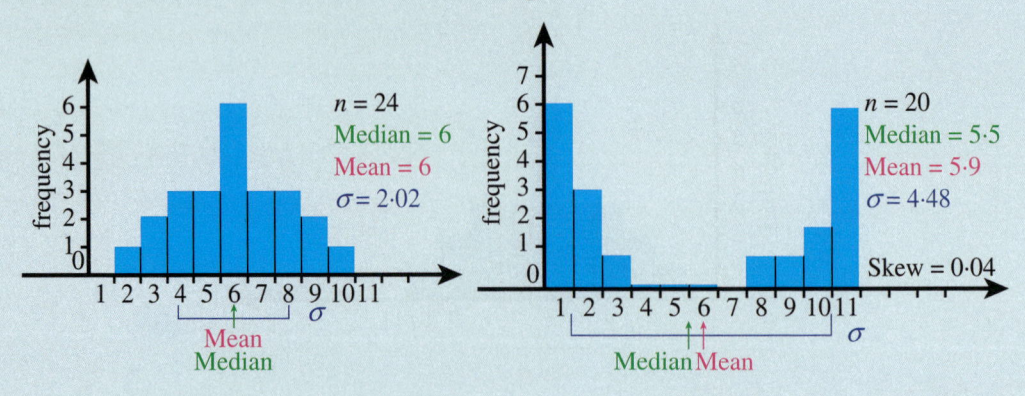

$n = 24$
Median = 6
Mean = 6
$\sigma = 2 \cdot 02$

$n = 20$
Median = 5·5
Mean = 5·9
$\sigma = 4 \cdot 48$
Skew = 0·04

Examples

The shapes of the histograms of four different sets of data are shown below.

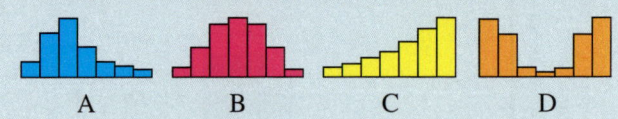

A   B   C   D

(a) Complete the table below, indicating whether the statement is correct (✓) or incorrect (✗) with respect to each data set.

	A	B	C	D
The data are skewed to the left				
The data are skewed to the right				
The mean is equal to the median				
The mean is greater than the median				
There is a single mode				

(b) Assume that the four histograms are drawn on the same scale.
State which of them has the largest standard deviation, and justify your answer.
(SEC Sample 2012)

Solutions

(a)

	A	B	C	D
The data are skewed to the left	✗	✗	✓	✗
The data are skewed to the right	✓	✗	✗	✗
The mean is equal to the median	✗	✓	✗	✓
The mean is greater than the median	✓	✗	✗	✗
There is a single mode	✓	✓	✓	✗

(b) Set D has the largest standard deviation. The data is more widely dispersed about the mean.

Bivariate data

Scatter plots (graphs)

A **scatter plot** (graph) is used to show whether there is a relationship between two sets of data (bivariate data), e.g. height and weight of students in a class.

We show these data points on a co-ordinate plane, without joining the points, and look for a pattern in the shape, spread and direction of the data points.

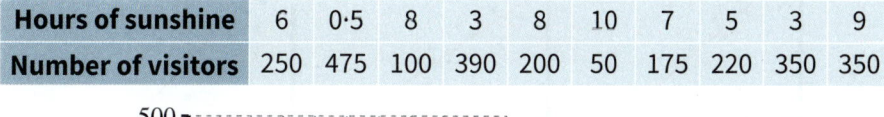

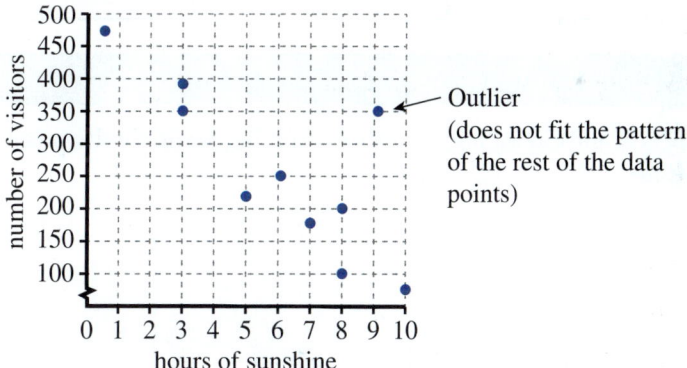

Hours of sunshine	6	0·5	8	3	8	10	7	5	3	9
Number of visitors	250	475	100	390	200	50	175	220	350	350

Outlier (does not fit the pattern of the rest of the data points)

Correlation

Correlation is a measure of the strength of a relationship between two sets of data. It reflects the spread and direction of a linear relationship.

A relationship between two data sets can be described as:
- a positive correlation: as one quantity increases so does the other
- a negative correlation: as one quantity increases the other decreases
- no correlation: there is no pattern in how one data set relates to the other.

9. Statistics 2   179

Positive correlation — sales of sun cream vs temperature

Negative correlation — value of car (€) vs age of car

No correlation — shoe size vs weekly income

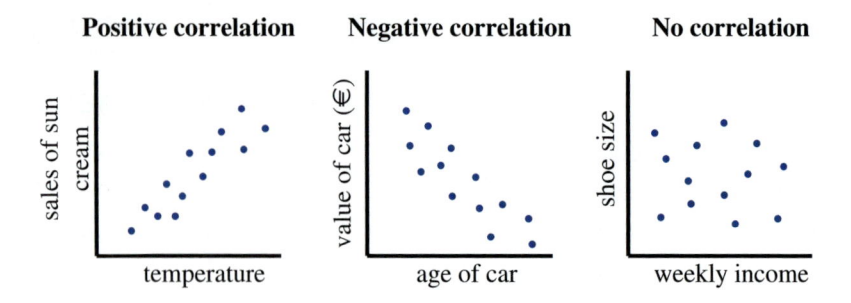

We can also comment on the strength of the correlation: very weak, weak, moderate, strong or very strong.

Strong positive

Moderate positive

Weak positive

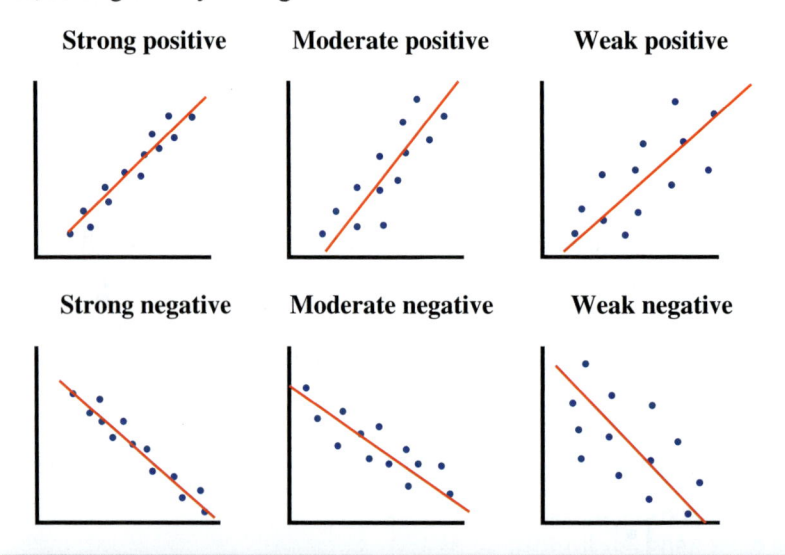

Strong negative

Moderate negative

Weak negative

Examples

State the type of correlation for each scatter graph below and write a sentence describing the relationship in each case.

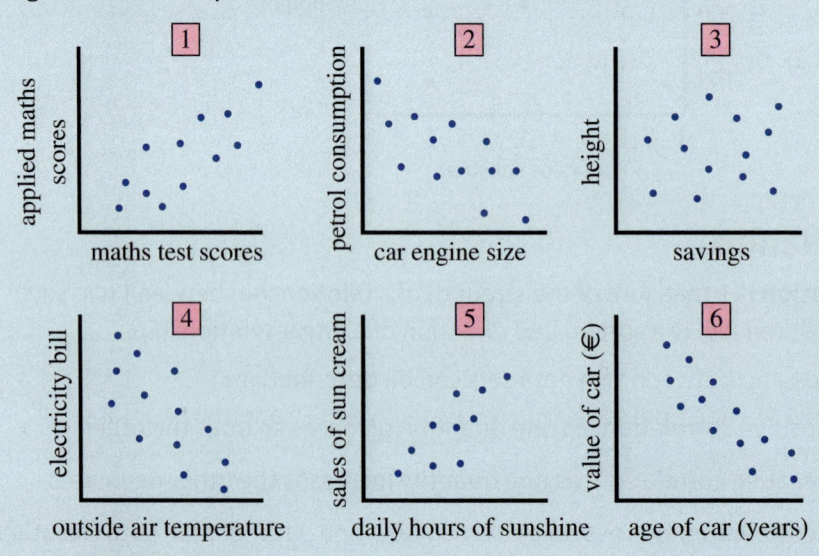

1. applied maths scores vs maths test scores
2. petrol consumption vs car engine size
3. height vs savings
4. electricity bill vs outside air temperature
5. sales of sun cream vs daily hours of sunshine
6. value of car (€) vs age of car (years)

Solutions

1. Positive correlation. Students with higher maths scores tend to get higher applied maths scores.
2. Negative correlation. As the engine size of cars increases they use more petrol.
3. No correlation. The value of a person's savings does not affect his or her height.
4. Negative correlation. As outside temperature increases electricity bills will be lower.
5. Positive correlation. People tend to buy sun cream when the weather is good.
6. Negative correlation. The value of a car tends to decrease as the car gets older.

We use the letter r to denote the **correlation coefficient** of a set of data points. r is a numerical measure of the direction and strength of a linear relationship.

Correlation coefficient r	Direction and strength
+1	Perfect positive linear correlation
0	Little or no correlation
−1	Perfect negative linear correlation
Close to 1	Strong positive linear correlation
Close to −1	Strong negative linear correlation

Point to note

$-1 \leq r \leq 1$

Line of best fit

The **line of best fit** is a line that best represents the data on a scatter plot. It can go through some, all, or none of the points.

The line of best fit has roughly the same number of points on either side of it. If there is a strong correlation the scatter points will lie very close to the line, and if there is a weak correlation the scatter points will lie far from the line.

Method for drawing line of best fit:

1. Draw a scatter plot.
2. Find the mean of the x values, $\bar{x}$.
3. Find mean of the y values, $\bar{y}$.
4. Plot $(\bar{x}, \bar{y})$.
5. Draw lines parallel to the x- and y-axes though $(\bar{x}, \bar{y})$ to divide the scatter plot into four quadrants.
6. Select the two quadrants with the most data points.
7. Draw the line of best fit through the point $(\bar{x}, \bar{y})$ and the two quadrants with the most data points.

> **Point to note**
>
> The line of best fit must contain the point $(\bar{x}, \bar{y})$.
>
> It should go through the two quadrants with most data points.
>
> It should have roughly the same number of points on either side of it.

To find the equation of the line of best fit:

1. Select two points on the line of best fit (you can use $(\bar{x}, \bar{y})$ as one of your points).
2. Find the slope of your line of best fit (m).
3. Use $y - y_1 = m(x - x_1)$ to find the equation of the line of best fit.

> **Point to note**
>
> The slope of the line of best fit is *not* equal to the correlation coefficient.
>
> The sign of the slope of the line of best fit will be the same as that of the correlation coefficient.

Examples

Over a period of three years, a company has been recording the number of units of output per quarter and the total cost of producing the units. The table below shows the data recorded.

(a) Draw a scatter plot to illustrate the data.

(b) Calculate the correlation coefficient and comment on the correlation for the scatter plot.

(c) Find the mean number of units of output and the mean total cost of producing the units.

(d) Draw the line of best fit.

(e) Find the equation of the line of best fit in the form $y = a + bx$. Explain what b represents in the context of the scatter plot.

(f) The selling price of each unit is €1·60. Use your graph to estimate the level of output at which the total income and the total costs are equal. Give a brief interpretation of this value.

Units of output (000s)	Total cost (€000s)
14	35
29	50
55	70
75	98
11	20
20	40
35	65
69	86
18	38
36	54
60	81
80	90

Solutions

(a)

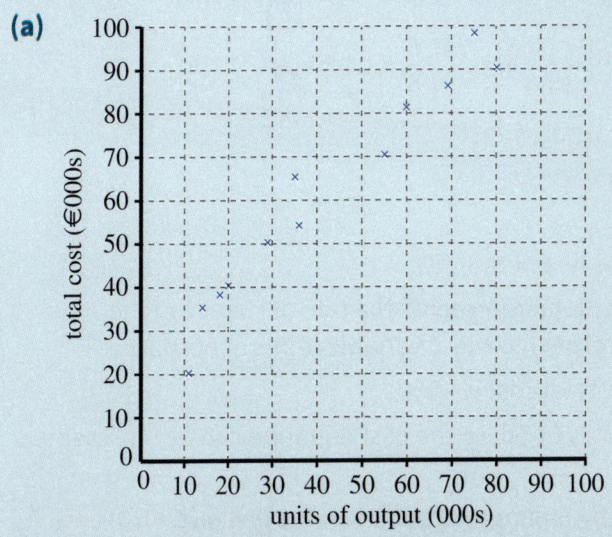

[Scatter plot: total cost (€000s) vs units of output (000s)]

(b) Correlation coefficient $r = 0.9742$

> **Top Tip**
> Practise using your calculator for statistical calculations.
> Look at the 'Learn to use calculators' section of the Project Maths website to see how to calculate the correlation coefficient and other statistical measures.

This is a very strong positive correlation. As the units of output increases so does the total cost.

(c) Mean number of outputs (from calculator) = 41·8 thousand.

Mean total cost (from calculator) = €60·6 thousand.

(d)

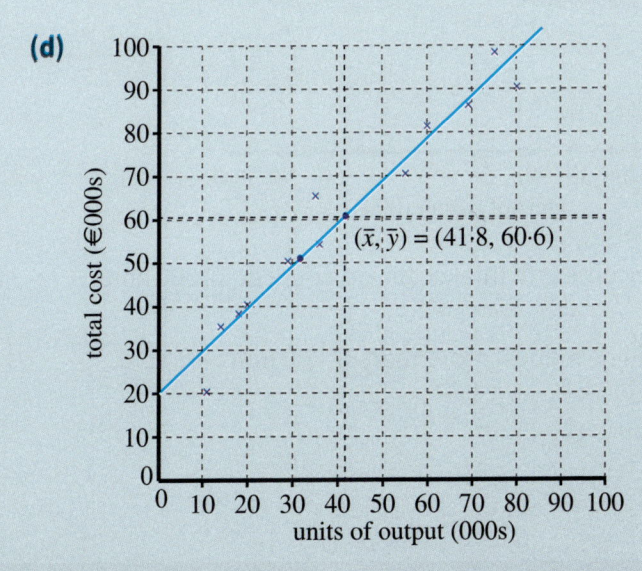

[Scatter plot with line of best fit; $(\bar{x}, \bar{y}) = (41·8, 60·6)$]

9. Statistics 2 — 183

(e) Use $(\bar{x}, \bar{y}) = (41·8, 60·6)$ as one point and $(0, 19·8)$ as another point.

Slope of line $= \dfrac{y_2 - y_1}{x_2 - x_1} = \dfrac{19·8 - 60·6}{0 - 41·8} = \dfrac{-40·8}{-41·8} = 0·98 = m$

Equation of line of best fit: $y - y_1 = m(x - x_1)$

$y - 19·8 = 0·98(x - 0)$

$\quad y = 19·8 + 0·98x$

b represents the slope of the line of best fit.

In the context of the scatter plot it represents the rate of change of the y variable (total cost) with respect to the x variable (units of output).

For 1000 units of output the total cost is €980.

(f) The selling price of each unit is €1·60, so the cost equation can be represented by $y = 1·6x$.

Draw this line on the graph by finding two points on the line (e.g. $(0, 0)$ and $(10, 16)$) and joining them. The point where this line crosses the line of best fit is the point where the total income and total costs are equal.

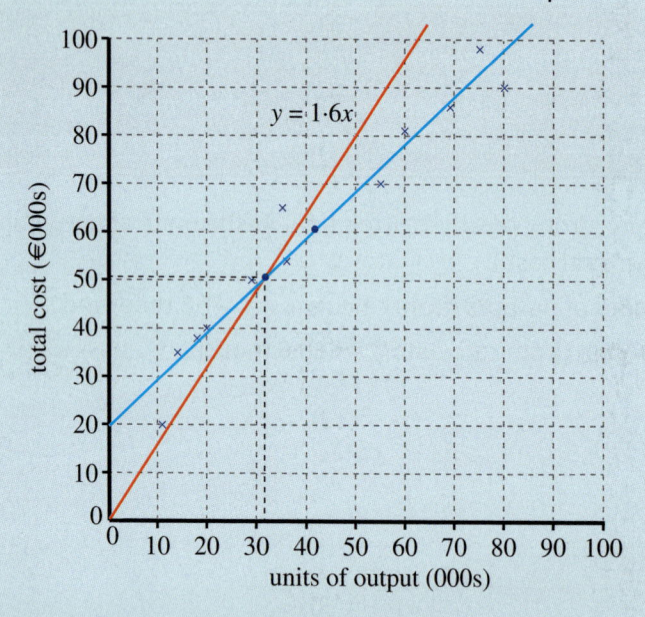

From the graph, the total income and total costs are equal at 32 000 units approximately.

This means that a profit will be made if more than 32 000 units are sold.

Examples

A person's *maximum heart rate* is the highest rate at which their heart beats during certain extreme kinds of exercise. It is measured in beats per minute (bpm). It can be measured under controlled conditions. As part of a study in 2001, researchers measured the maximum heart rate of 514 adults and compared it to each person's age. The results were like those shown in the scatter plot on the right.

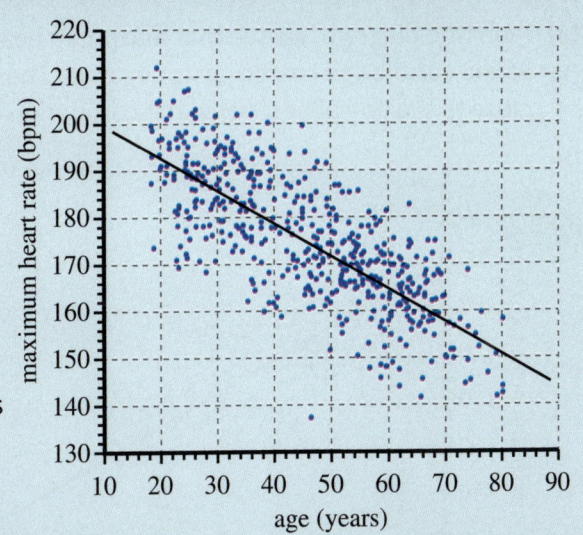

(Source: Simulated data based on: Tanaka H, Monaghan KD, and Seals DR. Age-predicted maximal heart rate revisited, J. Am. Coll. Cardiol. 2001;37:153–156.)

(a) From the diagram, estimate the correlation coefficient.

(b) Find the *outlier* on the diagram and write down the person's age and maximum heart rate.

(c) The line of best fit is shown on the diagram. Use the line of best fit to estimate the maximum heart rate of a 44-year-old person.

(d) By taking suitable readings from the diagram, calculate the slope of the line of best fit.

(e) Find the equation of the line of best fit and write it in the form:
MHR = a − b × (age), where MHR is the maximum heart rate.

(f) The researchers compared their new rule for estimating maximum heart rate to an older rule. The older rule is: MHR = 220 − age. The two rules can give different estimates of a person's maximum heart rate. Describe how the level of agreement between the two rules varies according to the age of the person. Illustrate your answer with two examples.

(g) A particular exercise programme is based on the idea that a person will get most benefit by exercising at 75% of their estimated *MHR*. A 65-year-old man has been following this programme, using the old rule for estimating *MHR*. If he learns about the researchers' new rule for estimating *MHR*, how should he change what he is doing?

(SEC 2010)

Solutions

(a) From the diagram, we see that maximum heart rate decreases as age increases, so the correlation coefficient is negative. The data is reasonably, but not very, close to the line of best fit, so the correlation coefficient is about −0·75.

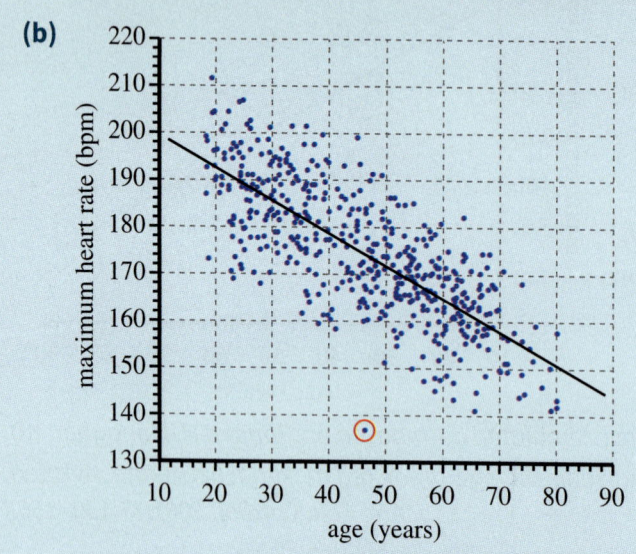

(b)

At the outlier, age = 47 years and maximum heart rate = 137 bpm.

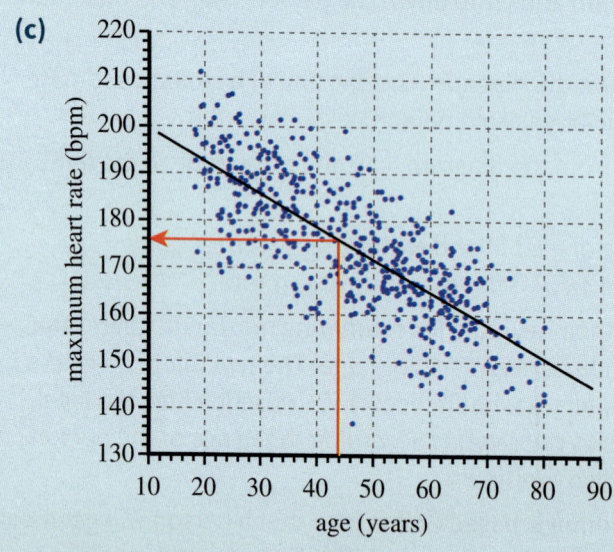

(c)

Maximum heart rate of a 44-year-old = 176 bpm.

(d) Use the readings (10, 200) and (90, 144), for example.

$$m = \frac{y_2 - y_1}{x_2 - x_1} = \frac{144 - 200}{90 - 10} = \frac{-56}{80} = \frac{-7}{10} \Rightarrow m = -0 \cdot 7$$

186 Revise Wise • Mathematics

(e) $y - y_1 = m(x - x_1) \Rightarrow y - 200 = -0.7(x - 10)$

$y = -0.7x + 207$

$MHR = 207 - 0.7 \times$ (age)

(f) For young adults the old rule gives a greater MHR than the new rule.

For example, for an adult aged 20:
- old rule gives $MHR = 220 - 20 = 200$ bpm
- new rule gives $MHR = 207 - 0.7(20) = 193$ bpm.

Towards middle age there is a greater agreement between the rules.

For older people the old rule gives a lower MHR than the new rule.

For example, for an adult aged 70:
- old rule gives $MHR = 220 - 70 = 150$ bpm
- new rule gives $MHR = 207 - 0.7(70) = 158$ bpm.

(g) He should exercise a bit more intensely.

Using the old rule he exercises to 75% of $(220 - 165) = 116$ bpm.

Using the new rule he can exercise to 75% of $(207 - (0.7)(165)) = 121$ bpm.

Examples

An economics student is interested in finding out whether the length of time people spend in education affects the income they earn. The student carries out a small study. Twelve adults are asked to state their annual income and the number of years they spent in full-time education. The data are given in the table below, and a scatter plot is given.

Years education	Annual income (€000s)
11	28
12	30
13	35
13	43
14	55
15	38
16	45
16	38
17	55
17	60
17	30
19	58

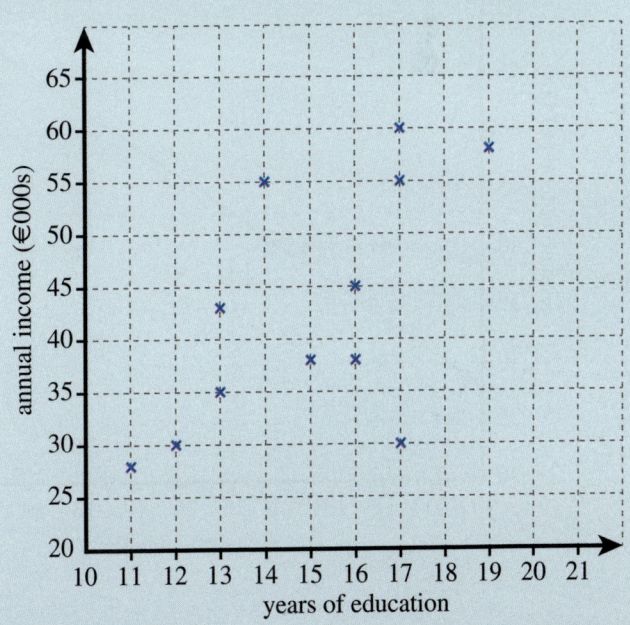

(a) Calculate the correlation coefficient.
(b) What can you conclude from the scatter plot and the correlation coefficient?
(c) Add the line of best fit to the completed scatter plot.
(d) Use the line of best fit to estimate the annual income of somebody who has spent 14 years in education.
(e) By taking suitable readings from your diagram, or otherwise, calculate the slope of the line of best fit.
(f) Explain how to interpret this slope in this context.
(g) The student collected the data using a telephone survey. Numbers were randomly chosen from the Dublin area telephone directory. The calls were made in the evenings, between 7 and 9 pm. If there was no answer, or if the person who answered did not agree to participate, then another number was chosen at random.

List three possible problems regarding the sample and how it was collected that might make the results of the investigation unreliable. In each case, state clearly why the issue you mention could cause a problem.

Solutions

(a) Correlation coefficient = 0·6232.
(b) There is a moderate positive correlation between years in education and salary.
(c) Calculate the mean: $(\bar{x}, \bar{y}) = (15, 42\cdot9)$.

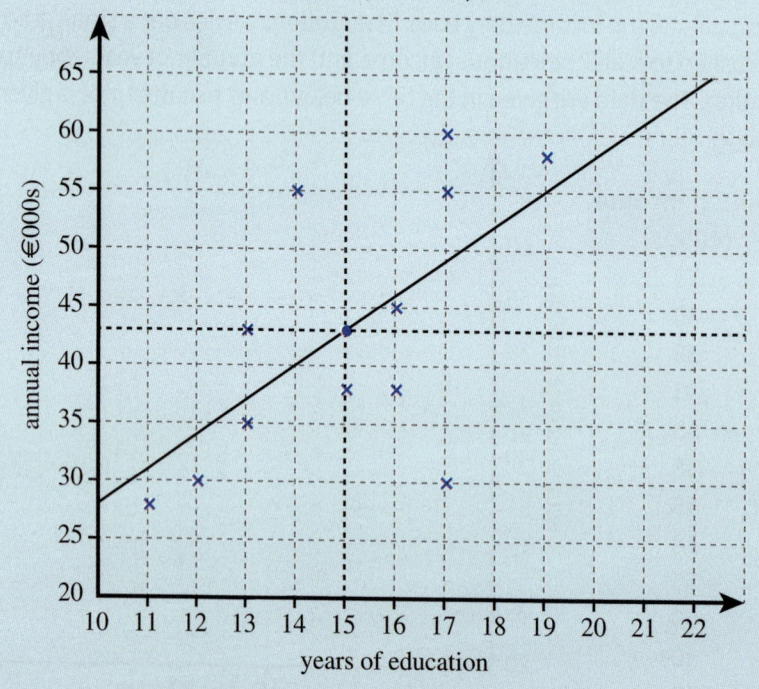

(d)

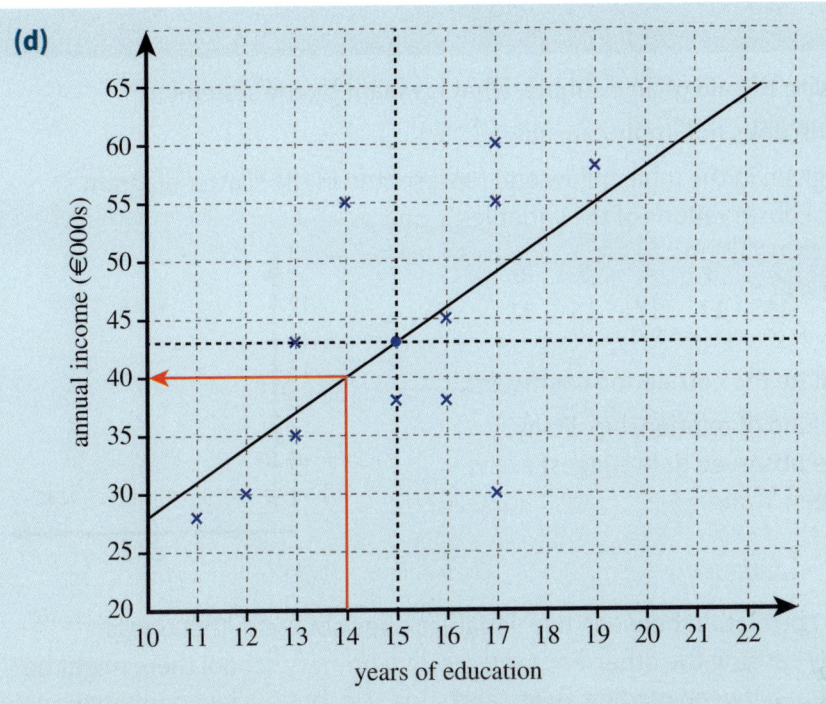

From the graph, annual income of somebody who has spent 14 years in education is about €40 000.

(e) Use the readings (15, 42·9) and (16, 46), for example.

$$m = \frac{y_2 - y_1}{x_2 - x_1} = \frac{46 - 42\cdot 9}{16 - 15} = 3\cdot 1 \approx 3$$

(f) Salary increases by approximately €3000 for every extra year spent in education.

(g) 1 The sample is only in the Dublin area. This might lead to bias as salary information might be different in different areas.

  2 The sample only includes people who are at home between 7 and 9 pm. This would exclude people who work at that time, which might lead to a low response rate or to biased data.

  3 The survey depends on people being listed in the telephone directory, which might lead to bias.

Correlation vs causation

Strong correlation between two variables does not mean that one causes the other. A consistently strong correlation may suggest causation, but it does not prove it.

A shop selling electrical goods might see a very strong correlation between sales of iPods and sales of iPads over a certain period. This doesn't mean that buying an iPad will cause a customer to buy an iPod. It is more likely that both sales trends are triggered by the same thing, e.g. a marketing campaign.

9. Statistics 2

Examples

(a) Explain, with the aid of an example, what is meant by the statement:
'Correlation does not imply causality.'

(b) The data given in the table below and represented in the scatter diagram are pairs of observations of the variables x and y.

x	1	2	3	4	5	6
y	11	15	17	17	15	11

(i) Calculate the correlation coefficient.

(ii) What kind of relationship, if any, do the observed data suggest exists between x and y? (SEC 2011)

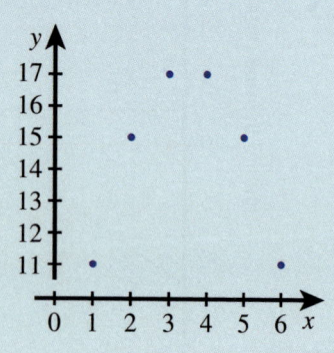

Solutions

(a) A positive correlation between two variables does not mean that one is necessarily causing the other. For example, in a primary school there might be a correlation between reading ability and shoe size, but big feet don't make you read better and reading doesn't make your feet grow! In this case, both variables are connected to age, which is a 'confounding factor'.

(b) (i) Correlation coefficient = 0.

(ii) There is no linear relationship, but the pattern suggests a quadratic relationship.

Checklist

✓ Practise finding the mean and standard deviation of a list of numbers and a frequency distribution on your calculator.

✓ Practise finding the correlation coefficient r on your calculator.

✓ Practise drawing histograms and line plots.

✓ Practise drawing and finding the equation of the line of best fit for scatter plots.

✓ Know how to find the three Ms – mode, mean and median.

✓ Know how to find the quartiles and percentiles of data.

✓ Recognise shapes of distributions – skewed and symmetric.

✓ Know what can affect the mean and standard deviation of a list of numbers.

Further Probability and Statistics

10

Learning objectives

In this chapter you will learn how to:

- Understand the concept of a probability distribution
- Calculate expected value and understand that this does not need to be one of the outcomes
- Recognise the role of expected value in decision making and explore the issue of fair games
- Apply an understanding of Bernoulli trials
- Solve problems involving up to three Bernoulli trials
- Calculate the probability that the first success occurs in the nth Bernoulli trial where n is specified
- Solve problems involving calculating the probability of k successes in n repeated Bernoulli trials (normal approximation not required)
- Calculate the probability that the kth success occurs on the nth Bernoulli trial
- Make decisions based on the empirical rule
- Solve problems involving reading probabilities from the normal distribution tables
- Calculate the margin of error $\left(\frac{1}{\sqrt{n}}\right)$ for a population proportion
- Build on the concept of margin of error and understand that increased confidence level implies wider intervals
- Construct 95% confidence intervals for the population proportion from a large sample using z tables
- Distinguish between sample proportion and sample means
- Construct 95% confidence intervals for the population mean from a large sample using z tables
- Perform univariate large sample tests of the population mean (two tailed z-test only)
- Conduct a hypothesis test on a population proportion using the margin of error
- Use and interpret p-values.

Probability distribution

Consider the sample space for an experiment: tossing a coin three times.
There are eight outcomes: TTT, TTH, THT, THH, HTT, HTH, HHT, HHH.
Let x be the number of heads obtained and $P(x)$ be the probability of getting x heads. Then we can form a **probability distribution table**.

x	0 (no head)	1 (1 head)	2 (2 heads)	3 (3 heads)
$P(x)$	$\frac{1}{8}$	$\frac{3}{8}$	$\frac{3}{8}$	$\frac{1}{8}$

> **Point to note**
> x is a random variable which can be discrete (as in the example) or continuous (heights, IQ, etc.).

> **Point to note**
> $P(x)$ is the probability that x happens, written as a fraction, decimal or percentage.

The following diagram shows a graph of the probability distribution for a coin tossed 6 times where x = number of heads obtained (discrete value) and $P(x)$ = probability of getting x heads as a percentage. We can see from the shape of the distribution that it is symmetric and similar to a normal distribution.

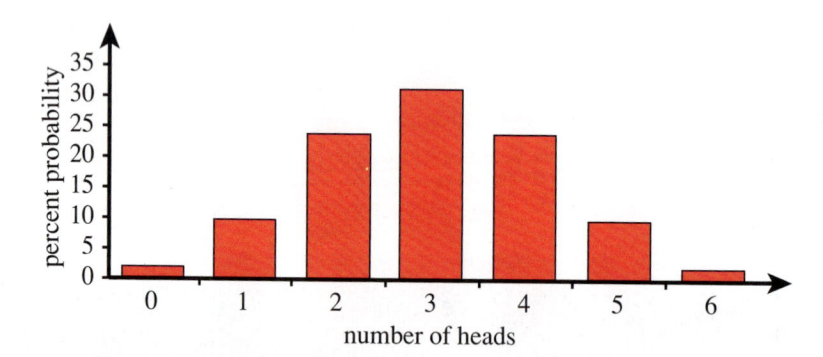

Expected value

Expected value ($E(X)$) can be thought of as the mean of a random variable. It represents the average of all the results obtained if the experiment is repeated over and over. The **expected outcome** is the average outcome you would expect from an experiment.

$$E(X) = \sum xP(x)$$

> **Point to note**
> $\sum xP(x)$ represents the sum of each possible outcome multiplied by the probability of that outcome occurring.

> **Point to note**
> The expected value need not be one of the outcomes.

Example

What is the expected value if a fair die is rolled?

Solution

Build a table of each outcome and its probability.

Outcome (x)	1	2	3	4	5	6
Probability $P(x)$	$\frac{1}{6}$	$\frac{1}{6}$	$\frac{1}{6}$	$\frac{1}{6}$	$\frac{1}{6}$	$\frac{1}{6}$
$xP(x)$	$\frac{1}{6}$	$\frac{1}{3}$	$\frac{1}{2}$	$\frac{2}{3}$	$\frac{5}{6}$	1

$$E(X) = \sum xP(x) = \frac{1}{6} + \frac{1}{3} + \frac{1}{2} + \frac{2}{3} + \frac{5}{6} + 1 = \frac{7}{2} = 3.5$$

The expected outcome is 3·5 (not one of the outcomes).

Fair games

To determine if a game is **fair** we need to know the cost of entry and the expected value of the game.

If expected value = 0 then the game is fair.

If expected value > 0 then the player will win in the long run.

If expected value < 0 then the player will lose in the long run, and the person running the game will win.

Examples

Two different games of chance, shown here, can be played at a charity fundraiser. In each game, the player spins an arrow on a wheel and wins the amount shown on the sector that the arrow stops in. Each game is fair in that the arrow is just as likely to stop in one sector as in any other sector on that wheel.

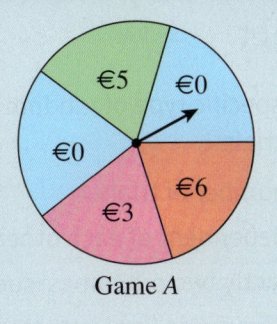

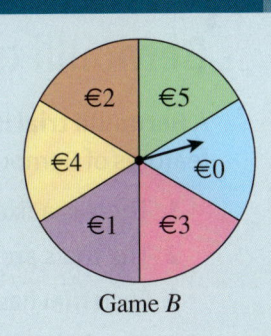

Game A

Game B

10. Further Probability and Statistics

(a) John plays Game A four times and tells us that he has won a total of €8. In how many different ways could he have done this?

(b) To spin either arrow once, the player pays €3. Which game of chance would you expect to be more successful in raising funds for the charity? Give a reason for your answer.

(c) Mary plays Game B six times. Find the probability that the arrow stops in the €4 sector exactly twice. (SEC 2014)

Solutions

(a) List the possible outcomes that give a win of €8.

5, 3, 0, 0	3, 5, 0, 0	0, 5, 3, 0	0, 3, 5, 0
5, 0, 3, 0	3, 0, 5, 0	0, 5, 0, 3	0, 3, 0, 5
5, 0, 0, 3	3, 0, 0, 5	0, 0, 5, 3	0, 0, 3, 5

There are 12 ways in which John could win €8.

(b) Work out the expected outcome $E(X) = \sum xP(x)$ for each game.

Game A: $E(x) = 0\left(\frac{2}{5}\right) + 3\left(\frac{1}{5}\right) + 5\left(\frac{1}{5}\right) + 6\left(\frac{1}{5}\right) = \frac{14}{5} = 2\frac{4}{5}$

Game B: $E(x) = 0\left(\frac{1}{6}\right) + 1\left(\frac{1}{6}\right) + 2\left(\frac{1}{6}\right) + 3\left(\frac{1}{6}\right) + 4\left(\frac{1}{6}\right) + 5\left(\frac{1}{6}\right) = \frac{15}{6} = 2\frac{3}{6} = 2\frac{1}{2}$

Game B would be more successful in raising money, because it pays out less money.

(c)

> **Remember**
> Recall from Chapter 17 of Book 1 that the probability of r successes in n trials is $P(X = r) = \binom{n}{r}p^r q^{n-r}$, where p = probability of success and q = probability of failure.

$n = 6$, $r = 2$, $p = P(€4) = \frac{1}{6}$, $q = P(\text{not } €4) = \left(\frac{5}{6}\right)$

$P(\text{stops in €4 sector exactly twice}) = \binom{6}{2}\left(\frac{1}{6}\right)^2\left(\frac{5}{6}\right)^4 = 0\cdot 2$

Bernoulli trials

A **Bernoulli trial** is a specific type of random experiment. There are four main features of Bernoulli trials.

1. There is a fixed number of trials.
2. The trials are independent of each other.
3. Each trial has exactly two outcomes: success or failure.
4. The probability of success (p) is constant in each trial.

Some examples of experiments involving Bernoulli trials are tossing a coin, hitting a target, and shooting free throws in a basketball game.

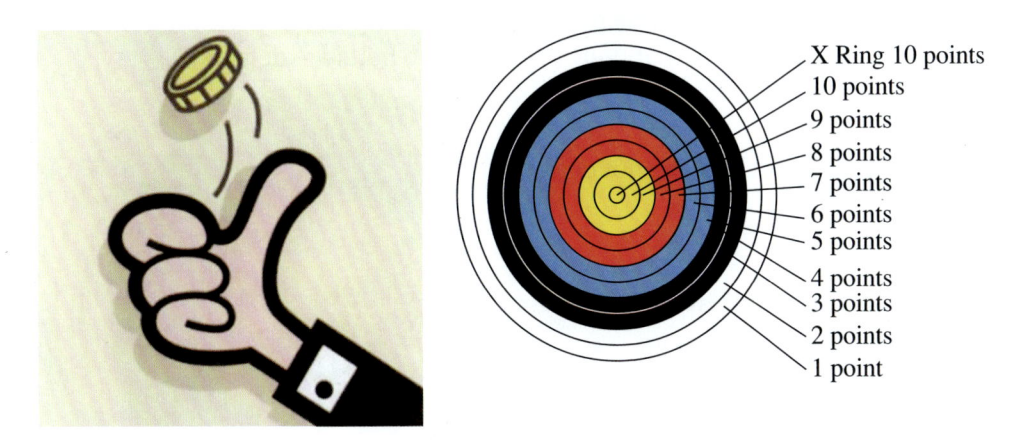

Bernoulli trials are based on a binomial distribution (because there are two outcomes: success and failure). We use the formula on page 33 of the *Formulae and Tables* booklet:

$$P(X = r) = \binom{n}{r} p^r q^{n-r}, \; r = 0, \ldots, n$$

where X is a discrete random variable

n is the total number of trials

p is the probability of success

q is the probability of failure ($q = 1 - p$)

r is the number of successes.

We have seen this already in Chapter 17 of Book 1.

Point to note
The sum of all probabilities = 1.

Example

A coin is tossed five times. What is the probability of getting four heads?

Solution

n = number of trials = 5

p = probability of success = 0·5

q = probability of failure = 0·5

r = number of successes = 4

$$P(X = 4) = \binom{5}{4}(0·5)^4(0·5)^{5-4} = 5(0·5)^4(0·5)^1 = 0·15625$$

Example

10% of the bolts produced by a machine are defective. Five bolts are chosen at random. Find the probability that none of the chosen bolts are defective.

Solution

Let X = number of bolts that are not defective

$r = 5$

$n = 5$

p = probability that a bolt is not defective = 0·9

q = probability that a bolt is defective = 0·1

$P(X = 5) = \binom{5}{5}(0.9)^5(0.1)^0 = (0.9)^5 = 0.59049$

Examples

A certain soccer player takes the free kicks for his team. The probability of him scoring from a free kick is 0·3. During a particular match he gets seven free kicks.

(a) Find the probability that he doesn't score from his seven free kicks.

(b) Find the probability that he scores from exactly three of his seven free kicks.

(c) Find the probability that he scores at most five times.

Solutions

(a) Let X = number of misses

$r = 7$

$n = 7$

p = probability of not scoring = 0·7

q = probability of scoring = 0·3

$P(X = 7) = \binom{7}{7}(0.7)^7(0.3)^0 = (0.7)^7 = 0.0823543$

(b) Let X = number of scores

$r = 3$

$n = 7$

p = probability of scoring = 0·3

q = probability of not scoring = 0·7

$P(X = 3) = \binom{7}{3}(0.3)^3(0.7)^4 = 0.2268945$

(c) Probability that he scores at most 5 means scoring 0 or 1 or 2 or 3 or 4 or 5.

It is easier to calculate scoring 6 or 7 times and subtract from 1, because the sum of all probabilities equals 1.

$P(X \geq 6) = P(X = 6) + P(X = 7)$

$P(X = 6) = \binom{7}{6}(0.3)^6(0.7)^1 = 0.0035721$

$P(X = 7) = \binom{7}{7}(0.3)^7(0.7)^0 = 0.0002187$

$P(X \leq 5) = 1 - P(X \geq 6) = 1 - (0.0035721 + 0.0002187) = 0.9962092$

Examples

A certain basketball player scores 60% of the free-throw shots she attempts. During a particular game, she gets six free throws.

(a) What assumption(s) must be made in order to regard this as a sequence of Bernoulli trials?

(b) Based on such assumption(s), find, correct to three decimal places, the probability that:

(i) she scores on exactly four of the six shots

(ii) she scores for the second time on the fifth shot.   (SEC 2012)

Solutions

(a) Remember the four features of Bernoulli trials.
1 There is a fixed number of trials.
2 The trials are independent of each other.
3 Each trial has exactly two outcomes: success or failure.
4 The probability of success (p) is constant in each trial.

In this case, 1 and 3 are given. We must assume that the trials are independent and that the probability of success is the same each time.

(b) (i) Let X = number of scores

$r = 4$

$n = 6$

p = probability of scoring = 0.6

q = probability of not scoring = 0.4

$P(X = 4) = \binom{6}{4}(0.6)^4(0.4)^2 = 0.31104 = 0.311$ to 3 decimal places

(ii) If she scores for the fifth time on the second shot, then she has exactly one success among the first four throws, AND a success on the fifth.
AND ⇒ MULTIPLY.

Probability of one success in first four throws:

$r = 1$

$n = 4$

$P(X = 1) = \binom{4}{1}(0{\cdot}6)^1(0{\cdot}4)^3 = 0{\cdot}31104 = 0{\cdot}5136$

Probability of a success on the fifth shot = 0·6

Probability of scoring for the second time on the fifth shot
= 0·5136 × 0·6 = 0·09216 = 0·092 to 3 decimal places.

Normal distribution

In the previous sections we worked with a discrete probability distribution where the possible outcomes can be listed and a probability is associated with each. For continuous variables such as height, weight and IQ scores, it is not possible to list all the outcomes. In this case we can represent the distribution with a **normal curve** or a **normal distribution**.

The main features of a normal curve or normal distribution are:

1. The curve is bell-shaped.
2. The curve is symmetrical about the mean, μ.
3. Mean = mode = median.
4. Area under normal curve = total of all probabilities = 1.
5. The width and height of the normal curve depends on the **variance** (how far a set of numbers are spread out) of the normal distribution.

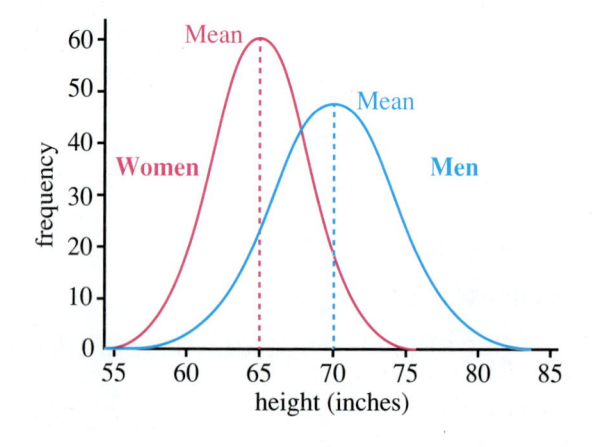

Empirical rule

> **Point to note**
>
> The **empirical rule** states that in any normal distribution:
>
> 1. Approximately 68% of the distribution lies within one standard deviation of the mean.
>   68% lies within the range $[\mu - \sigma, \mu + \sigma]$.
> 2. Approximately 95% of the distribution lies within two standard deviations of the mean.
>   95% lies within the range $[\mu - 2\sigma, \mu + 2\sigma]$.
> 3. Approximately 99·7% of the distribution lies within three standard deviations of the mean.
>   99·7% lies within the range $[\mu - 3\sigma, \mu + 3\sigma]$.

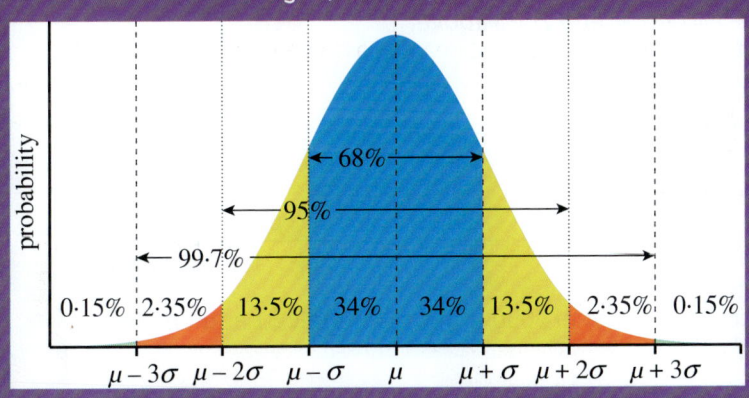

Examples

In a sample of 2050 adult males, the mean height was found to be 170 cm and the standard deviation was 4 cm. Assume the distribution is a normal distribution.

(a) How many adult males have a height between 166 cm and 174 cm?

(b) Find the range of heights for the central 95% of the distribution.

(c) How many adult males would you expect to be taller than 178 cm?

Solutions

(a) 166 cm is one standard deviation below the mean, and 174 cm is one standard deviation above. Approximately 68% of the distribution lies within one standard deviation of the mean.

68% of 2050 = 1394 adult males

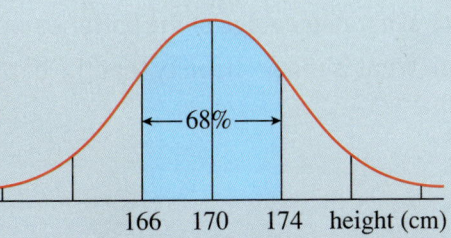

(b) Approximately 95% of the distribution lies within two standard deviations of the mean.

Two standard deviations below the mean is 170 − (2)(4) = 162.
Two standard deviations above the mean is 170 + (2)(4) = 178.

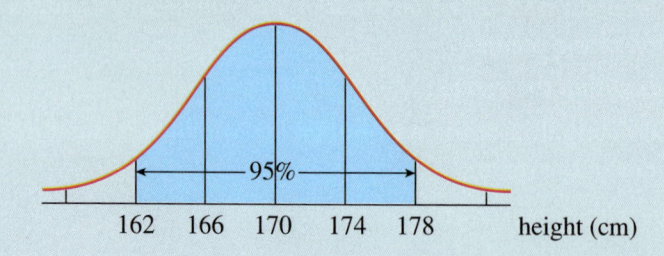

The range is 162 to 178 cm.

(c) 5% of heights are outside two standard deviations of the mean. That's 2·5% below, and 2·5% above.

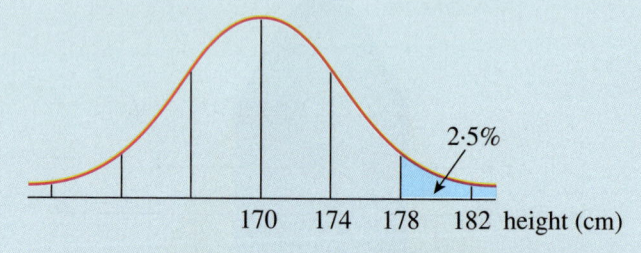

So we calculate 2·5% of 2050 = approximately 51 adult males.

Examples

The mean lifetime of a particular type of battery is 7·5 hours, with a standard deviation of 30 minutes. In a batch of 3000 batteries, assuming the lifetimes are normally distributed:

(a) How many of the batteries would you expect to last between 7 and 8 hours?

(b) How many of the batteries would you expect to last between 6·5 and 8·5 hours?

(c) What percentage of the batteries would last between 8·5 and 9 hours?

(d) What is the probability that the batteries would last between 8·5 and 9 hours?

Solutions

(a)

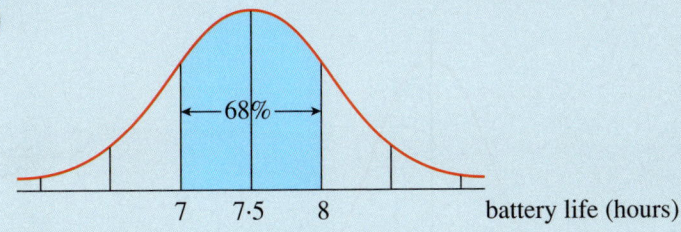

68% = 2040 batteries would last between 7 and 8 hours.

(b)

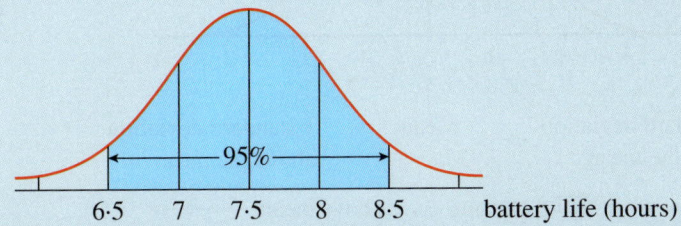

95% = 2850 batteries would last between 6·5 and 8·5 hours.

(c) 8·5 to 9 hours is between two and three standard deviations above the mean.

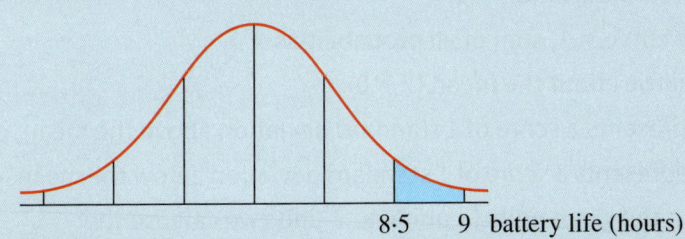

95% lies within two standard deviations of the mean, and 99·7% lies within three standard deviations, so 99·7 − 95 = 4·7% lies between two and three standard deviations.

We are only interested in the values above the mean, so $\frac{4·7}{2}$ = 2·35% would last between 8·5 and 9 hours.

(d) 2·35% last between 8·5 and 9 hours, so the probability is 0·0235.

Standard normal distribution

Normal distributions may have any mean and any standard deviation, as we have seen in the previous examples. We can convert a normal distribution to a **standard normal distribution** by using standard units.

The standard normal distribution has **a mean of 0 and a standard deviation of 1**. These standard units are called z **units**.

z scores define the position of a score compared to the mean (above or below) using the standard deviation as a unit of measurement.

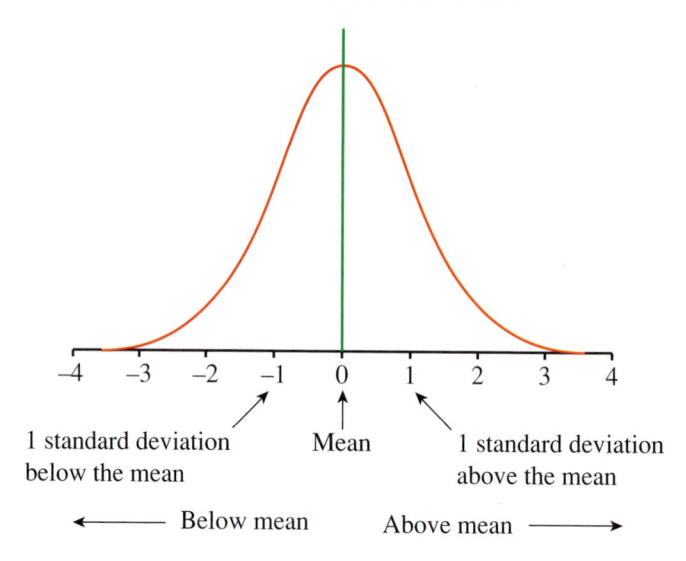

1 standard deviation below the mean • Mean • 1 standard deviation above the mean

Below mean • Above mean

The main features of a standard normal distribution are:

1. Mean = 0, standard deviation = 1.
2. Area under the curve = 1, sum of all probabilities = 1.
3. Curve is symmetric about the mean ($z = 0$).
4. z score of 1 represents a score of 1 standard deviation above the mean, etc.
5. z score of −1 represents a score of 1 standard deviation below the mean, etc.
6. To change from the given units (x units) to z units we can use the standardising formula on page 34 of the *Formulae and Tables* booklet:

$$z = \frac{x - \mu}{\sigma}$$

where x = given score, value or data point

μ = given mean (population mean)

σ = given standard deviation (standard deviation of the population).

Point to note

Probabilities for the standard normal distribution from $z = 0$ to $z = 3.09$ are given on pages 36 and 37 of the *Formulae and Tables* booklet.

The area under the curve to the left of a value p gives the probability that $z \leq p$. The area to the right gives the probability that $z \geq p$.

We need to know how to find the probabilities for the z scores at different positions on the curve.

1. To find the area to the left of z, when $z \geq 0$, we can read the value directly from the tables.

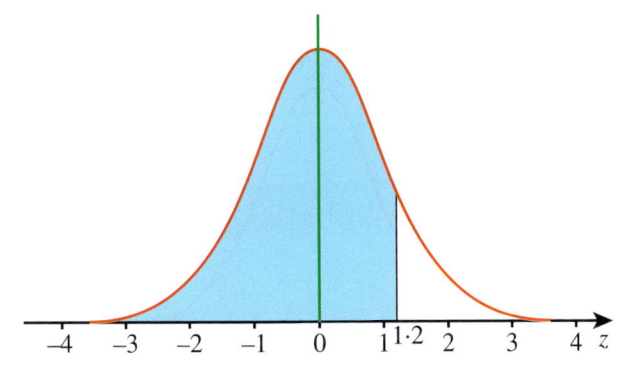

$P(z \leq 1\cdot2) = 0\cdot8849$

2. To find the area of the tail to the right of z, when $z > 0$, calculate $1 -$ area to the left of z.

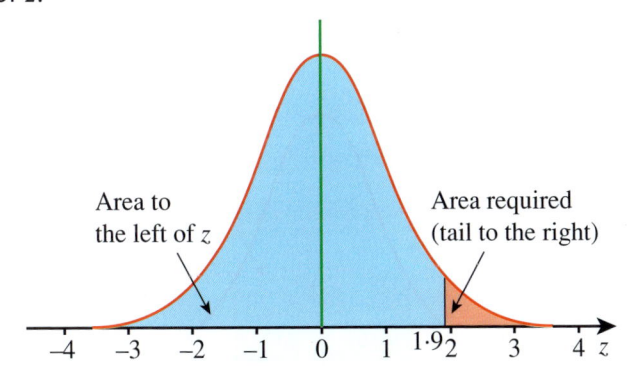

$P(z \geq 1\cdot9) = 1 - P(z \leq 1\cdot9)$
$= 1 - 0\cdot9713 = 0\cdot0287$

3. To find the area of the tail to the right of z, when $z < 0$, notice that the area to the right of a negative value is the same as the area to the left of the corresponding positive value. We can therefore read the value for $|z|$ directly from the tables.

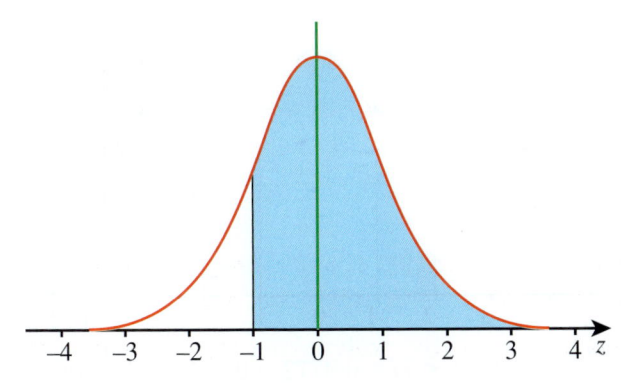

$P(z \geq -1) = P(z \leq 1) = 0\cdot8413$

4. To find the area of the tail to the left of z, when $z < 0$, notice that the area to the left of a negative value is the same as the area to the right of the corresponding positive value. Therefore, calculate 1 − area to the left of $|z|$.

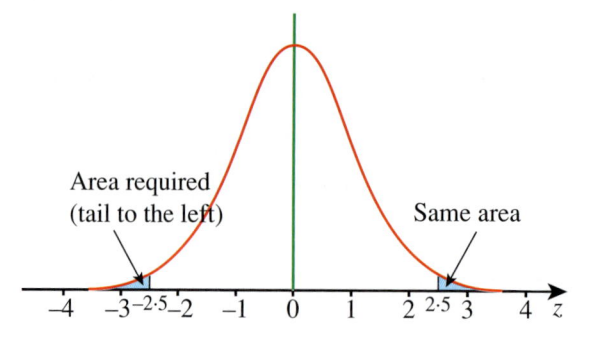

$P(z \leq -2\cdot 5) = P(z \geq 2\cdot 5) = 1 - P(z \leq 2\cdot 5)$
$= 1 - 0\cdot 9938 = 0\cdot 0062$

5. To find the area between z_1 and z_2, where z_1 is below the mean and z_2 is above the mean, calculate $P(z_2) - P(z_1) = P(z_2) - (1 - P(z_2))$.

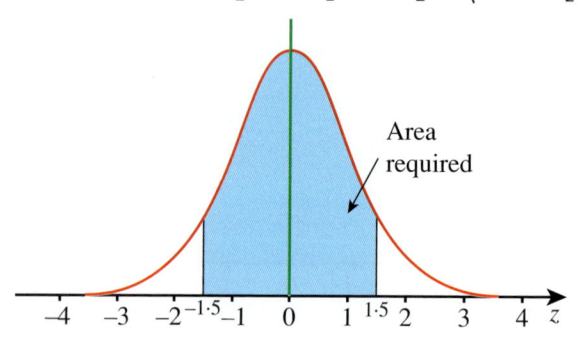

$P(-1\cdot 5 \leq z \leq 1\cdot 5) = P(z \leq 1\cdot 5) - (1 - P(z \leq 1\cdot 5))$
$= 0\cdot 9332 - (1 - 0\cdot 9332) = 0\cdot 8664$

6. To find the area between z_1 and z_2, where z_1 and z_2 are both above the mean and $z_2 > z_1$, calculate $P(z_2) - P(z_1)$.
If z_1 and z_2 are both below the mean and $z_1 > z_2$, calculate $P(|z_2|) - P(|z_1|)$.

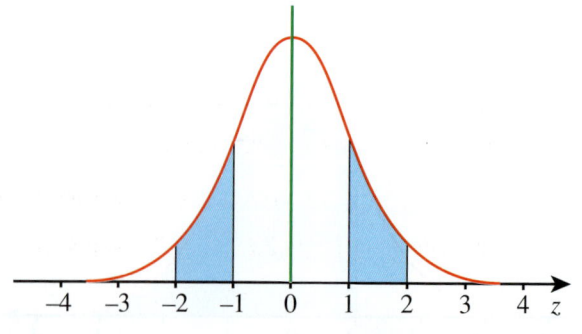

$P(-2 \leq z \leq -1) = P(1 \leq z \leq 2) = 0\cdot 9772 - 0\cdot 8413 = 0\cdot 1359$

Examples

The weight of product A is normally distributed with a mean of 25 g and a standard deviation of 3 g.

The weight of product B is normally distributed with a mean of 25 g and a standard deviation of 6 g.

X is a random variable which represents the weight of the product.

(a) Calculate for product A the probability that a product chosen at random has a weight between 22 g and 28 g using:
   (i) the empirical rule
   (ii) a standard normal distribution.
   (iii) Comment on your answers.

(b) Find $P(25 \leq X \leq 37)$ for product B using:
   (i) the empirical rule
   (ii) a standard normal distribution.

Solutions

(a) $P(22 \leq X \leq 28)$ for product A.

   (i) 22 g is one standard deviation below the mean, and 28 g is one standard deviation above. Using the empirical rule, 68% of items will be between 22 g and 28 g, so $P(22 \leq X \leq 28) = 0.68$.

   (ii) Convert to z units using the formula $z = \dfrac{x - \mu}{\sigma}$.

   $X = 22 \Rightarrow z = \dfrac{22 - 25}{3} = \dfrac{-3}{3} = -1$

   $X = 28 \Rightarrow z = \dfrac{28 - 25}{3} = \dfrac{3}{3} = 1$

   $P(-1 \leq z \leq 1) = P(z \leq 1) - (1 - P(z \leq 1))$

   Look the values up in the tables.

   $P(-1 \leq z \leq 1) = 0.8413 - (1 - 0.8413) = 0.6826$

   (iii) The standard normal distribution gives a greater degree of accuracy than the empirical rule.

(b) $P(25 \leq X \leq 37)$ for product B.

   (i) 25 g is the mean, and 37 g is two standard deviations above. Using the empirical rule, 95% of items are within two standard deviations of the mean, so $\dfrac{95}{2} = 47.5\%$ of items are between the mean and two standard deviations above. Therefore, $P(25 \leq X \leq 37) = 0.475$.

(ii) Convert to z units using the formula $z = \dfrac{x - \mu}{\sigma}$.

$X = 25 \Rightarrow z = \dfrac{25 - 25}{6} = \dfrac{0}{6} = 0$

$X = 37 \Rightarrow z = \dfrac{37 - 25}{6} = \dfrac{12}{6} = 2$

$P(0 \leq z \leq 2) = P(z \leq 2) - P(z \leq 0)$

Look the values up in the tables.

$P(0 \leq z \leq 2) = 0.9772 - 0.5 = 0.4772$

Examples

A random variable X follows a normal distribution with mean 60 and standard deviation 5.

(a) Find $P(X \leq 68)$.
(b) Find $P(52 \leq X \leq 68)$.

(SEC 2013)

Solutions

(a) Convert to a standard normal distribution.

$X = 68 \Rightarrow z = \dfrac{68 - 60}{5} = 1.6$

Read the probability value from the tables.

$P(z \leq 1.6) = 0.9452$

(b) $X = 52 \Rightarrow z = \dfrac{52 - 60}{5} = -1.6$

We need to find $P(-1.6 \leq z \leq 1.6)$. Draw a diagram to visualise the problem.

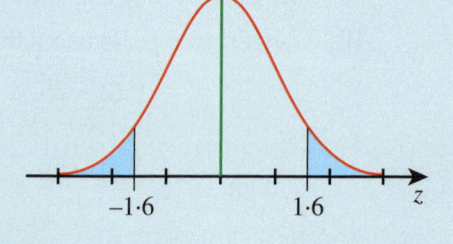

$P(-1.6 \leq z \leq 1.6) = P(z \leq 1.6) - P(z \leq -1.6)$

$ = P(z \leq 1.6) - (1 - P(z \leq 1.6))$

$ = 0.9452 - (1 - 0.9542) = 0.8904$

Examples

A company produces calculator batteries. The diameter of the batteries is supposed to be 20 mm. The tolerance is 0.25 mm. Any batteries outside this tolerance are rejected. You may assume that this is the only reason for rejecting the batteries.

(a) The company has a machine that produces batteries with diameters that are normally distributed with mean 20 mm and standard deviation 0.1 mm. Out of every 10 000 batteries produced by this machine, how many, on average, are rejected?

(b) A setting on the machine slips, so that the mean diameter of the batteries increases to 20·05 mm, while the standard deviation remains unchanged. Find the percentage increase in the rejection rate for batteries from this machine.

(SEC 2012)

Solutions

(a) A battery is rejected if its diameter is 0·25 mm smaller or larger than 20 mm. We need to find $P(|X - 20| > 0·25)$.

Convert to a standard normal distribution.

$X = 20·25 \Rightarrow z = \dfrac{20·25 - 20}{0·1} = 2·5$

$P(|X - 20| > 0·25) = P(|z| > 2·5)$

$P(|X - 20| > 0·25) = 2(1 - P(z \leq 2·5))$

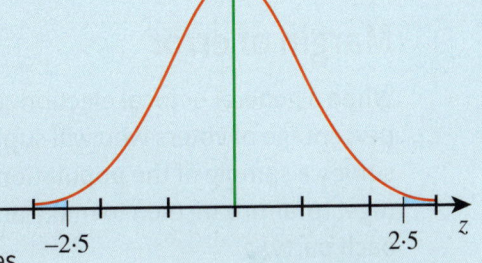

$\qquad = 2(1 - 0·9938)$

$\qquad = 0·0124$

On average, $10\,000 \times 0·0124 = 124$ batteries are rejected out of every 10 000.

(b) A battery is rejected if its diameter is smaller than 19·75 mm or larger than 20·25 mm.

Convert to a standard normal distribution using the new mean.

$X = 19·75 \Rightarrow z = \dfrac{19·75 - 20·05}{0·1} = -3$

$X = 20·25 \Rightarrow z = \dfrac{20·25 - 20·05}{0·1} = 2$

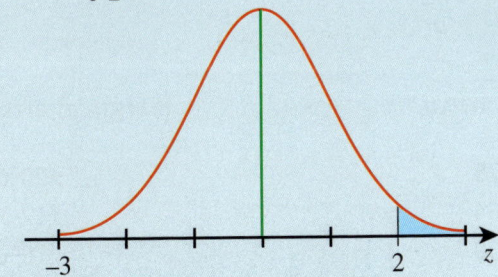

$P(|X - 20| > 0·25) = P(z \leq -3) + P(z \leq 2)$

$\qquad = 1 - P(z \leq 3) + 1 - P(z \leq 2)$

$\qquad = 1 - 0·9987 + 1 - 0·9772$

$\qquad = 2 - 1·9759 = 0·0241$

Compare this with the probability of rejection from part (a).

$\dfrac{0·0241}{0·0124} = 1·9435 \Rightarrow$ the rate of rejection has increased by 94·35%.

Confidence interval

When we are applying statistics we can use a sample of the population to draw conclusions about the population. This is known as **inferential statistics**. The size of the sample will determine the margin of error.

We can create a **confidence interval** (e.g. a 95% confidence interval or a 5% level of significance) so we can say that we are 95% confident that the true population lies within this interval.

We can use **hypothesis testing** to make a decision about a claim regarding a population based on a sample.

Margin of error

When a general or local election occurs, national newspapers publish a percentage of voters who will support each party. Market research companies survey a sample of the population, reflecting the demographic of the population (age, rural/urban, etc.) to make an estimate about the percentage support for each party.

There is of course a **margin of error** when making such predictions based on a sample.

Notation:

p = population proportion (a parameter)

$\hat{p}$ (p hat) = sample proportion (estimate of population proportion) (a statistic)

n = sample size

E = margin of error = $\dfrac{1}{\sqrt{n}}$.

Sample size n	Margin of error $E = \dfrac{1}{\sqrt{n}}$
25	±20%
64	±12·5%
100	±10%
400	±5%
625	±4%
1111	±3%
10 000	±1%

We can see clearly that the margin of error decreases as the sample size increases. The size of the population does not matter.

A sample size of approx. 1000 is very popular with market research companies, as the margin of error of ±3% is quite acceptable. Time and costs are important;

to survey, say, 10 000 people would take too long and be too costly. The opinions of the population might even change during the time it takes to conduct the survey.

If the sample size (n) for a survey is 1111 then the margin of error

$$E = \frac{1}{\sqrt{n}} = \frac{1}{\sqrt{1111}} \approx \pm 3\%$$

If the market research revealed 25% support ($\hat{p}$) for Party A from the sample, we can be reasonably confident that the proportion of the population who support Party A is between $25 - 3 = 22\%$ and $25 + 3 = 28\%$.

This leads to a confidence interval

$$[\hat{p} - E, \hat{p} + E] = \hat{p} \pm \frac{1}{\sqrt{n}}$$

We can also write this in this form

$$\hat{p} - \frac{1}{\sqrt{n}} < p < \hat{p} + \frac{1}{\sqrt{n}}$$

Sample proportion – margin of error < true proportion < sample proportion + margin of error.

> **Point to note**
>
> This confidence interval means that if many samples of 1111 voters were surveyed on the same day, the percentage support for Party A would be in the interval 22% to 28% in 95% of the samples.
>
> 95% of the time the true proportion is in this interval.

Examples

A survey is conducted to find the proportion of students who use the internet in a college. In a random sample of 625 students, 450 said that they use the internet for study on a regular basis.

(a) Calculate the sample proportion $\hat{p}$.
(b) Calculate the margin of error, at the 95% level of confidence.
(c) Construct a 95% confidence interval for the proportion of students who use the internet for study on a regular basis. Briefly explain what this means.
(d) How could the margin of error be reduced?

Solutions

(a) $\hat{p} = \dfrac{450}{625} = \dfrac{18}{25} = 0 \cdot 7$

(b) Margin of error $E = \dfrac{1}{\sqrt{n}} = \dfrac{1}{\sqrt{625}} = 0 \cdot 04$

(c) Confidence interval

$\hat{p} - E < p < \hat{p} + E$

$0.7 - 0.04 < p < 0.7 + 0.04$

$0.66 < p < 0.74$

$66\% < p < 74\%$

This means that we are 95% confident that the proportion of students in this college who use the internet on a regular basis lies between 66% and 74%.

(d) If the sample size is increased the margin of error is reduced. If the sample size is increased to 1000 the margin of error is reduced to ±3%.

Increasing the sample size might incur extra costs and it would take more time for the survey to be undertaken.

We can find a **more accurate confidence interval** by **using z scores**.

By the empirical rule, we know that the central 95% of the standard normal curve lies within two standard deviations of the mean.

Using z scores we can say that this interval lies within 1·96 standard deviations of the population proportion.

Keep in mind that we use a sample to construct a confidence interval. The standard deviation of the sampling distribution is called the standard error of the proportion. This formula is on page 34 of the *Formulae and Tables* booklet.

Standard error of the proportion $= \sigma_{\hat{p}} = \sqrt{\dfrac{p(1-p)}{n}}$

Since we don't know the value of p (the true proportion or population proportion) we must use $\hat{p}$ in place of p to calculate the standard error.

Standard error of $\hat{p} = \sigma_{\hat{p}} = \sqrt{\dfrac{\hat{p}(1-\hat{p})}{n}}$

> **Point to note**
>
> Using standard normal tables, the 95% confidence interval for a population proportion is
>
> $$\hat{p} \pm 1.96\sigma_{\hat{p}}$$
>
> This can also be written as
>
> $$\hat{p} - 1.96\sigma_{\hat{p}} < p < \hat{p} + 1.96\sigma_{\hat{p}}$$
>
> We get a more accurate confidence interval for a population proportion using this rather than the confidence interval on page 209.

Example

A certain company carries out a survey among its customers to determine if customers might buy its new product. In a survey of 1000 of its customers, 650 said they would be interested in buying the new product.

Using z scores, determine a 95% confidence interval based on this sample.

Solution

$n = 1000$, $\hat{p} = \dfrac{650}{1000} = 0.65$

Standard error $\sigma_{\hat{p}} = \sqrt{\dfrac{\hat{p}(1-\hat{p})}{n}} = \sqrt{\dfrac{0.65(1-0.65)}{1000}} = 0.0151$

Margin of error $= \pm 1.96\sigma_{\hat{p}} = \pm 1.96(0.0151) = \pm 0.0296$

95% confidence interval for sample: $0.65 - 0.0296 < p < 0.65 + 0.0296$

$0.6204 < p < 0.6796$

As a percentage, we can say that the company can be 95% confident that between 62.04% and 67.96% of its customers would be interested in buying its new product based on the sample survey.

Sampling

For Higher Level, you need to know two types of sampling:
- sample proportion (previous examples have used sample proportion)
- sample means.

Consider a population distribution with mean μ and standard deviation σ. The shape of the population distribution might be normal or skewed.

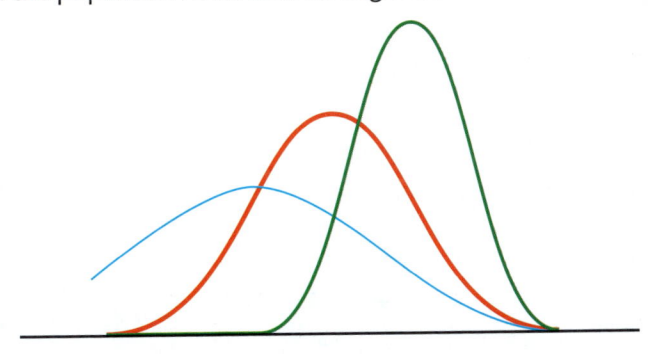

This diagram shows three normal curves with different means and standard deviations.

We take random samples from the population of size n. Each sample has its own mean and standard deviation.

10. Further Probability and Statistics

Population: mean = μ, standard deviation = σ

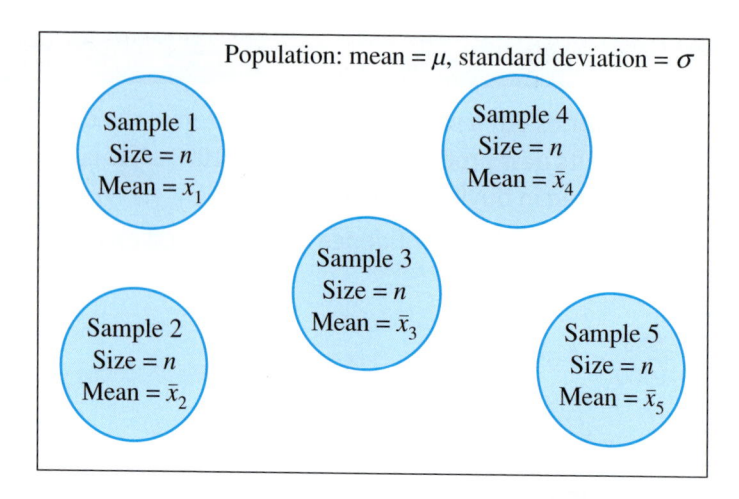

Sample 1
Size = n
Mean = $\bar{x}_1$

Sample 2
Size = n
Mean = $\bar{x}_2$

Sample 3
Size = n
Mean = $\bar{x}_3$

Sample 4
Size = n
Mean = $\bar{x}_4$

Sample 5
Size = n
Mean = $\bar{x}_5$

The different means of these samples are called the **sample means**.

These means will form their own distribution, which we call the **sampling distribution of the mean**.

Examples

A population consists of the age of 10 students:

13, 14, 15, 15, 16, 16, 17, 17, 19, 20

(a) Use a suitable diagram to plot the population distribution.
(b) Write down five possible random samples of size 7 from the population.
(c) Find the mean of each of these samples.
(d) Compare the mean of the population and the mean of the sample means. Comment on your answer.
(e) Find the standard deviation of the population σ.
(f) Find the standard deviation of the sample means and compare it to the standard deviation of the population.

Solutions

(a) A line plot is a good way to display this data.

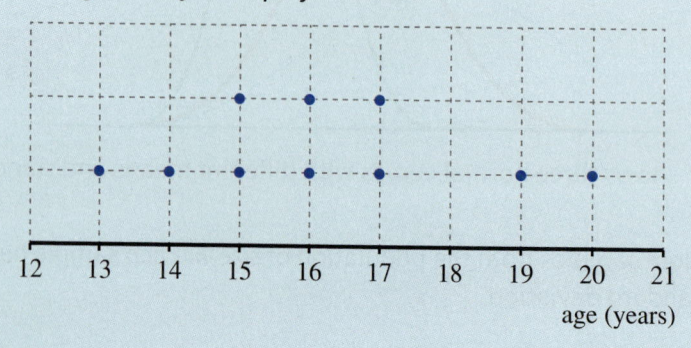

age (years)

(b) $S_1 = \{13, 15, 15, 16, 16, 17, 19\}$
$S_2 = \{13, 14, 15, 15, 16, 17, 19\}$
$S_3 = \{13, 15, 15, 16, 17, 19, 20\}$
$S_4 = \{13, 15, 15, 16, 17, 17, 20\}$
$S_5 = \{14, 15, 15, 16, 17, 17, 20\}$

(c) Mean of each sample:
$$\bar{x}_1 = \frac{13 + 15 + 15 + 16 + 16 + 17 + 19}{7} = 15.9$$
$\bar{x}_2 = 15.6$
$\bar{x}_3 = 16.4$
$\bar{x}_4 = 16.1$
$\bar{x}_5 = 16.3$

(d) Mean of population $\mu = \dfrac{13 + 14 + 15 + 15 + 16 + 16 + 17 + 17 + 19 + 20}{10} = 16.2$

Mean of sample means $= \dfrac{15.9 + 15.6 + 16.4 + 16.1 + 16.3}{5} = 16.06$

We can see that the mean of the sample means in this example is very close to the mean of the population (considering the size of the population is only 10 students).

(e) Using a calculator, standard deviation of the population $\sigma = 2.04$, correct to 2 decimal places.

(f) Using a calculator, standard deviation of the sample means $= 0.29$, correct to 2 decimal places.

Comparing standard deviations, we can see in this example that the standard deviation of the sample means is much smaller than the standard deviation of the population.

The interesting features in the example above regarding the mean and standard deviation of the population compared to the sample means leads to the central limit theorem.

Central limit theorem

The central limit theorem describes the relationship between the sampling distribution of sample means and the population that the samples are taken from.

Notation:

	Population	Large sample	Sample means
Mean	μ	$\bar{x}$	$\mu_{\bar{x}}$
Standard deviation	σ	s	$\sigma_{\bar{x}} = \dfrac{\sigma}{\sqrt{n}}$

> **Point to note**
> $\sigma_{\bar{x}}$ is known as the standard error of the mean. The formula is on page 34 of the *Formulae and Tables* booklet.

The central limit theorem states that:
- If the population is normally distributed, the sampling distribution of sample means is normally distributed for any sample size n.
- If the population is not normally distributed, the sampling distribution of sample means will approximate a normal distribution provided the sample size is large enough ($n \geq 30$).
- The mean of the sample means will be the same as the population mean μ.
- The standard deviation of the sample means will approach $\dfrac{\sigma}{\sqrt{n}}$.

To convert from x units to z units use the formula:

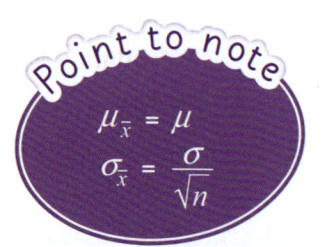

$$z = \dfrac{\bar{x} - \mu_{\bar{x}}}{\sigma_{\bar{x}}} = \dfrac{\bar{x} - \mu}{\dfrac{\sigma}{\sqrt{n}}} \quad (\mu_{\bar{x}} = \mu)$$

> **Point to note**
> $\mu_{\bar{x}} = \mu$
> $\sigma_{\bar{x}} = \dfrac{\sigma}{\sqrt{n}}$

Examples

A collection of glass bottles in a production line has a mean weight of 250 g and standard deviation 15 g.
A quality control is done to check the weight of bottles in production.
A sample of 200 bottles are chosen at random.
(a) Find the mean of the sample means.
(b) Find the standard error of the sample means or standard error of the mean.
(c) Given that the distribution of the sample means is normal, find the probability that the mean weight of the sample is less than 248 g.

Solutions

(a) Mean of sample means = mean of population (since n = sample size ≥ 30).
So mean of sample means = 250 g.

(b) Standard error of the mean:

$$\sigma_{\bar{x}} = \dfrac{\sigma}{\sqrt{n}} = \dfrac{15}{\sqrt{200}} = 1\cdot06$$

(c) We need to find $P(\bar{x} < 248)$.

$\sigma = 15$, $n = 200$, $\mu_{\bar{x}} = \mu = 250$

Convert to standard units using the formula $z = \dfrac{\bar{x} - \mu}{\frac{\sigma}{\sqrt{n}}}$.

$\bar{x} = 248 \Rightarrow z = \dfrac{248 - 250}{1 \cdot 06} = -1 \cdot 89$

$P(z < -1 \cdot 89) = 1 - P(z < 1 \cdot 89) = 1 - 0 \cdot 9706 = 0 \cdot 0294$

Hypothesis testing

Hypothesis testing is similar to making a decision in a trial based on the evidence given. In a trial, a jury must decide on two hypotheses:

The null hypothesis:

H_0: The defendant is innocent.

The alternative hypothesis:

H_1: The defendant is not innocent (guilty).

In statistics we need to make a decision about a population based on a population proportion (large sample) or a population mean based on the mean of random samples.

Hypothesis testing is based on a 95% confidence interval or a 5% level of significance.

To test a hypothesis based on the **population proportion**:

1. Write down the null hypothesis, H_0, and the alternative hypothesis, H_1.
2. Identify the sample proportion, $\hat{p}$, and the sample size, n, and calculate the margin of error.
3. Construct a 95% confidence interval for the population p.
4. If the value of $\hat{p}$ is within the confidence interval, accept H_0.
   If the value of $\hat{p}$ is outside the confidence interval, reject H_0 and accept H_1.

We have already seen examples for constructing a confidence interval for a population proportion. Now we go one step further and make a decision about a claim made by a company, manufacturer or newspaper based on the population proportion.

Examples

Go Fast Airlines provides internal flights in Ireland, short haul flights to Europe and long haul flights to America and Asia. On long haul flights the company sells economy class, business class and executive class tickets. All passengers have a baggage allowance of 20 kg and must pay a cost per kg for any weight over the 20 kg allowance.

Each month the company carries out a survey among 1000 passengers. Some of the results of the survey for May are shown below.

Gender	Male: 479	Female: 521
Previously flown with Go Fast Airlines	Yes: 682	No: 318
Would fly again with Go Fast Airlines	Yes: 913	No: 87
Passenger age	Mean age: 42 Median age: 31	
Spend on in-flight facilities	Mean spend: €18·65 Median spend: €32·18	

Was flight delayed	Yes	No	Don't know
	231	748	21

Passenger satisfaction with overall service	Satisfied	Not satisfied	Don't know
	664	238	98

(a) Go Fast Airlines used a **stratified random sample** to conduct the survey.
  (i) Explain what is meant by a stratified random sample.
  (ii) Write down four different passenger groups that the company might have included in their sample.

(b) What is the probability that a passenger selected at random from this sample:
  (i) had their flight delayed
  (ii) was not satisfied with the overall service?

(c) An employee suggests that the probability of selecting a passenger whose flight was delayed and who was not satisfied with the overall service should be equal to the product of the two probabilities in (b). Do you agree with the employee?

(d) Which of the graphs below do you think is most likely to represent the distribution of the weights of passenger baggage?

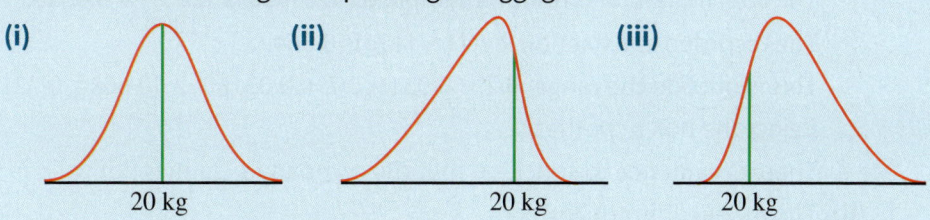

(i) 20 kg   (ii) 20 kg   (iii) 20 kg

(e) **(i)** Draw a sketch of the possible distribution of the ages of the passengers based on the data in the survey.
(ii) Explain your answer.

(f) **(i)** The company repeatedly asserts that 70% of their customers are satisfied with their overall service. Use a hypothesis test at the 5% level of significance to decide whether there is sufficient evidence to conclude that their claim is valid in May. State the null hypothesis and state your conclusion clearly.
(ii) A manager of the airline says: 'If we survey 2000 passengers from June on, we will halve the margin of error in our surveys.' Is the manager correct?
(SEC 2013)

Solutions

(a) **(i)** The population is divided into different subgroups which have common characteristics. Random samples are drawn from each subgroup according to their proportion of the population.
(ii) Some possibilities are long haul economy class passengers, long haul business class passengers, long haul executive class passengers and short haul passengers.

(b) **(i)** $P(\text{flight delayed}) = \dfrac{231}{1000} = 0 \cdot 231$

(ii) $P(\text{not satisfied}) = \dfrac{238}{1000} = 0 \cdot 238$

(c) I do not agree. If it was, this would imply that the events were independent. This is not likely since a passenger who had his flight delayed is likely to be not satisfied with the service.

(d) Graph (ii), because a lot of the passengers are likely to have baggage with a weight of less than the maximum 20 kg.

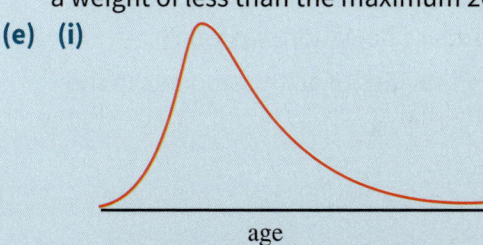

(e) **(i)**

age

(ii) The median is less than the mean so the graph is skewed to the right.

(f) (i) Null hypothesis: The satisfaction level is unchanged. $p = 0.7$

The 95% margin of error for a sample of size 1000 is $\dfrac{1}{\sqrt{1000}} = 0.0316$.

The recorded satisfaction level for May is 0·664.

This is outside the range $[0.7 - 0.0316, 0.7 + 0.03160] = [0.6684, 0.7316]$.

Reject the null hypothesis.

There is evidence to conclude that the company's claim is not valid in May.

(ii) The manager is not correct.

For a sample size of n, the margin of error is $\dfrac{1}{\sqrt{n}}$.

$\dfrac{1}{2}\dfrac{1}{\sqrt{1000}} \neq \dfrac{1}{\sqrt{2000}}$

To test a hypothesis based on a **population mean** we have to be careful, because we are dealing with a standard normal distribution and we are using z units and a more accurate confidence interval.

We have already used a confidence interval for a population proportion using standard normal tables: $\hat{p} - 1.96\sigma_{\hat{p}} < p < \hat{p} + 1.96\sigma_{\hat{p}}$

The confidence interval for a population mean involves working with **mean** values.

Notation:

μ = population mean

$\bar{x}$ = mean of random sample of size n

σ = standard deviation of population (we can use the standard deviation of the sample if the standard deviation of the population is not given)

$\sigma_{\bar{x}} = \dfrac{\sigma}{\sqrt{n}}$ = standard error of the mean.

We now can write confidence interval for the **population mean** as

$\bar{x} - 1.96\sigma_{\bar{x}} < \mu < \bar{x} + 1.96\sigma_{\bar{x}}$

This is also known as the 95% confidence interval for the population mean.

Example

A random sample of 60 students is chosen. Their weekly savings are recorded. Their mean savings was €10·50 and the standard deviation was €0·70.

Form a 95% confidence interval for the mean savings of all the students in the population.

Solution

> **Point to note**
> Note the key words in this question: 'mean of a sample' and '95% confidence interval'.

We are forming a confidence interval for the population mean of students.
$\bar{x} = €10·50$, $\sigma = €0·70$, $n = 60$

$$\sigma_{\bar{x}} = \frac{\sigma}{\sqrt{n}} = \frac{0·70}{\sqrt{60}} = 0·09$$

The 95% confidence interval is $\bar{x} - 1·96\sigma_{\bar{x}} < \mu < \bar{x} + 1·96\sigma_{\bar{x}}$

$10·50 - 1·96(0·09) < \mu < 10·50 + 1·96(0·09)$

$10·3236 < \mu < 10·6764$

This means that the confidence interval for μ is from €10·33 to €10·68. We are 95% confident that the mean savings of all the students in the population is between those figures.

To test a hypothesis based on a **population mean**:
1. Write down the null hypothesis, H_0, and the alternative hypothesis, H_1.
2. Identify μ, $\bar{x}$, σ and n.
3. Convert the observed results into z units (also known as a test statistic).
4. Draw a sketch and write down the critical values.

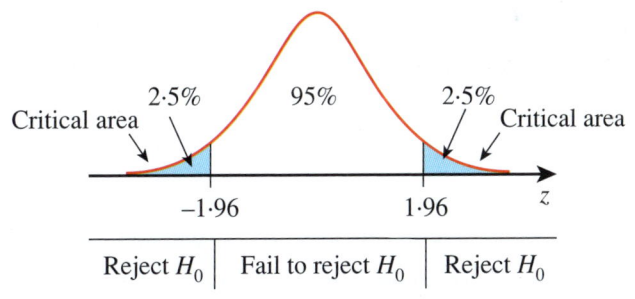

5. Reject H_0 if z is within the critical areas and accept H_1; otherwise fail to reject H_0.

Example

In a certain examination taken by a large number of students in a region, the mean mark was 52·3 and the standard deviation was 10·5. A random sample of 50 students was surveyed in a particular school and the mean mark for these students was 50.

At the 5% level of significance, test the school's claim that their students did as well as other students who did the exam. Clearly state your null hypothesis, your alternative hypothesis and your conclusion.

Solution

H_0: students in the school did as well as other students in the region.
H_1: students in the school did not do as well as other students in the region.

$\mu = 52\cdot3$, $\bar{x} = 50$, $\sigma = 10\cdot5$, $n = 50$

$$z = \frac{\bar{x} - \mu}{\frac{\sigma}{\sqrt{n}}} = \frac{50 - 52\cdot3}{\frac{10\cdot5}{\sqrt{50}}} = -1\cdot55$$

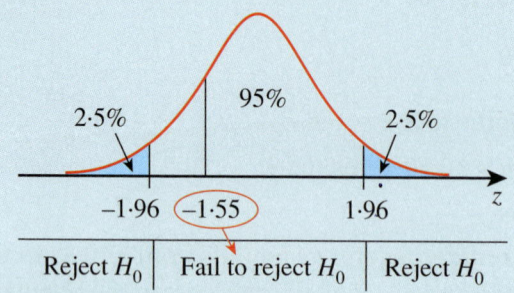

We fail to reject the null hypothesis and we can conclude that the students in the school did as well as other students in the region.

Examples

A car rental company has been using *Evertread* tyres on their fleet of economy cars. All cars in this fleet are identical. The company manages the tyres on each car in such a way that the four tyres all wear out at the same time. The company keeps a record of the lifespan of each set of tyres. The records show that the lifespan of these sets of tyres is normally distributed with mean 45 000 km and standard deviation 8000 km.

(a) A car from the economy fleet is chosen at random. Find the probability that the tyres on this car will last for at least 40 000 km.

(b) Twenty cars from the economy fleet are chosen at random. Find the probability that the tyres on at least eighteen of these cars will last for more than 40 000 km.

(c) The company is considering switching brands from *Evertread* tyres to *SafeRun* tyres, because they are cheaper. The distributors of *SafeRun* tyres claim that these tyres have the same mean lifespan as *Evertread* tyres. The car rental company wants to check this claim before they switch brands. They have enough data on *Evertread* tyres to regard these as a known population. They want to test a sample of *SafeRun* tyres against it.

The company selects 25 cars at random from the economy fleet and fits them with the new tyres. For these cars, it is found that the mean lifespan of the tyres is 43 850 km.

Assume that the lifespan of the sets of *SafeRun* tyres is normally distributed and has a standard deviation of 8000 km. Test, at the 5% level of significance, the hypothesis that the mean lifespan of *SafeRun* tyres is the same as the mean lifespan of *Evertread* tyres. State clearly what the company can conclude about the tyres.
(SEC Sample 2015)

Solutions

(a) Convert to z units

$$z = \frac{x - \mu}{\sigma}$$

$x = 40\,000$, $\mu = 45\,000$, $\sigma = 8000$

$$z = \frac{40\,000 - 45\,000}{8000} = -0.625$$

We need to find $P(X > 4000)$. Using z units, we need to find $P(z > -0.625) = P(z < 0.625)$.

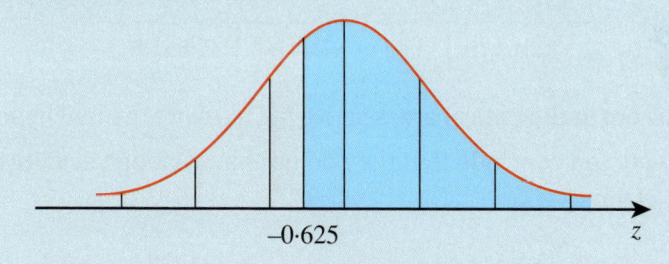

0·625 is not in the tables, so we need to take an average of the values for 0·62 and 0·63.

$$P(z > -0.625) = \frac{0.7324 + 0.7357}{2} = 0.734$$

The probability that the tyres last at least 40 000 km is 0·734.

(b) This scenario can be represented by a Bernoulli trial.
There are 20 trials, so $n = 20$.
p = probability of success = 0·734 (from part (a))
q = probability of failure = 1 − 0·734 = 0·266
Formula: $P(X = r) = \binom{n}{r} p^r q^{n-r}$

We need to find the probability that at least 18 of the cars will last more than 40 000 km. That is, 18 cars or 19 cars or 20 cars last that long.
We require $P(18) + P(19) + P(20)$.

$$P(18) = \binom{20}{18}(0.734)^{18}(0.266)^2 = 0.0514$$

$$P(19) = \binom{20}{19}(0.734)^{19}(0.266) = 0.0149$$

$$P(20) = \binom{20}{20}(0.734)^{20} = 0.0021$$

Adding these probabilities, we get 0·0684.

(c) This a hypothesis test for a population mean.

H_0: The mean lifespan of *SafeRun* tyres is 45 000 km

H_1: The mean lifespan of *SafeRun* tyres is not 45 000 km

$\mu = 45\,0000$, $\bar{x} = 43\,850$, $\sigma = 8000$, $n = 25$

$$\sigma_{\bar{x}} = \frac{\sigma}{\sqrt{n}} = \frac{8000}{\sqrt{25}} = 1600$$

Convert the observed results to z units

$$z = \frac{\bar{x} - \mu}{\sigma_{\bar{x}}} = \frac{43\,850 - 45\,000}{1600} = -0\cdot71875$$

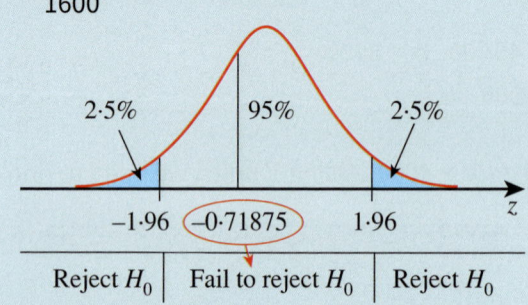

−0·71875 is not in the critical areas so we fail to reject the null hypothesis.

The company can conclude that they do not have enough evidence to dispute *SafeRun*'s claim.

p-values

A *p*-value is a probability.

The *p*-value is defined as the smallest level of significance at which the null hypothesis would be rejected. The *p*-value measures the strength of the evidence in the data against the null hypothesis.

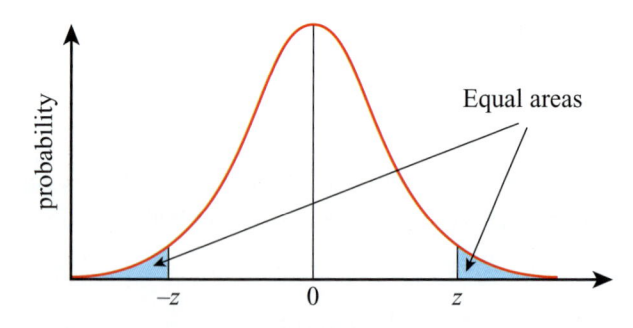

The *p*-value is the area of the two shaded regions.

Example

Calculate the p-value for the sample statistic $z = -2$.

Solution

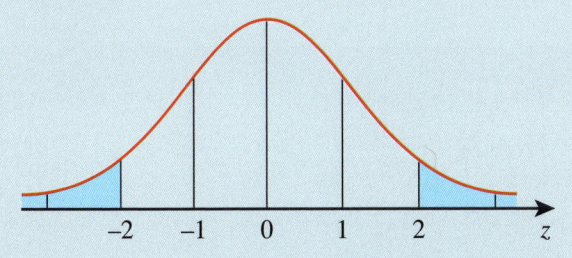

$P(z > 2) = 1 - P(z < 2) = 1 - 0.9772 = 0.0228$

p-value $= 2(0.0228) = 0.0456$

> **Point to note**
>
> The significance level is 5% = 0.05.
>
> $p \leq 0.05$ means that there is very strong evidence to reject H_0.
>
> $p > 0.05$ means that there is very strong evidence to fail to reject H_0.

Examples

(a) The mean lifetime of light bulbs produced by a company has, in the past, been 1500 hours. A sample of 100 bulbs, recently produced by the company, had a mean lifetime of 1475 hours with a standard deviation of 110 hours. Test the hypothesis that the mean lifetime of the bulbs has not changed, using a 0.05 level of significance.

(b) Find the p-value of the test you performed in part (a) above and explain what this value represents in the context of the question. *(SEC Sample 2015)*

Solutions

(a) H_0: The mean lifetime of the light bulbs is 1500 hours.

H_1: The mean lifetime of the light bulbs is not 1500 hours.

$\mu = 1500$, $\bar{x} = 1475$, $\sigma = 110$, $n = 100$

$$\sigma_{\bar{x}} = \frac{\sigma}{\sqrt{n}} = \frac{110}{\sqrt{100}} = 11$$

Convert the observed results to z units.

$$z = \frac{\bar{x} - \mu}{\sigma_{\bar{x}}} = \frac{1475 - 1500}{11} = -2.27$$

−2·27 is inside the critical area since −2·27 < −1·96.

We can reject the null hypothesis at the 5% level of significance.

There is enough evidence to say that the mean lifetime of the light bulbs has changed.

(b) The z score from part (a) is −2·27.

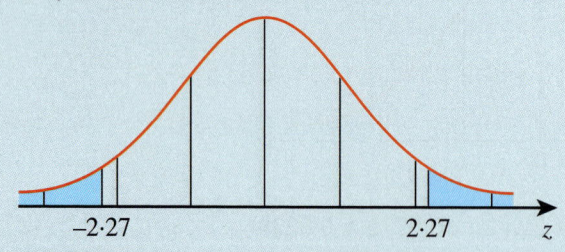

$P(z > 2·27) = 1 − P(z < 2·27) = 1 − 0·9884 = 0·0116$

p-value = $2(0·0116) = 0·02332$

A p-value ≤ 0·05 means that there is very strong evidence to reject the null hypothesis.

0·0232 ≤ 0·05

So the p-value means that there is very strong evidence to suggest that the mean lifetime of the light bulbs has changed.

Checklist

- ✓ Know how to calculate the expected value from a probability distribution.
- ✓ Practise solving problems involving Bernoulli trials.
- ✓ Know the empirical rule and how to use it to make decisions.
- ✓ Know how to calculate standard scores (z scores) and how to read the standard normal tables on pages 36 and 37 of the *Formulae and Tables* booklet.
- ✓ Know how to calculate the margin of error for a population proportion.
- ✓ Practise conducting hypothesis tests on a population proportion using the margin of error.
- ✓ Know how to construct 95% confidence intervals for the population mean from a large sample, and for the population proportion, in both cases using z tables.
- ✓ Practise hypothesis testing for population proportion and population mean.
- ✓ Know how to use and interpret p-values.

Questions to Practise

If you have a difficulty with a question do the following.

- Write the page number and the question number in the boxes provided.
- Practise the question. Each time you practise, tick a box.
- Usually, five ticks will indicate that you have mastered the difficulty.

This is a very efficient study method.

Page Number	Question Number						Page Number	Question Number					
		☐	☐	☐	☐	☐			☐	☐	☐	☐	☐
		☐	☐	☐	☐	☐			☐	☐	☐	☐	☐
		☐	☐	☐	☐	☐			☐	☐	☐	☐	☐
		☐	☐	☐	☐	☐			☐	☐	☐	☐	☐
		☐	☐	☐	☐	☐			☐	☐	☐	☐	☐
		☐	☐	☐	☐	☐			☐	☐	☐	☐	☐
		☐	☐	☐	☐	☐			☐	☐	☐	☐	☐
		☐	☐	☐	☐	☐			☐	☐	☐	☐	☐
		☐	☐	☐	☐	☐			☐	☐	☐	☐	☐
		☐	☐	☐	☐	☐			☐	☐	☐	☐	☐
		☐	☐	☐	☐	☐			☐	☐	☐	☐	☐
		☐	☐	☐	☐	☐			☐	☐	☐	☐	☐
		☐	☐	☐	☐	☐			☐	☐	☐	☐	☐
		☐	☐	☐	☐	☐			☐	☐	☐	☐	☐
		☐	☐	☐	☐	☐			☐	☐	☐	☐	☐

Page Number	Question Number					Page Number	Question Number				
		☐	☐	☐	☐			☐	☐	☐	☐
		☐	☐	☐	☐			☐	☐	☐	☐
		☐	☐	☐	☐			☐	☐	☐	☐
		☐	☐	☐	☐			☐	☐	☐	☐
		☐	☐	☐	☐			☐	☐	☐	☐
		☐	☐	☐	☐			☐	☐	☐	☐
		☐	☐	☐	☐			☐	☐	☐	☐
		☐	☐	☐	☐			☐	☐	☐	☐
		☐	☐	☐	☐			☐	☐	☐	☐
		☐	☐	☐	☐			☐	☐	☐	☐
		☐	☐	☐	☐			☐	☐	☐	☐
		☐	☐	☐	☐			☐	☐	☐	☐
		☐	☐	☐	☐			☐	☐	☐	☐
		☐	☐	☐	☐			☐	☐	☐	☐
		☐	☐	☐	☐			☐	☐	☐	☐
		☐	☐	☐	☐			☐	☐	☐	☐
		☐	☐	☐	☐			☐	☐	☐	☐
		☐	☐	☐	☐			☐	☐	☐	☐
		☐	☐	☐	☐			☐	☐	☐	☐
		☐	☐	☐	☐			☐	☐	☐	☐
		☐	☐	☐	☐			☐	☐	☐	☐
		☐	☐	☐	☐			☐	☐	☐	☐
		☐	☐	☐	☐			☐	☐	☐	☐
		☐	☐	☐	☐			☐	☐	☐	☐
		☐	☐	☐	☐			☐	☐	☐	☐
		☐	☐	☐	☐			☐	☐	☐	☐
		☐	☐	☐	☐			☐	☐	☐	☐
		☐	☐	☐	☐			☐	☐	☐	☐

Page Number	Question Number						Page Number	Question Number					
		☐	☐	☐	☐	☐			☐	☐	☐	☐	☐
		☐	☐	☐	☐	☐			☐	☐	☐	☐	☐
		☐	☐	☐	☐	☐			☐	☐	☐	☐	☐
		☐	☐	☐	☐	☐			☐	☐	☐	☐	☐
		☐	☐	☐	☐	☐			☐	☐	☐	☐	☐
		☐	☐	☐	☐	☐			☐	☐	☐	☐	☐
		☐	☐	☐	☐	☐			☐	☐	☐	☐	☐
		☐	☐	☐	☐	☐			☐	☐	☐	☐	☐
		☐	☐	☐	☐	☐			☐	☐	☐	☐	☐
		☐	☐	☐	☐	☐			☐	☐	☐	☐	☐
		☐	☐	☐	☐	☐			☐	☐	☐	☐	☐
		☐	☐	☐	☐	☐			☐	☐	☐	☐	☐
		☐	☐	☐	☐	☐			☐	☐	☐	☐	☐
		☐	☐	☐	☐	☐			☐	☐	☐	☐	☐
		☐	☐	☐	☐	☐			☐	☐	☐	☐	☐
		☐	☐	☐	☐	☐			☐	☐	☐	☐	☐
		☐	☐	☐	☐	☐			☐	☐	☐	☐	☐
		☐	☐	☐	☐	☐			☐	☐	☐	☐	☐
		☐	☐	☐	☐	☐			☐	☐	☐	☐	☐
		☐	☐	☐	☐	☐			☐	☐	☐	☐	☐
		☐	☐	☐	☐	☐			☐	☐	☐	☐	☐
		☐	☐	☐	☐	☐			☐	☐	☐	☐	☐
		☐	☐	☐	☐	☐			☐	☐	☐	☐	☐
		☐	☐	☐	☐	☐			☐	☐	☐	☐	☐
		☐	☐	☐	☐	☐			☐	☐	☐	☐	☐
		☐	☐	☐	☐	☐			☐	☐	☐	☐	☐
		☐	☐	☐	☐	☐			☐	☐	☐	☐	☐

Page Number	Question Number					Page Number	Question Number				
		☐	☐	☐	☐			☐	☐	☐	☐
		☐	☐	☐	☐			☐	☐	☐	☐
		☐	☐	☐	☐			☐	☐	☐	☐
		☐	☐	☐	☐			☐	☐	☐	☐
		☐	☐	☐	☐			☐	☐	☐	☐
		☐	☐	☐	☐			☐	☐	☐	☐
		☐	☐	☐	☐			☐	☐	☐	☐
		☐	☐	☐	☐			☐	☐	☐	☐
		☐	☐	☐	☐			☐	☐	☐	☐
		☐	☐	☐	☐			☐	☐	☐	☐
		☐	☐	☐	☐			☐	☐	☐	☐
		☐	☐	☐	☐			☐	☐	☐	☐
		☐	☐	☐	☐			☐	☐	☐	☐
		☐	☐	☐	☐			☐	☐	☐	☐
		☐	☐	☐	☐			☐	☐	☐	☐
		☐	☐	☐	☐			☐	☐	☐	☐
		☐	☐	☐	☐			☐	☐	☐	☐
		☐	☐	☐	☐			☐	☐	☐	☐
		☐	☐	☐	☐			☐	☐	☐	☐
		☐	☐	☐	☐			☐	☐	☐	☐
		☐	☐	☐	☐			☐	☐	☐	☐
		☐	☐	☐	☐			☐	☐	☐	☐
		☐	☐	☐	☐			☐	☐	☐	☐
		☐	☐	☐	☐			☐	☐	☐	☐
		☐	☐	☐	☐			☐	☐	☐	☐
		☐	☐	☐	☐			☐	☐	☐	☐
		☐	☐	☐	☐			☐	☐	☐	☐

Page Number	Question Number						Page Number	Question Number					
		☐	☐	☐	☐	☐			☐	☐	☐	☐	☐
		☐	☐	☐	☐	☐			☐	☐	☐	☐	☐
		☐	☐	☐	☐	☐			☐	☐	☐	☐	☐
		☐	☐	☐	☐	☐			☐	☐	☐	☐	☐
		☐	☐	☐	☐	☐			☐	☐	☐	☐	☐
		☐	☐	☐	☐	☐			☐	☐	☐	☐	☐
		☐	☐	☐	☐	☐			☐	☐	☐	☐	☐
		☐	☐	☐	☐	☐			☐	☐	☐	☐	☐
		☐	☐	☐	☐	☐			☐	☐	☐	☐	☐
		☐	☐	☐	☐	☐			☐	☐	☐	☐	☐
		☐	☐	☐	☐	☐			☐	☐	☐	☐	☐
		☐	☐	☐	☐	☐			☐	☐	☐	☐	☐
		☐	☐	☐	☐	☐			☐	☐	☐	☐	☐
		☐	☐	☐	☐	☐			☐	☐	☐	☐	☐
		☐	☐	☐	☐	☐			☐	☐	☐	☐	☐
		☐	☐	☐	☐	☐			☐	☐	☐	☐	☐
		☐	☐	☐	☐	☐			☐	☐	☐	☐	☐
		☐	☐	☐	☐	☐			☐	☐	☐	☐	☐
		☐	☐	☐	☐	☐			☐	☐	☐	☐	☐
		☐	☐	☐	☐	☐			☐	☐	☐	☐	☐
		☐	☐	☐	☐	☐			☐	☐	☐	☐	☐
		☐	☐	☐	☐	☐			☐	☐	☐	☐	☐
		☐	☐	☐	☐	☐			☐	☐	☐	☐	☐
		☐	☐	☐	☐	☐			☐	☐	☐	☐	☐
		☐	☐	☐	☐	☐			☐	☐	☐	☐	☐
		☐	☐	☐	☐	☐			☐	☐	☐	☐	☐

Appendix. Questions to Practise

Page Number	Question Number					Page Number	Question Number				
		☐	☐	☐	☐			☐	☐	☐	☐
		☐	☐	☐	☐			☐	☐	☐	☐
		☐	☐	☐	☐			☐	☐	☐	☐
		☐	☐	☐	☐			☐	☐	☐	☐
		☐	☐	☐	☐			☐	☐	☐	☐
		☐	☐	☐	☐			☐	☐	☐	☐
		☐	☐	☐	☐			☐	☐	☐	☐
		☐	☐	☐	☐			☐	☐	☐	☐
		☐	☐	☐	☐			☐	☐	☐	☐
		☐	☐	☐	☐			☐	☐	☐	☐
		☐	☐	☐	☐			☐	☐	☐	☐
		☐	☐	☐	☐			☐	☐	☐	☐
		☐	☐	☐	☐			☐	☐	☐	☐
		☐	☐	☐	☐			☐	☐	☐	☐
		☐	☐	☐	☐			☐	☐	☐	☐
		☐	☐	☐	☐			☐	☐	☐	☐
		☐	☐	☐	☐			☐	☐	☐	☐
		☐	☐	☐	☐			☐	☐	☐	☐
		☐	☐	☐	☐			☐	☐	☐	☐
		☐	☐	☐	☐			☐	☐	☐	☐
		☐	☐	☐	☐			☐	☐	☐	☐
		☐	☐	☐	☐			☐	☐	☐	☐
		☐	☐	☐	☐			☐	☐	☐	☐
		☐	☐	☐	☐			☐	☐	☐	☐
		☐	☐	☐	☐			☐	☐	☐	☐
		☐	☐	☐	☐			☐	☐	☐	☐
		☐	☐	☐	☐			☐	☐	☐	☐

Page Number	Question Number						Page Number	Question Number					
		☐	☐	☐	☐	☐			☐	☐	☐	☐	☐
		☐	☐	☐	☐	☐			☐	☐	☐	☐	☐
		☐	☐	☐	☐	☐			☐	☐	☐	☐	☐
		☐	☐	☐	☐	☐			☐	☐	☐	☐	☐
		☐	☐	☐	☐	☐			☐	☐	☐	☐	☐
		☐	☐	☐	☐	☐			☐	☐	☐	☐	☐
		☐	☐	☐	☐	☐			☐	☐	☐	☐	☐
		☐	☐	☐	☐	☐			☐	☐	☐	☐	☐
		☐	☐	☐	☐	☐			☐	☐	☐	☐	☐
		☐	☐	☐	☐	☐			☐	☐	☐	☐	☐
		☐	☐	☐	☐	☐			☐	☐	☐	☐	☐
		☐	☐	☐	☐	☐			☐	☐	☐	☐	☐
		☐	☐	☐	☐	☐			☐	☐	☐	☐	☐
		☐	☐	☐	☐	☐			☐	☐	☐	☐	☐
		☐	☐	☐	☐	☐			☐	☐	☐	☐	☐
		☐	☐	☐	☐	☐			☐	☐	☐	☐	☐
		☐	☐	☐	☐	☐			☐	☐	☐	☐	☐
		☐	☐	☐	☐	☐			☐	☐	☐	☐	☐
		☐	☐	☐	☐	☐			☐	☐	☐	☐	☐
		☐	☐	☐	☐	☐			☐	☐	☐	☐	☐
		☐	☐	☐	☐	☐			☐	☐	☐	☐	☐
		☐	☐	☐	☐	☐			☐	☐	☐	☐	☐
		☐	☐	☐	☐	☐			☐	☐	☐	☐	☐
		☐	☐	☐	☐	☐			☐	☐	☐	☐	☐
		☐	☐	☐	☐	☐			☐	☐	☐	☐	☐
		☐	☐	☐	☐	☐			☐	☐	☐	☐	☐
		☐	☐	☐	☐	☐			☐	☐	☐	☐	☐

Appendix. Questions to Practise

Page Number	Question Number					Page Number	Question Number				
		☐	☐	☐	☐			☐	☐	☐	☐
		☐	☐	☐	☐			☐	☐	☐	☐
		☐	☐	☐	☐			☐	☐	☐	☐
		☐	☐	☐	☐			☐	☐	☐	☐
		☐	☐	☐	☐			☐	☐	☐	☐
		☐	☐	☐	☐			☐	☐	☐	☐
		☐	☐	☐	☐			☐	☐	☐	☐
		☐	☐	☐	☐			☐	☐	☐	☐
		☐	☐	☐	☐			☐	☐	☐	☐
		☐	☐	☐	☐			☐	☐	☐	☐
		☐	☐	☐	☐			☐	☐	☐	☐
		☐	☐	☐	☐			☐	☐	☐	☐
		☐	☐	☐	☐			☐	☐	☐	☐
		☐	☐	☐	☐			☐	☐	☐	☐
		☐	☐	☐	☐			☐	☐	☐	☐
		☐	☐	☐	☐			☐	☐	☐	☐
		☐	☐	☐	☐			☐	☐	☐	☐
		☐	☐	☐	☐			☐	☐	☐	☐
		☐	☐	☐	☐			☐	☐	☐	☐
		☐	☐	☐	☐			☐	☐	☐	☐
		☐	☐	☐	☐			☐	☐	☐	☐
		☐	☐	☐	☐			☐	☐	☐	☐
		☐	☐	☐	☐			☐	☐	☐	☐
		☐	☐	☐	☐			☐	☐	☐	☐
		☐	☐	☐	☐			☐	☐	☐	☐
		☐	☐	☐	☐			☐	☐	☐	☐
		☐	☐	☐	☐			☐	☐	☐	☐
		☐	☐	☐	☐			☐	☐	☐	☐